2nd Workshop on Speech and Language Processing for Assistive Technologies 2011

(SLPAT 2011)

AA004570

Held at EMNLP 2011

Edinburgh, Scotland, UK
30 July 2011

ISBN: 978-1-61839-254-1

Printed from e-media with permission by:

Curran Associates, Inc.
57 Morehouse Lane
Red Hook, NY 12571

proceedings.com

Some format issues inherent in the e-media version may also appear in this print version.

Copyright© (2011) by the Association for Computational Linguistics
All rights reserved.

Printed by Curran Associates, Inc. (2011)

For permission requests, please contact the Association for Computational Linguistics
at the address below.

Association for Computational Linguistics
209 N. Eighth Street
Stroudsburg, Pennsylvania 18360

Phone: 1-570-476-8006
Fax: 1-570-476-0860

acl@aclweb.org

Additional copies of this publication are available from:

Curran Associates, Inc.
57 Morehouse Lane
Red Hook, NY 12571 USA
Phone: 845-758-0400
Fax: 845-758-2634
Email: curran@proceedings.com
Web: www.proceedings.com

Introduction

We are pleased to bring you these Proceedings of the Second Workshop on Speech and Language Processing for Assistive Technologies (SLPAT), held in Edinburgh, Scotland on 30 July, 2011. We received 19 paper submissions, of which 9 were chosen for oral presentation and another 6 for poster presentation – all 15 papers are included in this volume. In addition, five demo proposals were accepted, and short abstracts of these demos are also included here.

This workshop was intended to bring researchers from all areas of speech and language technology with a common interest in making everyday life more accessible for people with physical, cognitive, sensory, emotional or developmental disabilities. This workshop builds on the first such workshop (co-located with NAACL HLT 2010); it provides an opportunity for individuals from research communities, and the individuals with whom they are working, to share research findings, and to discuss present and future challenges and the potential for collaboration and progress.

While Augmentative and Alternative Communication (AAC) is a particularly apt application area for speech and Natural Language Processing (NLP) technologies, we purposefully made the scope of the workshop broad enough to include assistive technologies (AT) as a whole, even those falling outside of AAC. While we encouraged work that validates methods with human experimental trials, we also accepted work on basic-level innovations and philosophy, inspired by AT/AAC related problems. Thus we have aimed at broad inclusivity, which is also manifest in the diversity of our Program Committee.

We are very excited to have four invited speakers. Sylvia Grant, Darryal Stark and Greg McMurchie will speak on their experiences and perspectives as users of AAC technology. Norman Alm will chair this expert panel and facilitate discussion between the panel and workshop participants. Norman has a wealth of research experience in applying NLP technologies to AAC and we look forward to a truly interactive and informative session. We would like to thank all four speakers for taking the time to participate and provide their collective insight to the workshop.

We would also like to thank the members of the Program Committee for completing their reviews promptly, and for providing useful feedback for deciding on the program and preparing the final versions of the papers. Thanks also to Marie Candito, Bonnie Webber and Miles Osborne for assistance with logistics and to Brian Roark for his guidance and support. Finally, thanks to the authors of the papers, for submitting such interesting and diverse work, and to the presenters of demos and commercial exhibitions.

Melanie Fried-Oken, Peter Ljunglöf, Kathy McCoy and Annalu Waller

Co-organizers of the workshop

Organizers:

Melanie Fried-Oken, Oregon Health & Science University
Peter Ljunglöf, University of Gothenburg & Chalmers University of Technology
Kathleen F. McCoy, University of Delaware
Annalu Waller, University of Dundee

Program Committee:

Jan Alexandersson, German Research Center for Artificial Intelligence
Norman Alm, University of Dundee
John Arnott, University of Dundee
Melanie Baljko, York University, Canada
Jan Bedrosian, Western Michigan University
Rolf Black, University of Dundee
Torbjørg Breivik, the Language Council of Norway
Tim Bunnell, University of Delaware
Rob Clark, University of Edinburgh
Ann Copestake, University of Cambridge
Stuart Cunningham, University of Sheffield
Rickard Domeij, Stockholm, University
Alistair D.N. Edwards, University of York
Michael Elhadad, Ben-Gurion University
Björn Granström, Royal Institute of Technology, Stockholm
Phil Green, Sheffield University
Mark Hasegawa-Johnson, University of Illinois
Per-Olof Hedvall, Lund University
Graeme Hirst, University of Toronto
Linda Hoag, Kansas State University
Harry Howard, Tulane University
Matt Huenerfauth, CUNY
Sofie Johansson Kokkinakis, University of Gothenburg
Simon Judge, Barnsley NHS & Sheffield University
Simon King, University of Edinburgh
Greg Lesher, Dynavox Technologies, Inc.
Jeremy Linskell, Electronic Assistive Technology Service, Tayside NHS
Mats Lundälv, DART, Gothenburg, Sweden
Ornella Mich, Foundazione Bruno Kessler
Yael Netzer, Ben-Gurion University
Alan Newell, University of Dundee
Torbjørn Nordgård, Lingit A/S, Norway
Helen Petrie, University of York
Karen Petrie, University of Dundee
Ehud Reiter, University of Aberdeen
Bitte Rydeman, Lund University
Howard Shane, Children's Hospital Boston
Fraser Shein, Bloorview Kids Rehab, Canada
Richard Sproat, Oregan Health and Science University
Kumiko Tanaka-Ishii, University of Tokyo
Nava Tintarev, University of Aberdeen
Tonio Wandmacher, Commissariat á l'énergie atomique, France
Jan-Oliver Wuelfing, Fraunhofer Centre Birlinghoven, Germany

Table of Contents

Workshop Program

Saturday, July 30

08:15–08:45 Registration

08:45–09:00 Opening remarks

Session: Speech impairment

09:00–09:30 *An on-line system for remote treatment of aphasia*
Anna Pompili, Alberto Abad, Isabel Trancoso, José Fonseca, Isabel Pavão Martins, Gabriela Leal and Luisa Farrajota

09:30–10:00 *Acoustic transformations to improve the intelligibility of dysarthric speech*
Frank Rudzicz

10:00–10:30 *Towards technology-assisted co-construction with communication partners*
Brian Roark, Andrew Fowler, Richard Sproat, Christopher Gibbons and Melanie Fried-Oken

10:30–11:00 Coffee break

Session: Access for physical impairment

11:00–11:30 *Trap Hunting: Finding Personal Data Management Issues in Next Generation AAC Devices*
Joseph Reddington and Lizzie Coles-Kemp

User panel, Posters and Demonstrations

11:30–12:40 Invited user panel, chaired by Norman Alm

12:40–14:00 Lunch, Posters and Demonstrations

Saturday, July 30 (continued)

Session: Visual impairment

14:00–14:30 *Asynchronous fixed-grid scanning with dynamic codes*
Russ Beckley and Brian Roark

14:30–15:00 *Improving the Accessibility of Line Graphs in Multimodal Documents*
Charles Greenbacker, Peng Wu, Sandra Carberry, Kathleen McCoy, Stephanie Elzer, David McDonald, Daniel Chester and Seniz Demir

15:00–15:30 *Indian Language Screen Readers and Syllable Based Festival Text-to-Speech Synthesis System*
Anila Susan Kurian, Badri Narayan, Nagarajan Madasamy, Ashwin Bellur, Raghava Krishnan, Kasthuri G, Vinodh M. Vishwanath, Kishore Prahallad and Hema A. Murthy

15:30–16:00 Coffee break, Posters and Demonstrations

Session: Language simplification / hearing impairments

16:00–16:30 *READ–IT: Assessing Readability of Italian Texts with a View to Text Simplification*
Felice Dell'Orletta, Simonetta Montemagni and Giulia Venturi

16:30–17:00 *Source Language Categorization for improving a Speech into Sign Language Translation System*
Verónica López-Ludeña, Rubén San-Segundo, Syaheerah Lufti, Juan Manuel Lucas-Cuesta, Julián David Echevarry and Beatriz Martínez-González

17:00–17:45 Review of workshop and discussion on future SLPAT activities

Poster papers

What does it mean to communicate (not) emotionally?
Jan-Oliver Wülfing and Lisa Hoffmann

Arabic Text to Arabic Sign Language Translation System for the Deaf and Hearing-Impaired Community
Abdulaziz Almohimeed, Mike Wald and R.I. Damper

Lekbot: A talking and playing robot for children with disabilities
Peter Ljunglöf, Britt Claesson, Ingrid Mattsson Müller, Stina Ericsson, Cajsa Ottesjö, Alexander Berman and Fredrik Kronlid

Using lexical and corpus resources for augmenting the AAC-lexicon
Katarina Heimann Mühlenbock and Mats Lundälv

Saturday, July 30 (continued)

An on-line system for remote treatment of aphasia

Anna Pompili, Alberto Abad, Isabel Trancoso
L[2]F - Spoken Language Systems Lab
INESC-ID/IST, Lisbon, Portugal
{anna,alberto,imt}@l2f.inesc-id.pt

José Fonseca, Isabel P. Martins, Gabriela Leal, Luisa Farrajota
LEL - Language Research Laboratory
Lisbon Faculty of Medicine, Portugal
jfonseca@fm.ul.pt

Abstract

Aphasia treatment for the recovery of lost communication functionalities is possible through frequent and intense speech therapy sessions. In this sense, speech and language technology may provide important support in improving the recovery process. The aim of the project Vithea (Virtual Therapist for Aphasia Treatment) is to develop an on-line system designed to behave as a virtual therapist, guiding the patient in performing training exercises in a simple and intuitive fashion. In this paper, the fundamental components of the Vithea system are presented, with particular emphasis on the speech recognition module. Furthermore, we report encouraging automatic word naming recognition results using data collected from speech therapy sessions.

1 Introduction

Aphasia is a communication disorder that can affect various aspects of language, including hearing comprehension, speech production, and reading and writing fluency. It is caused by damage to one or more of the language areas of the brain. Many times the cause of the brain injury is a cerebral vascular accident (CVA), but other causes can be brain tumors, brain infections and severe head injury due to an accident. Unfortunately, in the last decades the number of individuals that suffer CVAs has dramatically increased, with an estimated 600.000 new cases each year in the EU. Typically, a third of these cases present language deficiencies (Pedersen et al., 1995). This kind of language disorder involves countless professional, family and economic problems, both from the point of view of the individual and the society. In this context, two remarkable considerations have led to the development of the Portuguese national project Vithea (Virtual Therapist for Aphasia treatment).

First are the enormous benefits that speech and language technology (SLT) may bring to the daily lives of people with physical impairment. Information access and environment control are two areas where SLT has been beneficially applied, but SLT also has great potential for diagnosis, assessment and treatment of several speech disorders (Hawley et al., 2005). For instance, a method for speech intelligibility assessment using both automatic speech recognition and prosodic analysis is proposed in (Maier et al., 2009). This method is applied to the study of patients that have suffered a laryngotomy and to children with cleft lip and palate. (Castillo-Guerra and Lovey, 2003) presents a method for dysarthria assessment using features extracted from pathological speech signals. In (Yin et al., 2009), the authors describe an approach to pronunciation verification for a speech therapy application.

The second reason for undertaking the Vithea project is that several aphasia studies have demonstrated the positive effect of speech therapy activities for the improvement of social communication abilities. These have focused on specific linguistic impairments at the phonemic, semantic or syntactic levels (Basso, 1992). In fact, it is believed more and more that the intensity of speech therapy positively influences language recovery in aphasic patients (Bhogal et al., 2003).

These compelling reasons have motivated the de-

Proceedings of the 2nd Workshop on Speech and Language Processing for Assistive Technologies, pages 1–10,
Edinburgh, Scotland, UK, July 30, 2011. ©2011 Association for Computational Linguistics

velopment of an on-line system for the treatment of aphasic patients incorporating recent advances in speech and language technology in Portuguese. The system will act as a "virtual therapist", simulating an ordinary speech therapy session, where by means of the use of automatic speech recognition (ASR) technology, the virtual therapist will be able to recognize what was said by the patient and to validate if it was correct or not. As a result of this novel and specialized stimulation method for the treatment of aphasia, patients will have access to word naming exercises from their homes at any time, which will certainly cause an increase in the number of training hours, and consequently it has the potential to bring significant improvements to the rehabilitation process.

In section 2 we provide a brief description of different aphasia syndromes, provide an overview of the most commonly adopted therapies for aphasia, and describe the therapeutic focus of our system. Section 3 is devoted to an in depth description of the functionalities that make up the system, while section 4 aims at detailing its architecture. Finally, section 5 describes the automatic speech recognition module and discusses the results achieved within the automatic naming recognition task.

2 About the aphasia disorder

2.1 Classification of aphasia

It is possible to distinguish two different types of aphasia on the basis of the fluency of the speech produced: fluent and non-fluent aphasia. The speech of someone with fluent aphasia has normal articulation and rhythm, but is deficient in meaning. Typically, there are word-finding problems that most affect nouns and picturable action words. Non-fluent aphasic speech is slow and labored, with short utterance length. The flow of speech is more or less impaired at the levels of speech initiation, the finding and sequencing of articulatory movements, and the production of grammatical sequences. Speech is choppy, interrupted, and awkwardly articulated.

Difficulty of recalling words or names is the most common language disorder presented by aphasic individuals (whether fluent or non-fluent). In fact, it can be the only residual defect after rehabilitation of aphasia (Wilshire and Coslett, 2000).

2.2 Common therapeutic approaches

There are several therapeutic approaches for the treatment of the various syndromes of aphasia. Often these methods are focused on treating a specific disorder caused from aphasia. The most commonly used techniques are output focused, such as the stimulation method and the Melodical Intonation Therapy (MIT) (Albert et al., 1994). Other methods are linguistic-oriented learning approaches, such as the lexical-semantic therapy or the mapping technique for the treatment of agrammatism. Still, several non-verbal methods for the treatment of some severe cases of non-fluent aphasia, such as the visual analog communication, iconic communication, visual action and drawing therapies, are currently used (Sarno, 1981; Albert, 1998).

Although there is an extensive list of treatments specifically designed to recover from particular disorders caused by aphasia, one class of rehabilitation therapy especially important aims to improve the recovery from word retrieval problems, given the widespread difficulty of recalling words or names. Naming ability problems are typically treated with semantic exercises like *Naming Objects* or *Naming common actions* (Adlam et al., 2006). The approach typically followed is to subject the patient to a set of exercises comprising a set of stimuli in a variety of tasks. The stimuli are chosen based on their semantic content. The patient is asked to name the subject that has been shown.

2.3 Therapeutic focus of the Vithea system

The focus of the Vithea system is on the recovery of word naming ability for aphasic patients. So far, experiments have only been made with fluent aphasia patients, but even for this type of aphasia, major differences may be found. Particularly, patients with Transcortical sensorial aphasia, Conduction aphasia and Anomic aphasia (Goodglass, 1993) have been included in our studies.

Although the system has been specifically designed for aphasia treatment, it may be easily adapted to the treatment or diagnosis of other disorders in speech production. In fact, two of the patients that have participated in our experimental study were diagnosed with acquired apraxia of speech (AOS), which typically results from a stroke,

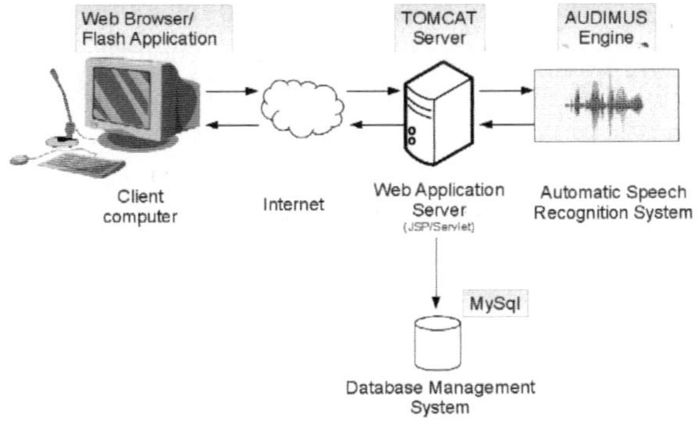

Figure 1: Comprehensive overview of the Vithea system.

tumor, or other known neurological illness or injury, and is characterized by inconsistent articulatory errors, groping oral movements to locate the correct articulatory position, and increasing errors with increasing word and phrase length.

3 The Vithea System

The overall flow of the system can be described as follows: when a therapy session starts, the virtual therapist will show to the patient, one at a time, a series of visual or auditory stimuli. The patient is required to respond verbally to these stimuli by naming the contents of the object or action that is represented. The utterance produced is recorded, encoded and sent via network to the server side. Here, a web application server receives the audio file via a servlet that serves as an interface to the ASR system, which takes as input the audio file encoding the patient's answer and generates a textual representation of it. This result is then compared with a set of predetermined textual answers (for that given question, of course) in order to verify the correctness of the patient's input. Finally, feedback is sent back to the patient. Figure 1 shows a comprehensive view of this process.

The system comprises two specific modules, dedicated respectively to the patients for carrying out the therapy sessions and to the clinicians for the administration of the functionalities related to them. The two modules adhere to different requirements that have been defined for the particular class of user for which they have been developed. Nonetheless they share the set of training exercises, that are built by the clinicians and performed by the patients.

3.1 Speech therapy exercises

Following the common therapeutic approach for treatment of word finding difficulties, a training exercise is composed of several semantic stimuli items. The stimuli may be of several different types: text, audio, image and video. Like in ordinary speech therapy sessions, the patient is asked to respond to the stimuli verbally, describing the imaging he/she sees or completing a popular saying (which was presented verbally or in text).

Exercise categories

The set of therapeutic exercises integrated in Vithea has been designed by the Language Research Laboratory of the Department of Clinical Neuroscience of the Lisbon Faculty of Medicine (LEL). LEL has provided a rich battery of exercises that can be classified into two macro-categories according to the main modality of the stimulus, namely:

A) Image or video: *Naming object picture, Naming of verbs with action pictures, and Naming verbs given pictures of objects.*

B) Text or speech: *Responsive Naming, Complete Sayings, Part-whole Associations, What name is given to..., Generic Designation, Naming by function, Phonological Evocation, and Semantics Evocation.*

Exercises can be also classified according to *Themes*, in order to immerse the individual in a pragmatic, familiar environment: a) *Home b) Animals c) Tools d) Food e) Furniture f) Professions g) Appliances h) Transportation i) Alive/Not Alive j) Manipulable/Not Manipulable k) Clothing l) Random.*

Evaluation exercises

In addition to the set of training exercises, which are meant to be used on a daily basis by the aphasic patient, the Vithea system also supports a different class of exercises: Evaluation Exercises. Unlike training exercises, evaluation exercises are used by human therapists to periodically assess the patient's progress and his/her current degree of aphasia via an objective metric denoted as Aphasia Quotient (AQ). Evaluation exercises are chosen from a subset of the previously mentioned classes of therapeutic exercises, namely: *Naming object picture*, *Naming of verbs with action pictures*, and *Naming verbs given pictures of objects*.

3.2 Patient Module

The patient module is meant to be used by aphasic individuals to perform the therapeutic exercises.

Visual design considerations

Most of the users for whom this module is intended have had a CVA. Because of this, they may have some forms of physical disabilities such as reduced arm mobility, and therefore they may experience problems using a mouse. Acknowledging this eventuality, particular attention has been given to the design of the graphical user interface (GUI) for this module, making it simple to use both at the presentation level and in terms of functionality provided. Driven by the principle of accessibility, we designed the layout in an easy to use and understand fashion, such that the interaction should be predictable and unmistakable.

Moreover, even though aphasia is increasing in the youngest age groups, it still remains a predominant disorder among elderly people. This age group is prone to suffer from visual impairments. Thus, we carefully considered the graphic elements chosen, using big icons for representing our interface elements. Figure 2 illustrates some screenshots of the Patient Module on the top.

Exercise protocol

Once logged into the system, the virtual therapist guides the patient in carrying out the training sessions, providing a list of possible exercises to be performed. When the patient choses to start a training exercise, the system will present target stimuli one at a time in a random way. After the evaluation of the patient's answer by the system, the patient can listen again to his/her previous answer, record again an utterance (up to a number of times chosen before starting the exercise) or pass to the next exercise.

Patient tracking

Besides permitting training sessions, the patient module has the responsibility of storing statistical and historical data related to user sessions. User utterances and information about each user access to the system are stored in a relational database. Particularly, start and end time of the whole training session, of a training exercise, and of each stimulus are collected. On the one hand, we log every access in order to evaluate the impact and effectiveness of the program by seeing the frequency with which it is used. On the other hand, we record the total time needed to accomplish a single stimulus or to end a whole exercise in order to estimate user performance improvements.

3.3 Clinician Module

The clinician module is specifically designed to allow clinicians to manage patient data, to regulate the creation of new stimuli and the alteration of the existing ones, and to monitor user performance in terms of frequency of access to the system and user progress. The module is composed by three submodules: **User, Exercise, Statistic**.

User sub-module

This module allows the management of a knowledge base of patients. Besides basic information related to the user personal profile, the database also stores for each individual his/her type of aphasia, his/her aphasia severity (7-level subjective scale) and AQ information.

Exercise sub-module

This module allows the clinician to create, update, preview and delete stimuli from an exercise. An exercise is composed of a varying number of stimuli. In addition to the canonical valid answer, the system accepts for each stimulus an extended word list comprising three extra valid answers. This list allows the system to consider the most frequent synonyms and diminutives.

Since the stimuli are associated with a wide assortment of multimedia files, besides the management of the set of stimuli, the sub-module also provides a rich Web based interface to manage the database of multimedia resources used within the stimuli. Figure 2c shows a screenshot listing some multimedia files. From this list, it is possible to select a desired file in order to edit or delete it.

In this context, a preview feature has also been provided. The system is capable of handling a wide range of multimedia encoding: audio (accepted file

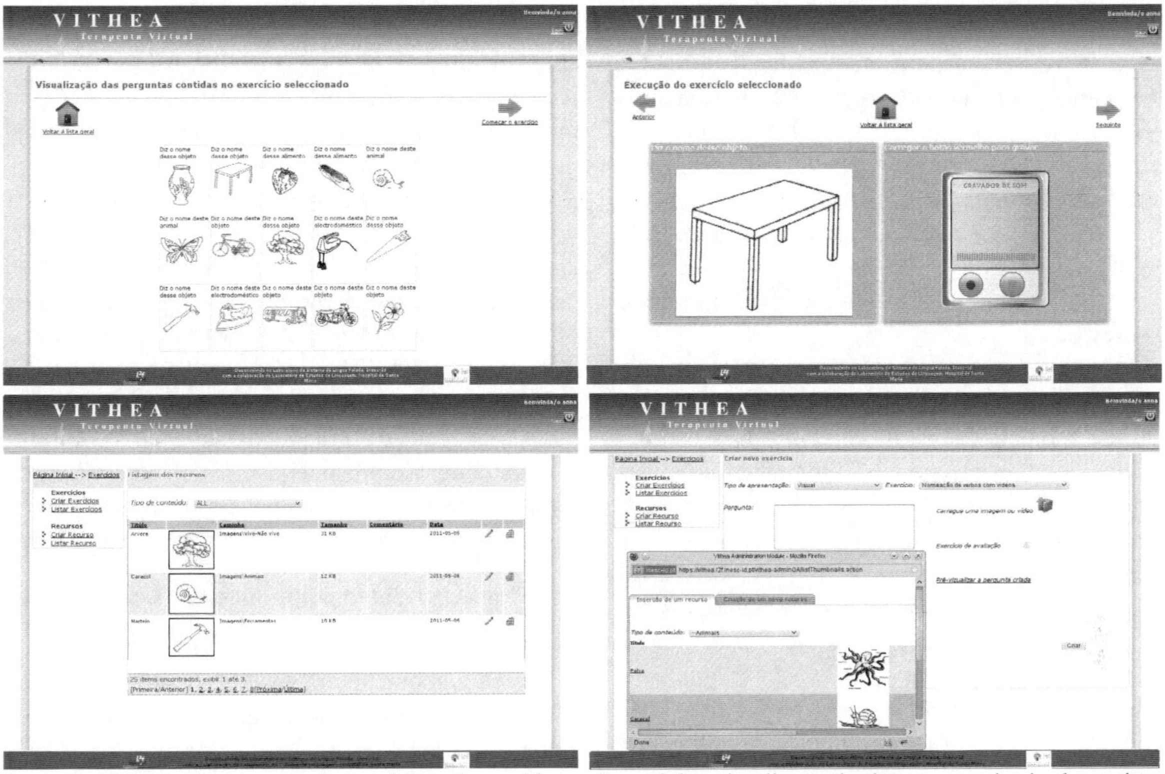

Figure 2: Vithea system screenshots: a) Interface with preview of the stimuli constituting an exercise in the patients module (top-left), b) interface for performing a specific stimulus in the patients module (top-right), c) interface for the management of multimedia resources in the clinician module (bottom-left) and d) interface for the creation of new stimulus in the clinician module (bottom-right).

types: *wav, mp3*), video (accepted file types: *wmv, avi, mov, mp4, mpe, mpeg, mpg, swf*), and images (accepted file types: *jpe, jpeg, jpg, png, gif, bmp, tif, tiff*).

Given the diversity of the various file types accepted by the system, a conversion to a unique file type was needed, in order to show them all with only one external tool. Audio files are therefore converted to *mp3* file format, while video files are converted to *flv* file format.

Finally, a custom functionality has been designed to create new stimuli in an intuitive fashion similar in style to a WYSIWYG editor. Figure 2d illustrates the stimuli editor, showing how to insert a multimedia resource.

Statistics sub-module

This module allows the clinician both to monitor statistical information related to user-system interactions and to access the utterances produced by the patient during the therapeutic sessions. The statistical information comprises data related to the user's progress and to the frequency with which users access the system. On the one hand, we provide all the attempts recorded by the patients in order to allow a re-evaluation by clinicians. This data can be used to identify possible weaknesses or errors from the recognition engine. On the other hand, we thought that monitoring the utilization of the application from the users could be an important piece of feedback about the system's feasibility. This is motivated by common concerns about the fact that some users abandon their therapeutic sessions when they are not able to see quick results in terms of improvements.

4 Architectural Overview

Considering the aforementioned requirements and features that will make up the system, Learning Management Systems (LMSs) software applications were initially considered. LMSs automate the administration of training events, manage the log-in of registered users, manage course catalog, record data from learners and provide reports to the management (Aydin and Tirkes, 2010). Thus, an in-depth evaluation of the currently widespread solutions was carried out (Pompili, 2011). Concretely, eight different LMSs (Atutor, Chamilo, Claroline, eFront, Ilias, Moodle, Olat, Sakai) were studied in detail. Unfortunately, the outcome of this study revealed important drawbacks.

The main problem noticed is that LMSs are typically feature-rich tools that try to be of general purpose use, sometimes resulting in the loss of their usefulness to the average user. Often the initial user reaction to the interface of these tools is confusion: the most disorienting challenge is figuring out where to get the information needed. As previously mentioned, patients who have had a CVA may experience physical deficiencies, thus the Vithea system needs an easy to use and understandable interface. We dedicated some effort trying to personalize LMS solutions, but most of them do not allow easy simplification of the presentation layout.

Moreover, while there were several differences between the functionalities that the evaluated LMSs provided in terms of training exercises, they all presented various limitations in their implementation. Eventually, we had to acknowledge that it would have been extremely complex to customize the evaluated frameworks to meet the Vithea project requirements without introducing major structural changes to the code.

Besides, the average user for whom the Vithea system is intended is not necessarily accustomed with computers and even less with these tools, which in most cases are developed for environments such as universities or huge organizations. This means that our users may lack the technical skills necessary to work with an LMS, and the extra effort of understanding the system would result in a loss of motivation.

Therefore, considering the conclusions from this study, we have opted to build a modular, portable application which will totally adhere to our requirements. With these purposes in mind, the system has been designed as a multi-tier web application, being accessible everywhere from a web browser. The implementation of the whole system has been achieved by integrating different technologies of a heterogeneous nature. In fact, the presentation tier exploits Adobe®Flash®technology in order to support rich multimedia interaction. The middle tier comprises the integration of our own speech recognition system, AUDIMUS, and some of the most advanced open source frameworks for the development of web applications, Apache Tiles, Apache Struts 2, Hibernate and Spring. In the data tier, the persistence of the application data is delegated to the relational database MySQL. This is where the system maintains information related to patient clinical data, utterances produced during therapeutic sessions, training exercises, stimuli and statistical data related both to the frequency with which the system is used, and to the patient progress.

4.1 Speech-related components of the system

Audio Recorder

In order to record the patient's utterances, the Vithea system takes advantage of opportunities offered by Adobe®Flash®technology. This allows easy integration in most browsers without any required extra plugin, while avoiding the need for security certificates to attest to the reliability of an external component running in the client machine within the browser. This choice was mainly motivated from the particular kind of users who will use the system, allowing them to enjoy the advantages of the virtual therapist without the frustration of additional configuration. A customized component has been developed following the aforementioned principles of usability in terms of designing the user interface. Keeping simplicity and understandability as our main guidelines, we used a reduced set of large symbols and we tried to keep the number of interactions required to a bare minimum. Therefore, recording and sending an utterance to the server requires only that the patient starts the recording when ready, and then stops it when finished. Another action is required to play back the recorded audio.

Automatic Speech Recognition Engine

AUDIMUS is the Automatic Speech Recognition engine integrated into the Vithea system. The AUDIMUS framework has been developed during the last years of research at the Spoken Language Processing Lab of INESC-ID (L^2F), it has been successfully used for the development of several ASR applications such as the recognition of Broadcast News (BN) (Meinedo et al., 2010). It represents an essential building block, being the component in charge of receiving the patient answers and validating the correctness of the utterances with respect to the therapeutic exercises. In the following section, this specific module of the Vithea architecture is assessed and described in more detail.

5 The Vithea speech recognition module

5.1 The AUDIMUS hybrid speech recognizer

AUDIMUS is a hybrid recognizer that follows the connectionist approach (Boulard and Morgan, 1993; Boulard and Morgan, 1994). It combines the temporal modeling capacity of Hidden Markov Models (HMMs) with the pattern discriminative classification of multilayer perceptrons (MLP). A Markov process is used to model the basic temporal nature of the speech signal, while an artificial neural network is used to estimate posterior phone probabilities given the acoustic data at each frame. Each MLP is trained on distinct feature sets resulting from different feature extraction processes, namely Perceptual Linear Predictive (PLP), log-RelAtive SpecTrAl PLP (RASTA-PLP) and Modulation SpectroGram (MSG).

The AUDIMUS decoder is based on the Weighted Finite State Transducer (WFST) approach to large vocabulary speech recognition (Mohri et al., 2002).

The current version of AUDIMUS for the European Portuguese language uses an acoustic model trained with 57 hours of downsampled Broadcast News data and 58 hours of mixed fixed-telephone and mobile-telephone data (Abad and Neto, 2008).

5.2 Word Naming Recognition task

We refer to *word recognition* as the task that performs the evaluation of the utterances spoken by the patients, in a similar way to the role of the therapist in a rehabilitation session. This task represents the main challenge addressed by the virtual therapist system. Its difficulty is related to the utterances produced by aphasic individuals that are frequently interleaved with disfluencies like hesitation, repetitions, and doubts. In order to choose the best approach to accomplish this critical task, preliminary evaluations were performed with two sub-sets of the Portuguese Speech Dat II corpus. These consist of word spotting phrases using embedded keywords: the development set is composed of 3334 utterances, while the evaluation set comprises 481 utterances. The number of keywords is 27. Two different approaches were compared: the first based on large vocabulary continuous speech recognition (LVCSR), the second based on the acoustic matching of speech with keyword models in contrast to a background model. Experimental results showed promising performance indicators by the latter approach, both in terms of Equal Error Rate (EER), False Alarm (FA) and False Rejection (FR). Thus, on the basis of these outcomes, background modeling based keyword spotting (KWS) was considered more appropriate for this task.

Background modeling based KWS

In this work, an equally-likely 1-gram model formed by the possible target keywords and a competing background model is used for word detection. While keyword models are described by their sequence of phonetic units provided by an automatic grapheme-to-phoneme module, the problem of background modeling must be specifically addressed. The most common method consists of building a new phoneme classification network that in addition to the conventional phoneme set, also models the posterior probability of a background unit representing "general speech". This is usually done by using all the training speech as positive examples for background modeling and requires retraining the acoustic networks. Alternatively, the posterior probability of the background unit can be estimated based on the posterior probabilities of the other phones (Pinto et al., 2007). We followed the second approach, estimating the posterior probability of a garbage unit as the mean probability of the top-6 most likely outputs of the phonetic network at each time frame. In this way there is no need for acoustic network re-training. Then, a likelihood-dependent decision threshold (determined with telephonic data for development) is used to prune the best recognition hypotheses to a reduced set of sentences where the target keyword is searched for.

5.3 Experiments with real data

Corpus of aphasic speech

A reduced speech corpus composed of data collected during therapy sessions of eight different patients has been used to assess the performance of the speech recognition module. As explained above, two of them (patients 2 and 7) were diagnosed with AOS. Each of the sessions consists of naming exercises with 103 objects per patient. Each object is shown with an interval of 15 seconds from the previous. The objects and the presentation order are the same for all patients. Word-level transcription and segmentation were manually produced for the patient excerpts in each session, totaling 996 segments. The complete evaluation corpus has a duration of approximately 1 hour and 20 minutes.

Evaluation criteria

A word naming exercise is considered to be completed correctly whenever the targeted word is said by the patient (independently of its position, amount of silence before the valid answer, etc...). It is worth noticing that this is not necessarily the criterion followed in therapy tests by speech therapists. In fact, doubts, repetitions, corrections, approximation strategies and other similar factors are usually considered unacceptable in word naming tests, since their presence is an indicator of speech pathologies. However, for the sake of comparability between a human speech therapist evaluation and an automatic evaluation, we keep this simplified evaluation criterion. In addition to the canonical valid answer to every exercise, an extended word list containing the most frequent synonyms and diminutives has been defined, for a total KWS vocabulary of 252 words. Only answers included in this list have been accepted as correct in both manual and automatic evaluation.

Results

Word naming scores are calculated for each speaker as the number of positive word detections divided by the total number of exercises (leftmost plot of Figure 3). The correlation between the human evaluation assessed during ordinary therapeutic sessions and the automatic evaluation assessed with the word recognition task has resulted in a Person's coefficient of 0.9043. This result is considered quite promising in terms of global evaluation. As concerning individual evaluations (rightmost plot of Figure 3), it can be seen that the system shows remarkable performance variability in terms of false alarms and misses depending on the specific patient. In this sense, the adaptation to the specific user profile may be interesting in terms of adjusting the system's operation point to the type and level of aphasia. As a preliminary attempt to tackle the customization issue, the word detector has been individually calibrated for each speaker following a 5-fold cross-validation strategy with the corresponding patient exercises. The calibration is optimized to the minimum false alarm operation point for patients with high false-alarm rates (2, 3, 4, 5 and 8) and to the minimum miss rate for patients with a high number of misses (1, 6 and 7). Figure 4 shows results for this customized detector. In this case, the correlation between human and automatic evaluation is 0.9652 and a more balanced performance (in terms of false alarm and false rejection ratios) is observed for most speakers.

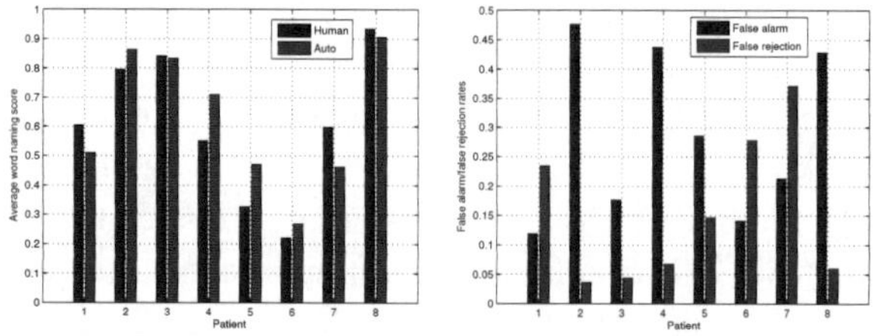

Figure 3: *On the left side, average word naming scores of the human and automatic evaluations. On the right side, false alarm and false rejection rates.*

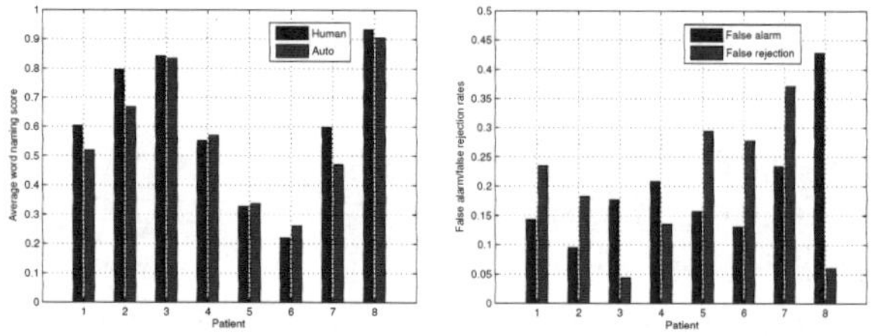

Figure 4: *On the left side, average word naming scores of the human and automatic evaluations with the customized detector. On the right side, false alarm and false rejection rates of the customized detector.*

Analysis of word detection errors

The most common cause for false alarms is the presence of many "invented" nonexistent words without semantic meaning, which are very often phonetically very close to the target words. These paraphasic errors were present in all types of fluent aphasia and AOS that we have observed, but not for all patients. In many of these errors, the stressed syllable is often pronounced right, or at least its rhyme. As the typical stress pattern in Portuguese is in the penultimate syllable, most often the last syllable is also pronounced correctly (e.g. borco / porco). In patients that try to say the word by approximation, that is, by successive attempts to get closer to the target word, but using only existent words, the differences between the percentages of miss and false alarms are not so remarkable.

One characteristic of aphasic patients that sometimes causes keywords to be missed (both when correctly or incorrectly pronounced) is pauses in between syllables. This may justify the inclusion of alternative pronunciations, in case such pronunciations are considered acceptable by therapists. Additionally, more sophisticated speech tools may also be integrated, such as tools for computing the goodness of pronunciation (Witt, 1999). This would allow a different type of assessment of the pronunciation errors, which may provide useful feedback for the therapist and the patients.

6 Conclusions and future work

6.1 Conclusions

This paper described how automatic speech recognition technology has contributed to build up a system that will act as a virtual therapist, being capable of facilitating the recovery of people who have a particular language disorder: aphasia. Early experiments conducted to evaluate ASR performance with speech from aphasic patients yielded quite promising results.

The virtual therapist has been designed following relevant accessibility principles tailored to the particular category of users targeted by the system. Special attention has been devoted to the user interface design: web page layout and graphical elements have been chosen keeping in mind the possibility that a user may experience reduced arm mobility and the technology that has been integrated was selected with the idea of minimizing possible difficulties in using the system. A pedagogical approach has been followed in planning the functionalities of the virtual therapist. This has been mainly driven by the fundamental idea of avoiding an extra feature rich tool which could have resulted in frustration for some patients, who seek help for recovery and do not need to learn how to use complex software.

Overall, since the system is a web application, it allows therapy sessions anywhere at anytime. Thus, we expect that this will bring significant improvements to the quality of life of the patients allowing more frequent, intense rehabilitation sessions and thus a faster recovery.

6.2 Future work

The Vithea system has recently achieved the first phase of a project which still entails several improvements. Even though, *Naming objects* and *Naming common actions* are the most commonly used exercises during the rehabilitation therapies, the system has been designed to allow a more comprehensive set of therapeutic exercises which will be implemented during the next refinement phase. Also, at this stage, we plan to make available the current version of the system to real patients in order to receive effective feedback on the system.

In the subsequent improvement phase, we will integrate the possibility of providing help, both semantic and phonological to the patient whenever the virtual therapist is asked for. Hints could be given both in the form of a written solution or as a speech synthesized production based on Text To Speech (TTS). Furthermore, we are considering the possibility of incorporating an intelligent animated agent that together with the exploitation of synthesized speech, will behave like a sensitive and effective clinician, providing positive encouragements to the user.

Acknowledgements

This work was funded by the FCT project RIPD/ADA/109646/2009, and partially supported by FCT (INESC-ID multiannual funding) through the PIDDAC Program funds. The authors would like to thank to Prof. Dr. M. T. Pazienza, A. Costa and the reviewers for their precious comments.

References

A. Abad and J. P. Neto. 2008. International Conference on Computational Processing of Portuguese Language, Portugal. *Automatic classification and transcription of telephone speech in radio broadcast data.*

A. L. R. Adlam, K. Patterson, T. T. Rogers, P. J. Nestor, C. H. Salmond, J. Acosta-Cabronero and J. R. Hodges. 2006. Brain. *Semantic dementia and Primary Progressive Aphasia: two side of the same coin?*, 129:3066–3080.

M. L. Albert, R. Sparks and N. A. Helm. 1994. Neurology. *Report of the Therapeutics and Technology Assessment Subcommittee of the American Academy of Neurology. Assesment: melodic intonation therapy*, 44:566–568.

M. L. Albert. 1998. Arch Neurol-Chicago *Treatment of aphasia*, 55:1417–1419.

C. C. Aydin and G. Tirkes. 2010. Education Engineering. *Open source learning management systems in e-learning and Moodle*, 54:593–600.

A. Basso. 1992. Aphasiology. *Prognostic factors in aphasia*, 6(4):337–348.

S. K. Bhogal, R. Teasell and M. Speechley. 2003. Stroke. *Intensity of aphasia therapy, impact on recovery*, 34:987–993.

H. Bourlard and N. Morgan. 1993. IEEE Transactions on Neural Networks. *Continuous speech recognition by connectionist statistical methods*, 4(6):893–909.

H. Bourlard and N. Morgan. 1994. Springer. *Connectionist speech recognition: a hybrid approach.*

D. Caseiro, I. Trancoso, C. Viana and M. Barros. 2003. International Congress of Phonetic Sciences, Barcelona, Spain. *A Comparative Description of GtoP Modules for Portuguese and Mirandese Using Finite State Transducers.*

E. Castillo-Guerra and D. F. Lovey. 2003. 25th Annual Conference IEEE Engineering in Medicine and Biology Society. *A Modern Approach to Dysarthria Classification.*

H. Goodglass. 1993. *Understanding aphasia: technical report.* Academy Press, University of Califórnia. San Diego.

M. S. Hawley, P. D. Green, P. Enderby, S. P. Cunningham and R. K. Moore. 2005. Interspeech. *Speech technology for e-inclusion of people with physical disabilities and disordered speech*, 445–448.

A. Maier, T. Haderlein, U. Eysholdt, F. Rosanowski, A. Batliner, M. Schuster and E. Nöth. 2009. Speech Communication. *PEAKS - A System for the Automatic Evaluation of Voice and Speech Disorders*, 51(5):425–437.

H. Meinedo and J. P. Neto. 2000. International Conference on Spoken Language Processing, Beijing, China. *Combination Of Acoustic Models In Continuous Speech Recognition Hybrid Systems*, 2:931–934.

H. Meinedo, A. Abad, T. Pellegrini, I. Trancoso and J. P. Neto. 2010. Fala 2010, Vigo, Spain. *The L2F Broadcast News Speech Recognition System.*

M. Mohri, F. Pereira and M. Riley. 2002. Computer Speech and Language. *Weighted Finite-State Transducers in Speech Recognition*, 16:69–88.

P. M. Pedersen, H. S. Jørgensen, H. Nakayama, H. O. Raaschou and T. S. Olsen. 1995. Ann Neurol *Aphasia in acute stroke: incidence, determinants, and recovery*, 38(4):659–666.

J. Pinto, A. Lovitt and H. Hermansky. 2007. Interspeech. *Exploiting Phoneme Similarities in Hybrid HMM-ANN Keyword Spotting*, 1817–1820.

A. Pompili. 2011. Thesis, Department of Computer Science, University of Rome. *Virtual therapist for aphasia treatment.*

M. T. Sarno. 1981. *Recovery and rehabilitation in aphasia*, 485–530. Acquired Aphasia, Academic Press, New York.

C. E. Wilshire and H. B. Coslett. 2000. *Disorders of word retrieval in aphasia theories and potential applications*, 82–107. Aphasia and Language: Theory to practice, The Guilford Press, New York.

S. M. Witt. 1999. *Use of speech recognition in Computer assisted Language Learning.* PhD thesis, Department of Engineering, University of Cambridge.

S. -C. Yin, R. Rose, O. Saz and E. Lleida. 2009. IEEE International Conference on Acoustics, Speech and Signal Processing. *A study of pronunciation verification in a speech therapy application*, 4609–4612.

Acoustic transformations to improve the intelligibility of dysarthric speech

Frank Rudzicz
University of Toronto, Department of Computer Science
6 King's College Road
Toronto, Ontario, Canada
frank@cs.toronto.edu

Abstract

This paper describes modifications to acoustic speech signals produced by speakers with dysarthria in order to make those utterances more intelligible to typical listeners. These modifications include the correction of tempo, the adjustment of formant frequencies in sonorants, the removal of aberrant voicing, the deletion of phoneme insertion errors, and the replacement of erroneously dropped phonemes. Through simple evaluations of intelligibility with naïve listeners, we show that the correction of phoneme errors results in the greatest increase in intelligibility and is therefore a desirable mechanism for the eventual creation of augmentative application software for individuals with dysarthria.

1 Introduction

Dysarthria is a set of neuromotor disorders that impair the physical production of speech. These impairments reduce the normal control of the primary vocal articulators but do not affect the regular comprehension or production of meaningful, syntactically correct language. For example, damage to the recurrent laryngeal nerve reduces control of vocal fold vibration (i.e., phonation), which can result in aberrant voicing. Inadequate control of soft palate movement caused by disruption of the vagus cranial nerve may lead to a disproportionate amount of air being released through the nose during speech (i.e., hypernasality). The lack of articulatory control also leads to various involuntary non-speech sounds including velopharyngeal or glottal noise (Rosen and Yampolsky, 2000). More commonly, a lack of tongue and lip dexterity often produces heavily slurred speech and a more diffuse and less differentiable vowel target space (Kent and Rosen, 2004).

The neurological damage that causes dysarthria usually affects other physical activity as well which can have a drastically adverse affect on mobility and computer interaction. For instance, severely dysarthric speakers are 150 to 300 times slower than typical users in keyboard interaction (Hosom et al., 2003; Hux et al., 2000). However, since dysarthric speech is often only 10 to 17 times slower than that of typical speakers (Patel, 1998), speech is a viable input modality for computer-assisted interaction.

Consider a dysarthric individual who must travel into a city by public transportation. This might involve purchasing tickets, asking for directions, or indicating intentions to fellow passengers, all within a noisy and crowded environment. A personal portable communication device in this scenario (either hand-held or attached to a wheelchair) would transform relatively unintelligible speech spoken into a microphone to make it more intelligible before being played over a set of speakers. Such a system could facilitate interaction and overcome difficult or failed attempts at communication in daily life.

We propose a system that avoids drawbacks of other voice-output communication aids that output only synthetic speech. Before software for such a device is designed, our goal is to establish and evaluate a set of modifications to dysarthric speech to produce a more intelligible equivalent. Understanding the utility of each of these techniques will be crucial to effectively designing the proposed system.

Proceedings of the 2nd Workshop on Speech and Language Processing for Assistive Technologies, pages 11–21,
Edinburgh, Scotland, UK, July 30, 2011. ©2011 Association for Computational Linguistics

2 Background and related work

Hawley et al. (2007) described an experiment in which 8 dysarthric individuals (with either cerebral palsy or multiple sclerosis) controlled non-critical devices in their home (e.g., TV) with automatic speech recognition. Command vocabularies consisted of very simple phrases (e.g., "*TV channel up*", "*Radio volume down*") and feedback was provided to the user either by visual displays or by auditory cues. This speech-based environmental control was compared with a 'scanning' interface in which a button is physically pressed to iteratively cycle through a list of alternative commands, words, or phrases. While the speech interface made more errors (between 90.8% and 100% accuracy after training) than the scanning interface (100% accuracy), the former was significantly faster (7.7s vs 16.9s, on average). Participants commented that speech was significantly less tiring than the scanning interface, and just as subjectively appealing (Hawley et al., 2007). Similar results were obtained in other comparisons of speech and scanning interfaces (Havstam, Buchholz, and Hartelius, 2003), and command-and-control systems (Green et al., 2003). Speech is a desirable method of expression for individuals with dysarthria. There are many augmentative communication devices that employ synthetic text-to-speech in which messages can be written on a specialized keyboard or played back from a repository of pre-recorded phrases (Messina and Messina, 2007). This basic system architecture can be modified to allow for the replacement of textual input with spoken input. However, such a scenario would involve some degree of automatic speech recognition, which is still susceptible to fault despite recent advances (Rudzicz, 2011). Moreover, the type of synthetic speech output produced by such systems often lacks a sufficient degree of individual affectation or natural expression that one might expect in typical human speech (Kain et al., 2007). The use of prosody to convey personal information such as one's emotional state is generally not supported by such systems but is nevertheless a key part of a general communicative ability.

Transforming one's speech in a way that preserves the natural prosody will similarly also preserve extra-linguistic information such as emotions, and is therefore a pertinent response to the limitations of current technology. Kain et al. (2007) proposed the voice transformation system shown in figure 1 which produced output speech by concatenating together original unvoiced segments with synthesized voiced segments that consisted of a superposition of the original high-bandwidth signal with synthesized low-bandwidth formants. These synthesized formants were produced by modifications to input energy, pitch generation, and formant modifications. Modifications to energy and formants were performed by Gaussian mixture mapping, as described below, in which learned relationships between dysarthric and target acoustics were used to produce output closer to the target space. This process was intended to be automated, but Kain et al. (2007) performed extensive hand-tuning and manually identified formants in the input. This will obviously be impossible in a real-time system, but these processes can to some extent be automated. For example, voicing boundaries can be identified by the weighted combination of various acoustic features (e.g., energy, zero-crossing rate) (Kida and Kawahara, 2005; Hess, 2008), and formants can be identified by the Burg algorithm (Press et al., 1992) or through simple linear predictive analysis with continuity constraints on the identified resonances between adjacent frames (O'Shaughnessy, 2008).

Spectral modifications traditionally involve filtering or amplification methods such as spectral subtraction or harmonic filtering (O'Shaughnessy, 2000), but these are not useful for dealing with more serious mispronounciations (e.g., $/t/$ for $/n/$). Hosom et al. (2003) showed that Gaussian mixture mapping can be used to transform audio from one set of spectral acoustic features to another. During analysis, context-independent frames of speech are analyzed for bark-scaled energy and their 24th order cepstral coefficients.

For synthesis, a cepstral analysis approximates the original spectrum, and a high-order linear predictive filter is applied to each frame, and excited by impulses or white noise (for voiced and unvoiced segments). Hosom et al. (2003) showed that given 99% human accuracy in recognizing normal speech data, this method of reconstruction gave 93% accuracy on the same data. They then trained a transformative model between dysarthric and regular speech

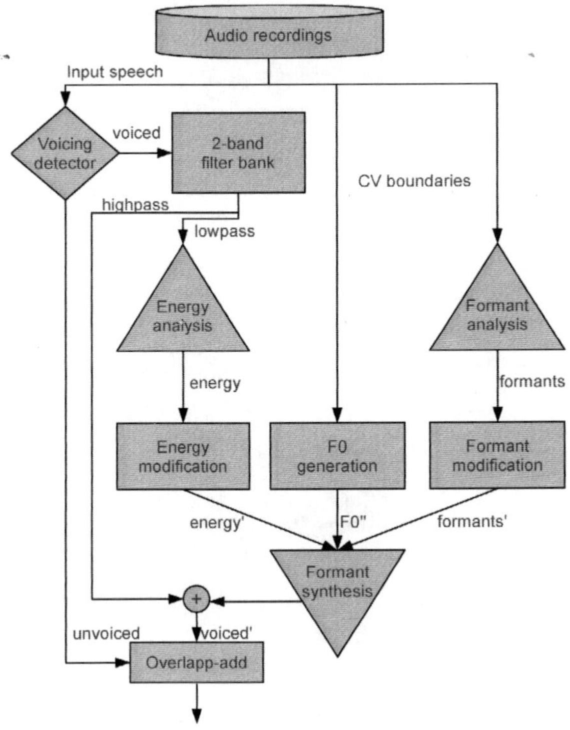

Figure 1: Voice transformation system proposed by Kain et al. (2007).

using aligned, phoneme-annotated, and orthographically identical sentences spoken by dysarthric and regular speakers, and a Gaussian Mixture Model (GMM) to model the probability distribution of the dysarthric source spectral features x as the sum of D normal distributions with mean vector μ, diagonal covariance matrix Σ, and prior probability α:

$$p(x) = \sum_{d=1}^{D} \alpha_d \mathbf{N}(x; \mu_d, \Sigma_d). \quad (1)$$

The GMM parameters were trained in an unsupervised mode using the expectation-maximization algorithm and 1, 2, 4, 8, and 16 mixture components, with $D = 4$ apparently being optimal. A probabilistic least-squares regression mapped the source features x onto the target (regular speaker) features y, producing the model $W_d(x) + b_d$ for each class, and a simple spectral distortion is performed to produce regularized versions of dysarthic speech $\hat{y}$:

$$\hat{y}(x) = \sum_{d=1}^{D} h_d(x)\,(W_d(x) + b_d) \quad (2)$$

for posterior probabilities $h_d(x)$. This model is interesting in that it explicitly maps the acoustic differences for different features between disordered and regular speech[1]. Reconstructing the dysarthric spectrum in this way to sound more 'typical' while leaving pitch (F_0), timing, and energy characteristics intact resulted in a 59.4% relative error rate reduction (68% to 87% accuracy) among a group of 18 naive human listeners each of whom annotated a total of 206 dysarthric test words (Hosom et al., 2003).

3 The TORGOMorph transformations

TORGOMorph encapsulates of a number of transformations of the acoustics uttered by speakers with dysarthria. Each modification is implemented in reaction to a particular effect of dysarthria on intelligibility as determined by observations on the TORGO database of dysarthric speech (Rudzicz, Namasivayam, and Wolff, 2011). Currently, these modifications are uniformly preceded by noise reduction using spectral subtraction and either phonological or phonemic annotations. This latter step is currently necessary, since certain modifications require either knowledge of the manner of articulation or the identities of the vowel segments, as explained below. The purpose of this exercise is to determine which modifications result in the most significant improvements to intelligibility, so the correct annotation sequence is vital to avoid the introduction of an additional dimension of error. Therefore, the annotations used below are extracted directly from the professional markup in the TORGO database. In practice, however, phonemic annotations determined automatically by speech recognition would be imperfect, which is why investigations of this type often forgo that automation altogether (e.g., see Kain et al. (2007)). Possible alternatives to full ASR are discussed in section 5.

In some cases, the dysarthric speech must be compared or supplemented with another vocal source. Here, we synthesize segments of speech using a text-to-speech application developed by Black and Lenzo (2004). This system is based on the University of Edinburgh's Festival tool and synthesizes phonemes using a standard method based on lin-

[1] This model can also be used to measure the difference between any two types of speech.

ear predictive coding with a pronunciation lexicon and part-of-speech tagger that assists in the selection of intonation parameters (Taylor, Black, and Caley, 1998). This system is invoked by providing the expected text uttered by the dysarthic speaker. In order to properly combine this purely synthetic signal and the original waveforms we require identical sampling rates, so we resample the former by a rational factor using a polyphase filter with low-pass filtering to avoid aliasing (Hayes, 1999). Since the discrete phoneme sequences themselves can differ, we find an ideal alignment between the two by the Levenshtein algorithm (Levenshtein, 1966), which provides the total number of insertion, deletion, and substitution errors.

The following sections detail the components of TORGOMorph, which is outlined in figure 2. These components allow for a cascade of one transformation followed by another, although we can also perform these steps independently to isolate their effects. In all cases, the spectrogram is derived with the fast Fourier transform given 2048 bins on the range of 0–5 kHz. Voicing boundaries are extracted in a unidimensional vector aligned with the spectrogram using the method of Kida and Kawahara (2005) which uses GMMs trained with zero-crossing rate, amplitude, and the spectrum as input parameters. A pitch (F_0) contour is also extracted from the source by the method proposed by Kawahara et al. (2005), which uses a Viterbi-like potential decoding of F_0 traces described by cepstral and temporal features. That work showed an error rate of less than 0.14% in estimating F_0 contours as compared with simultaneously-recorded electroglottograph data. These contours are not in general modified by the methods proposed below, since Kain et al. (2007) showed that using original F_0 results in the highest intelligibility among alternative systems. Over a few segments, however, these contours can sometimes be decimated in time during the modification proposed in section 3.3 and in some cases removed entirely (along with all other acoustics) in the modification proposed in section 3.2.

3.1 High-pass filter on unvoiced consonants

The first acoustic modification is based on the observation that unvoiced consonants are improperly voiced in up to 18.7% of plosives (e.g. */d/* for */t/*)

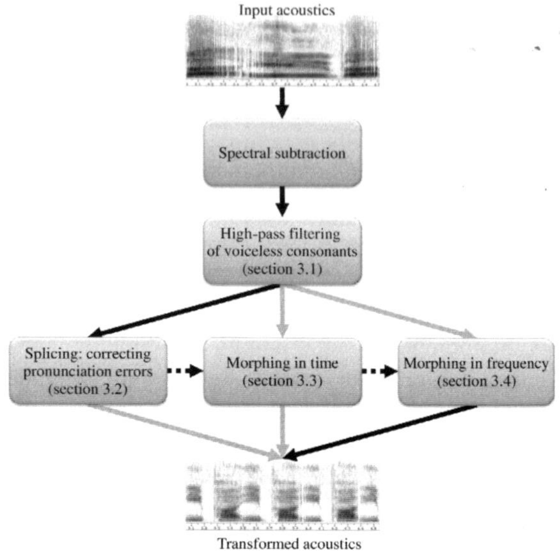

Figure 2: Outline of the TORGOMorph system. The black path indicates the cascade to be used in practice. Solid arrows indicate paths taken during evaluation.

and up to 8.5% of fricatives (e.g. */v/* for */f/*) in dysarthric speech in the TORGO database. Voiced consonants are typically differentiated from their unvoiced counterparts by the presence of the *voice bar*, which is a concentration of energy below 150 Hz indicative of vocal fold vibration that often persists throughout the consonant or during the closure before a plosive (Stevens, 1998). Empirical analysis of TORGO data suggests that for at least two male dysarthric speakers this voice bar extends considerably higher, up to 250 Hz.

In order to correct these mispronunciations, the voice bar is filtered out of all acoustic sub-sequences annotated as unvoiced consonants. For this task we use a high-pass Butterworth filter, which is "maximally flat" in the passband[2] and monotonic in magnitude in the frequency domain (Butterworth, 1930). Here, this filter is computed on a normalized frequency range respecting the Nyquist frequency, so that if a waveform's sampling rate is 16 kHz, the normalized cutoff frequency for this component is $f^*_{Norm} = 250/(1.6 \times 10^4/2) = 3.125 \times 10^{-2}$. The Butterworth filter is an all-pole transfer function between signals, and we use the 10th-order low-pass

[2]The passband is the frequency range in which the component magnitudes in the original signal should not be changed.

Butterworth filter whose magnitude response is

$$|\mathcal{B}(z;10)|^2 = |H(z;10)|^2 = \frac{1}{1+\left(jz/jz^*_{Norm}\right)^{2\times 10}} \tag{3}$$

where z is the complex frequency in polar coordinates and z^*_{Norm} is the cutoff frequency in that domain (Hayes, 1999). This allows the transfer function

$$\mathcal{B}(z;10) = H(z;10) = \frac{1}{1+z^{10}+\sum_{i=1}^{10} c_i z^{10-i}} \tag{4}$$

whose poles occur at known symmetric intervals around the unit complex-domain circle (Butterworth, 1930). These poles are then transformed by the Matlab function `zp2ss`, which produces the state-space coefficients α_i and β_i that describe the output signal resulting from applying the low-pass Butterworth filter to the discrete signal $x[n]$. These coefficients are further converted by

$$\begin{aligned} \vec{a} &= z^*_{Norm}\vec{\alpha}^{-1} \\ \vec{b} &= -z^*_{Norm}\left(\vec{\alpha}^{-1}\vec{\beta}\right) \end{aligned} \tag{5}$$

giving the high-pass Butterworth filter with the same cutoff frequency of z^*_{Norm}. This continuous system is converted to the discrete equivalent through the impulse-invariant discretization method and is implemented by the difference equation

$$y[n] = \sum_{k=1}^{10} a_k y[n-k] + \sum_{k=0}^{10} b_k x[n-k]. \tag{6}$$

As previously mentioned, this equation is applied to each acoustic sub-sequence annotated as unvoiced consonants, thereby smoothly removing the energy below 250 Hz.

3.2 Splicing: correcting dropped and inserted phoneme errors

The Levenshtein algorithm finds a best possible alignment of the phoneme sequence in actually uttered speech and the expected phoneme sequence, given the known word sequence. Isolating phoneme insertions and deletions are therefore a simple matter of iteratively adjusting the source speech according to that alignment. There are two cases where action is required:

insertion error In this case a phoneme is present where it ought not be. In the TORGO database, these insertion errors tend to be repetitions of phonemes occurring in the first syllable of a word, according to the International Speech Lexicon Dictionary (Hasegawa-Johnson and Fleck, 2007). When an insertion error is identified the entire associated segment of the signal is simply removed. In the case that the associated segment is not surrounded by silence, adjacent phonemes can be merged together with time-domain pitch-synchronous overlap-add (Moulines and Charpentier, 1990).

deletion error The vast majority of accidentally deleted phonemes in the TORGO database are fricatives, affricates, and plosives. Often, these involve not properly pluralizing nouns (e.g., *book* instead of *books*). Given their high preponderance of error, these phonemes are the only ones we insert into the dysarthric source speech. Specifically, when the deletion of a phoneme is recognized with the Levenshtein algorithm, we simply extract the associated segment from the aligned synthesized speech and insert it into the appropriate spot in the dysarthric speech. For all unvoiced fricatives, affricates, and plosives no further action is required. When these phonemes are voiced, however, we first extract and remove the F_0 curve from the synthetic speech, linearly interpolate the F_0 curve from adjacent phonemes in the source dysarthric speech, and resynthesize with the synthetic spectrum and interpolated F_0. If interpolation is not possible (e.g., the synthetic voiced phoneme is to be inserted beside an unvoiced phoneme), we simply generate a flat F_0 equal to the nearest natural F_0 curve.

3.3 Morphing in time

Figure 3 exemplifies that vowels uttered by dysarthric speakers are significantly slower than those uttered by typical speakers. In fact, sonorants can be twice as long in dysarthric speech, on average (Rudzicz, Namasivayam, and Wolff, 2011). In this modification, phoneme sequences identified as sonorant are simply contracted in time in order to be equal in extent to the greater of half their original

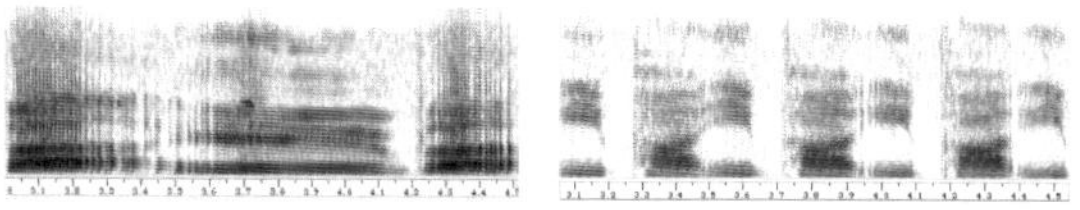

(a) (b)

Figure 3: Repetitions of */iy p ah/* over 1.5s by (a) a male speaker with athetoid CP, and (b) a female control in the TORGO database. Dysarthric speech is notably slower and more strained than regular speech.

length or the equivalent synthetic phoneme's length. In all cases this involved shortening the dysarthric source sonorant.

Since we wish to contract the length of a signal segment here without affecting its pitch or frequency characteristics, we use a phase vocoder based on digital short-time Fourier analysis (Portnoff, 1976). Here, Hamming-windowed segments of the source phoneme are analyzed with a z-transform giving both frequency and phase estimates for up to 2048 frequency bands. During pitch-preserving time-scaled warping, we specify the magnitude spectrum directly from the input magnitude spectrum with phase values chosen to ensure continuity (Sethares, 2007). Specifically, for the frequency band at frequency F and frames j and $k > j$ in the modified spectrogram, the phase θ is predicted by

$$\theta_k^{(F)} = \theta_j^{(F)} + 2\pi F(j-k). \quad (7)$$

In our case the discrete warping of the spectrogram involves simple decimation by a constant factor. The spectrogram is then converted into a time-domain signal modified in tempo but not in pitch relative to the original phoneme segment. This conversion is accomplished simply through the inverse Fourier transform.

3.4 Morphing in frequency

Formant trajectories inform the listener as to the identities of vowels, but the vowel space of dysarthric speakers tends to be constrained (Kain et al., 2007). In order to improve a listener's ability to differentiate between the vowels, this modification component identifies formant trajectories in the acoustics and modifies these according to the known vowel identity of a segment. Here, formants are identified with a 14th-order linear-predictive coder with continuity constraints on the identified resonances between adjacent frames (Snell and Milinazzo, 1993; O'Shaughnessy, 2008). Bandwidths are determined by the negative natural logarithm of the pole magnitude, as implemented in the STRAIGHT analysis system (Banno et al., 2007; Kawahara, 2006).

For each identified vowel in the dysarthric speech[3], formant candidates are identified at each frame in time up to 5 kHz. Only those time frames having at least 3 such candidates within 250 Hz of expected values are considered. The expected values of formants are derived from analyses performed by Allen et al. (1987). Given these subsets of candidate time frames in the vowel, the one having the highest spectral energy within the middle 50% of the length of the vowel is established as the *anchor position*, and the three formant candidates within the expected ranges are established as the *anchor frequencies* for formants F_1 to F_3. If more than one formant candidate falls within expected ranges, the one with the lowest bandwidth becomes the anchor frequency.

Given identified anchor points and target sonorant-specific frequencies and bandwidths, there are several methods to modify the spectrum. The most common may be to learn a statistical conversion function based on Gaussian mixture mapping, as described earlier, typically preceded by alignment of sequences using dynamic time warping (Stylianou, 2008). Here, we use the STRAIGHT morphing implemented by Kawahara and Matsui (2003), among others. The transformation of a frame of speech x_A for speaker A is performed with a multivariate frequency-transformation function $T_{A\beta}$ given known targets β using

$$\begin{aligned} T_{A\beta}(x_A) &= \int_0^{x_A} \exp\left(\log\left(\frac{\delta T_{A\beta}(\lambda)}{\delta\lambda}\right)\right)\delta\lambda \\ &= \int_0^{x_A} \exp\left((1-r)\log\left(\frac{\delta T_{AA}(\lambda)}{\delta\lambda}\right)\right. \\ &\quad \left. + r\log\left(\frac{\delta T_{A\beta}(\lambda)}{\delta\lambda}\right)\right)\delta\lambda \\ &= \int_0^{x_A}\left(\frac{\delta T_{A\beta}(\lambda)}{\delta\lambda}\right)^r \delta\lambda, \end{aligned} \quad (8)$$

[3] Accidentally inserted vowels are also included here, unless previously removed by the splicing technique in section 3.2.

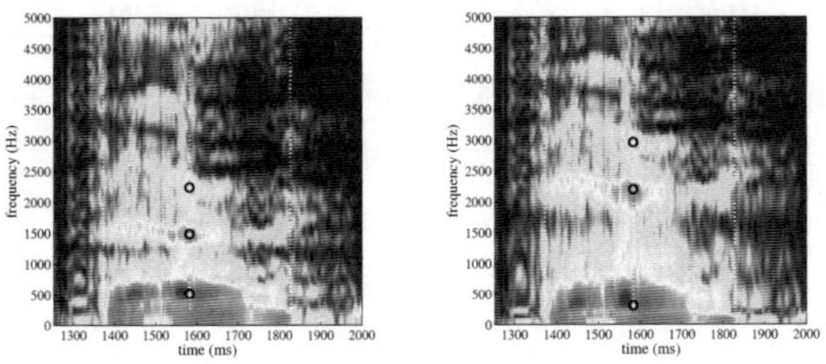

(a) (b)

Figure 4: Spectrograms for (a) the dysarthric original and (b) the frequency-modified renditions of the word *fear*. Circles represent indicative formant locations.

where λ is the frame-based time dimension and where $0 \leq r \leq 1$ is an interpolative rate at which to perform morphing (i.e., $r = 1$ implies complete conversion of the parameters of speaker A to parameter set β and $r = 0$ implies no conversion.) (Kawahara et al., 2009). An example of the results of this morphing technique is shown in figure 4 in which the three identified formants are shifted to their expected frequencies.

This method tracks formants and warps the frequency space automatically, whereas Kain et al. (2007) perform these functions manually. A future implementation may use Kalman filters to reduce the noise inherent in trajectory tracking. Such an approach has shown significant improvements in formant tracking, especially for F_1 (Yan et al., 2007).

4 Intelligibility experiments with TORGOMorph

The intelligibility of both purely synthetic and modified speech signals can be measured objectively by simply having a set of participants transcribe what they hear from a selection of word, phrase, or sentence prompts (Spiegel et al., 1990), although no single standard has emerged as pre-eminent (Schroeter, 2008). Hustad (2006) suggested that orthographic transcriptions provide a more accurate predictor of intelligibility among dysarthric speakers than the more subjective estimates used in clinical settings, e.g., Enderby (1983). That study had 80 listeners who transcribed audio (which is an atypically large group for this task) and showed that intelligibility increased from 61.9% given only acoustic stimuli to 66.75% given audiovisual stimuli on the transcription task in normal speech. In the current work, we modify only the acoustics of dysarthric speech; however future work might consider how to prompt listeners in a more multimodal context.

In order to gauge the intelligibility of our modifications, we designed a simple experiment in which human listeners attempt to identify words in sentence-level utterances under a number of acoustic scenarios. Sentences are either uttered by a speaker with dysarthria, modified from their original source acoustics, or manufactured by a text-to-speech synthesizer. Each participant is seated at a personal computer with a simple graphical user interface with a button which plays or replays the audio (up to 5 times), a text box in which to write responses, and a second button to submit those responses. Audio is played over a pair of headphones. The participants are told to only transcribe the words with which they are reasonably confident and to ignore those that they cannot discern. They are also informed that the sentences are grammatically correct but not necessarily semantically coherent, and that there is no profanity. Each participant listens to 20 sentences selected at random with the constraints that at least two utterances are taken from each category of audio, described below, and that at least five utterances are also provided to another listener, in order to evaluate inter-annotator agreement. Participants are self-selected to have no extensive prior experience in speaking with individuals with dysarthria, in order to reflect the general population. Although dysarthric utterances are likely to be contextualized within meaningful conversations in real-world situations, such pragmatic aspects of discourse are not considered here in order to concentrate on acoustic effects alone. No cues as to the topic or semantic context of the sentences are given, as there is no evidence that such aids to comprehension affect intelligibility (Hustad and Beukelman, 2002). In this study we use sentence-level utterances uttered by male speakers from the TORGO database.

Baseline performance is measured on the original dysarthric speech. Two other systems are used for reference:

Synthetic Word sequences are produced by the Cepstral commercial text-to-speech system using the U.S. English voice 'David'. This system is based on Festival in almost every respect, including its use of linguistic pre-processing (e.g., part-of-speech tagging) and rule-based generation (Taylor, Black, and Caley, 1998). This approach has the advantage that every aspect of the synthesized speech (e.g., the word sequence) can be controlled although here, as in practice, synthesized speech will not mimic the user's own acoustic patterns, and will often sound more 'mechanical' due to artificial prosody (Black and Lenzo, 2007).

GMM This system uses the Gaussian mixture mapping type of modification suggested by Toda, Black, and Tokuda (2005) and Kain et al. (2007). Here, we use the FestVox implementation of this algorithm, which includes pitch extraction, some phonological knowledge (Toth and Black, 2005), and a method for resynthesis. Parameters for this model are trained by the FestVox system using a standard expectation-maximization approach with 24th-order cepstral coefficients and 4 Gaussian components. The training set consists of all vowels uttered by a male speaker in the TORGO database and their synthetic realizations produced by the method above.

Performance is evaluated on the three other acoustic transformations, namely those described in sections 3.2, 3.3, and 3.4 above. Tables 1 and 2 respectively show the percentage of words and phonemes correctly identified by each listener relative to the expected word sequence under each acoustic condition. In each case, annotator transcriptions were aligned with the 'true' or expected sequences using the Levenshtein algorithm described in section 3. Plural forms of singular words, for example, are considered incorrect in word alignment although one obvious spelling mistake (i.e., 'skilfully') is corrected before evaluation. Words are split into component phonemes according to the CMU dictionary, with words having multiple pronunciations given the first decomposition therein.

In these experiments there is not enough data from which to make definitive claims of statistical significance, but it is clear that the purely synthetic speech has a far greater intelligibility than other approaches, more than doubling the average accuracy of the

	Orig.	GMM	Synth.	Splice	Time	Freq.
L01	22.1	15.6	82.0	40.2	34.7	35.2
L02	27.8	12.2	75.5	44.9	39.4	33.8
L03	38.3	14.8	76.3	37.5	12.9	21.4
L04	24.7	10.8	72.1	32.6	22.2	18.4
Avg.	28.2	13.6	76.5	38.8	27.3	27.2

Table 1: Percentage of *words* correctly identified by each listener (L0*) relative to the expected sequence. Sections 3.2, 3.3, and 3.4 discuss the 'Splice', 'Time', and 'Freq.' techniques, respectively.

	Orig.	GMM	Synth.	Splice	Time	Freq.
L01	52.0	43.1	98.2	64.7	47.8	55.1
L02	57.8	38.2	92.9	68.9	50.6	53.3
L03	50.1	41.4	96.8	57.1	30.7	46.7
L04	51.6	33.8	88.7	51.9	43.2	45.0
Avg.	52.9	39.1	94.2	60.7	43.1	50.0

Table 2: Percentage of *phonemes* correctly identified by each listener relative to the expected sequence. Sections 3.2, 3.3, and 3.4 discuss the 'Splice', 'Time', and 'Freq.' techniques, respectively.

TORGOMorph modifications. The GMM transformation method proposed by Kain et al. (2007) gave poor performance, although our experiments are distinguished from theirs in that our formant traces are detected automatically, rather than by hand. The relative success of the synthetic approach is not an argument against the type of modifications proposed here and by Kain et al. (2007), since our aim is to avoid the use of impersonal and invariant utterances. Indeed, future study in this area should incorporate subjective measures of 'naturalness'. Further uses of acoustic modifications not attainable by text-to-speech synthesis are discussed in section 5.

In all cases, the splicing technique of removing accidentally inserted phonemes and inserting missing ones gives the highest intelligibility relative to all acoustic transformation methods. Although more study is required, this result emphasizes the importance of lexically correct phoneme sequences. In the word-recognition experiment, there are an average of 5.2 substitution errors per sentence in the unmodified dysarthric speech against 2.75 in the synthetic speech. There are also 2.6 substitution errors on average per sentence for the speech modified in frequency, but 3.1 deletion errors, on average, against 0.24 in synthetic speech. No correlation is found between the 'loudness' of the speech (determined by the overall energy in the sonorants) and intelligibility results, although this might change with the acquisition of more data. Neel (2009), for instance, found that loud or amplified speech from individuals with Parkinson's disease was more intelligible to human listeners than quieter speech.

Our results are comparable in many respects to the experiments of Kain et al. (2007), although they only looked at simple consonant-vowel-consonant stimuli. Their results showed an average of 92% correct synthetic vowel recognition (compared with 94.2% phoneme recognition in table 2) and 48% correct dysarthric vowel recognition (compared with 52.9% in table 2). Our results, however, show that modified timing and modified frequencies do not actually benefit intelligibility in either the word or phoneme cases. This disparity may in part be due to the fact that our stimuli are much more complex (quicker sentences do not necessarily improve intelligibility).

5 Discussion

This work represents an inaugural step towards speech modification systems for human-human and human-computer interaction. Tolba and Torgoman (2009) claimed that significant improvements in automatic recognition of dysarthric speech are attainable by modifying formants F_1 and F_2 to be more similar to expected values. In that study, formants were identified using standard linear predictive coding techniques, although no information was provided as to how these formants were modified nor how their targets were determined. However, they claimed that modified dysarthric speech resulted in 'recognition rates' (by which they presumably meant word-accuracy) of 71.4% in the HTK speech recognition system, as compared with 28% on the unmodified dysarthric speech from 7 individuals. The results in section 4 show that human listeners are more likely to correctly identify utterances in which phoneme insertion and deletion errors are corrected than those in which formant frequencies are adjusted. Therefore, one might hypothesize that such pre-processing might provide even greater gains than those reported by Tolba and Torgoman (2009). Ongoing work ought to confirm or deny this hypothesis.

A prototypical client-based application based on our research for unrestricted speech transformation of novel sentences is currently in development. Such work will involve improving factors such as accuracy and accessibility for individuals whose neuromotor disabilities limit the use of modern speech recognition, and for whom alternative interaction modalities are insufficient. This application is being developed under the assumption that it will be used in a mobile device embeddable within a wheelchair. If word-prediction is to be incorporated, the predicted continuations of uttered sentence fragments can be synthesized without requiring acoustic input.

In practice, the modifications presented here will have to be based on automatically-generated annotations of the source audio. This is especially important to the 'splicing' module in which word-identification is crucial. There are a number of techniques that can be exercised in this area. Czyzewski, Kaczmarek, and Kostek (2003) apply both a variety of neural networks and rough sets to the task of classifying segments of speech according to the presence of stop-gaps, vowel prolongations, and incorrect syllable repetitions. In each case, input includes source waveforms and detected formant frequencies. They found that stop-gaps and vowel prolongations could be detected with up to 97.2% accuracy and that vowel repetitions could be detected with up to 90% accuracy using the rough set method. Accuracy was similar although slightly lower using traditional neural networks (Czyzewski, Kaczmarek, and Kostek, 2003). These results appear generally invariant even under frequency modifications to the source speech. Arbisi-Kelm (2010), for example, suggest that disfluent repetitions can be identified reliably through the use of pitch, duration, and pause detection (with precision up to 93% (Nakatani, 1993)). If more traditional models of speech recognition are to be deployed to identify vowels, the probabilities that they generate across hypothesized words might be used to weight the manner in which acoustic transformations are made.

The use of one's own voice to communicate is a desirable goal, and continuations of this research are therefore focused on the practical aspects of this research towards usable and portable systems.

References

Allen, Jonathan, M. Sharon Hunnicutt, Dennis H. Klatt, Robert C. Armstrong, and David B. Pisoni. 1987. *From text to speech: the MITalk system*. Cambridge University Press, New York, NY, USA.

Arbisi-Kelm, Timothy. 2010. Intonation structure and disfluency detection in stuttering. *Laboratory Phonology 10*, 4:405–432.

Banno, Hideki, Hiroaki Hata, Masanori Morise, Toru Takahashi, Toshio Irino, and Hideki Kawahara. 2007. Implementation of realtime STRAIGHT speech manipulation system: Report on its first implementation. *Acoustical Science and Technology*, 28(3):140–146.

Black, Alan W. and Kevin A. Lenzo. 2004. Multilingual text-to-speech synthesis. In *2004 IEEE International Conference on Acoustics, Speech, and Signal Processing (ICASSP 2004)*.

Black, Alan W. and Kevin A. Lenzo. 2007. Building synthetic voices. `http://www.festvox.org/festvox/bsv.ps.gz`.

Butterworth, Stephen. 1930. On the theory of filter amplifiers. *Experimental Wireless and the Wireless Engineer*, 7:536–541.

Czyzewski, Andrzej, Andrzej Kaczmarek, and Bozena Kostek. 2003. Intelligent processing of stuttered speech. *Journal of Intelligent Information Systems*, 21(2):143–171.

Enderby, Pamela M. 1983. *Frenchay Dysarthria Assessment*. College Hill Press.

Green, Phil, James Carmichael, Athanassios Hatzis, Pam Enderby, Mark Hawley, and Mark Parker. 2003. Automatic speech recognition with sparse training data for dysarthric speakers. In *Proceedings of Eurospeech 2003*, pages 1189–1192, Geneva.

Hasegawa-Johnson, Mark and Margaret Fleck. 2007. International Speech Lexicon Project. `http://www.isle.illinois.edu/dict/`.

Havstam, Christina, Margret Buchholz, and Lena Hartelius. 2003. Speech recognition and dysarthria: a single subject study of two individuals with profound impairment of speech and motor control. *Logopedics Phoniatrics Vocology*, 28:81–90(10), August.

Hawley, Mark S., Pam Enderby, Phil Green, Stuart Cunningham, Simon Brownsell, James Carmichael, Mark Parker, Athanassios Hatzis, Peter O'Neill, and Rebecca Palmer. 2007. A speech-controlled environmental control system for people with severe dysarthria. *Medical Engineering & Physics*, 29(5):586–593, June.

Hayes, Monson H. 1999. *Digital Signal Processing*. Schaum's Outlines. McGraw Hill.

Hess, Wolfgang J. 2008. Pitch and voicing determination of speech with an extension toward music signal. In Jacob Benesty, M. Mohan Sondhi, and Yiteng Huang, editors, *Speech Processing*. Springer.

Hosom, John-Paul, Alexander B. Kain, Taniya Mishra, Jan P. H. van Santen, Melanie Fried-Oken, and Janice Staehely. 2003. Intelligibility of modifications to dysarthric speech. In *Proceedings of the IEEE International Conference on Acoustics, Speech, and Signal Processing (ICASSP '03)*, volume 1, pages 924–927, April.

Hustad, Katherine C. 2006. Estimating the intelligibility of speakers with dysarthria. *Folia Phoniatrica et Logopaedica*, 58(3):217–228.

Hustad, Katherine C. and David R. Beukelman. 2002. Listener comprehension of severely dysarthric speech: Effects of linguistic cues and stimulus cohesion. *Journal of Speech, Language, and Hearing Research*, 45:545–558, June.

Hux, Karen, Joan Rankin-Erickson, Nancy Manasse, and Elizabeth Lauritzen. 2000. Accuracy of three speech recognition systems: Case study of dysarthric speech. *Augmentative and Alternative Communication (AAC)*, 16(3):186 –196, January.

Kain, Alexander B., John-Paul Hosom, Xiaochuan Niu, Jan P.H. van Santen, Melanie Fried-Oken, and Janice Staehely. 2007. Improving the intelligibility of dysarthric speech. *Speech Communication*, 49(9):743–759, September.

Kawahara, H. and H. Matsui. 2003. Auditory morphing based on an elastic perceptual distance metric in an interference-free time-frequency representation. In *Acoustics, Speech, and Signal Processing, 2003. Proceedings. (ICASSP '03). 2003 IEEE International Conference on*, volume 1, pages I–256 – I–259 vol.1, April.

Kawahara, H., R. Nisimura, T. Irino, M. Morise, T. Takahashi, and H. Banno. 2009. Temporally variable multi-aspect auditory morphing enabling extrapolation without objective and perceptual breakdown. In *Proceedings of IEEE International Conference on Acoustics, Speech and Signal Processing (ICASSP 2009)*, pages 3905–3908, April.

Kawahara, Hideki. 2006. STRAIGHT, exploitation of the other aspect of VOCODER: Perceptually isomorphic decomposition of speech sounds. *Acoustical Science and Technology*, 27(6):349–353.

Kawahara, Hideki, Alain de Cheveigné, Hideki Banno, Toru Takahashi, and Toshio Irino. 2005. Nearly Defect-Free F0 Trajectory Extraction for Expressive Speech Modifications Based on STRAIGHT. In *Proceedings of INTERSPEECH 2005*, pages 537–540, September.

Kent, Ray D. and Kristin Rosen. 2004. Motor control perspectives on motor speech disorders. In Ben

Maassen, Raymond Kent, Herman Peters, Pascal Van Lieshout, and Wouter Hulstijn, editors, *Speech Motor Control in Normal and Disordered Speech*. Oxford University Press, Oxford, chapter 12, pages 285–311.

Kida, Yusuke and Tatsuya Kawahara. 2005. Voice activity detection based on optimally weighted combination of multiple features. In *Proceedings of INTERSPEECH-2005*, pages 2621–2624.

Levenshtein, Vladimir I. 1966. Binary codes capable of correcting deletions, insertions, and reversals. *Cybernetics and Control Theory*, 10(8):707–710.

Messina, James J. and Constance M. Messina. 2007. Description of AAC devices. `http://www.coping.org/specialneeds/assistech/aacdev.htm`, April.

Moulines, Eric and Francis Charpentier. 1990. Pitch-synchronous waveform processing techniques for text-to-speech synthesis using diphones. *Speech Communication*, 9:453–467, December.

Nakatani, Christine. 1993. A speech-first model for repair detection and correction. In *Proceedings of the 31st Annual Meeting of the Association for Computational Linguistics*, pages 46–53.

Neel, Amy T. 2009. Effects of loud and amplified speech on sentence and word intelligibility in parkinson disease. *Journal of Speech, Language, and Hearing Research*, 52:1021–1033, August.

O'Shaughnessy, Douglas. 2000. *Speech Communications – Human and Machine*. IEEE Press, New York, NY, USA.

O'Shaughnessy, Douglas. 2008. Formant estimation and tracking. In Jacob Benesty, M. Mohan Sondhi, and Yiteng Huang, editors, *Speech Processing*. Springer.

Patel, Rupal. 1998. Control of prosodic parameters by an individual with severe dysarthria. Technical report, University of Toronto, December.

Portnoff, Michael R. 1976. Implementation of the digital phase vocoder using the fast Fourier transform. *IEEE Transactions on Acoustics, Speech and Signal Processing*, 24(3):243–248.

Press, William H., Saul A. Teukolsky, William T. Vetterling, and Brian P. Flannery. 1992. *Numerical Recipes in C: the art of scientific computing*. Cambridge University Press, second edition.

Rosen, Kristin and Sasha Yampolsky. 2000. Automatic speech recognition and a review of its functioning with dysarthric speech. *Augmentative & Alternative Communication*, 16(1):48–60, Jan.

Rudzicz, Frank. 2011. *Production knowledge in the recognition of dysarthric speech*. Ph.D. thesis, University of Toronto, Department of Computer Science.

Rudzicz, Frank, Aravind Kumar Namasivayam, and Talya Wolff. 2011. The TORGO database of acoustic and articulatory speech from speakers with dysarthria. *Language Resources and Evaluation*, (in press).

Schroeter, Juergen. 2008. Basic principles of speech synthesis. In Jacob Benesty, M. Mohan Sondhi, and Yiteng Huang, editors, *Speech Processing*. Springer.

Sethares, William Arthur. 2007. *Rhythm and Transforms*. Springer.

Snell, Roy C. and Fausto Milinazzo. 1993. Formant Location from LPC Analysis Data. *IEEE Transactions on Speech and Audio Processing*, 1(2), April.

Spiegel, Murray F., Mary Jo Altom, Marian J. Macchi, and Karen L. Wallace. 1990. Comprehensive assessment of the telephone intelligibility of synthesized and natural speech. *Speech Communication*, 9(4):279 – 291.

Stevens, Kenneth N. 1998. *Acoustic Phonetics*. MIT Press, Cambridge, Massachussetts.

Stylianou, Yannis. 2008. Voice transformation. In Jacob Benesty, M. Mohan Sondhi, and Yiteng Huang, editors, *Speech Processing*. Springer.

Taylor, Paul, Alan W. Black, and Richard Caley. 1998. The architecture of the Festival speech synthesis system. In *Proceedings of the 3rd ESCA Workshop on Speech Synthesis*, pages 147–151, Jenolan Caves, Australia.

Toda, Tomoki, Alan W. Black, and Keiichi Tokuda. 2005. Spectral conversion based on maximum likelihood estimation considering global variance of converted parameter. In *Proceedings of the 2005 International Conference on Acoustics, Speech, and Signal Processing (ICASSP 2005)*, Philadelphia, Pennsylvania.

Tolba, Hesham and Ahmed S. El Torgoman. 2009. Towards the improvement of automatic recognition of dysarthric speech. In *International Conference on Computer Science and Information Technology*, pages 277–281, Los Alamitos, CA, USA. IEEE Computer Society.

Toth, Arthur R. and Alan W. Black. 2005. Cross-speaker articulatory position data for phonetic feature prediction. In *Proceedings of Interspeech 2005*, Lisbon, Portugal.

Yan, Qin, Saeed Vaseghi, Esfandiar Zavarehei, Ben Milner, Jonathan Darch, Paul White, and Ioannis Andrianakis. 2007. Formant tracking linear prediction model usng HMMs and Kalman filters for noisy speech processing. *Computer Speech and Language*, 21:543–561.

Towards technology-assisted co-construction with communication partners

Brian Roark[†], **Andrew Fowler**[†], **Richard Sproat**[†], **Christopher Gibbons**[°], **Melanie Fried-Oken**[°]
[†]Center for Spoken Language Understanding [°]Child Development & Rehabilitation Center
Oregon Health & Science University
{roark,fowlera,sproatr}@cslu.ogi.edu {gibbons,mfo}@ohsu.edu

Abstract

In this paper, we examine the idea of technology-assisted co-construction, where the communication partner of an AAC user can make guesses about the intended messages, which are included in the user's word completion/prediction interface. We run some human trials to simulate this new interface concept, with subjects predicting words as the user's intended message is being generated in real time with specified typing speeds. Results indicate that people can provide substantial keystroke savings by providing word completion or prediction, but that the savings are not as high as n-gram language models. Interestingly, the language model and human predictions are complementary in certain key ways – humans doing a better job in some circumstances on contextually salient nouns. We discuss implications of the enhanced co-construction interface for real-time message generation in AAC direct selection devices.

1 Introduction

Individuals who cannot use standard keyboards for text entry because of physical disabilities have a number of alternative text entry methods that permit typing. Referred to as keyboard emulation within augmentative and alternative communication (AAC), there are many different access options for the user, ranging from direct selection of letters with any anatomical pointer (e.g., head, eyes) to use of a binary switch – triggered by button-press, eye-blink or even through event related potentials (ERP) such as the P300 detected in EEG signals. These options allow the individual to indirectly select a symbol based on some process for scanning through alternatives (Lesher et al., 1998). Typing speed is a challenge, yet is critically important for usability, and as a result there is a significant line of research into the utility of statistical language models for improving typing speed (McCoy et al., 2007; Koester and Levine, 1996; Koester and Levine, 1997; Koester and Levine, 1998). Methods of word, symbol, phrase and message prediction via statistical language models are widespread in both direct selection and scanning devices (Darragh et al., 1990; Li and Hirst, 2005; Trost et al., 2005; Trnka et al., 2006; Trnka et al., 2007; Wandmacher and Antoine, 2007; Todman et al., 2008). To the extent that the predictions are accurate, the number of keystrokes required to type a message can be dramatically reduced, greatly speeding typing.

AAC devices for spontaneous and novel text generation are intended to empower the user of the system, to place them in control of their own communication, and reduce their reliance on others for message formulation. As a result, *all* such devices (much like standard personal computers) are built for a single user, with a single keyboard and/or alternative input interface, which is driven by the user of the system. The unilateral nature of these high technology solutions to AAC stands in contrast to common low technology solutions, which rely on collaboration between the individual formulating the message and their communication partner. Many adults with acquired neurological conditions rely on communication partners for co-construction of messages (Beukelman et al., 2007).

One key reason why low-tech co-construction may be preferred to high-tech stand-alone AAC system solutions is the resulting speed of communication. Whereas spoken language reaches more than one hundred words per minute and an average speed typist using standard touch typing will achieve approximately 35 words per minute, a user of an AAC device will typically input text in the 3-10 words per minute range. With a communication partner guess-

Proceedings of the 2nd Workshop on Speech and Language Processing for Assistive Technologies, pages 22–31,
Edinburgh, Scotland, UK, July 30, 2011. ©2011 Association for Computational Linguistics

ing the intended message and requesting confirmation, the communication rate can speed up dramatically. For face-to-face communication – a modality that is currently very poorly served by AAC devices – such a speedup is greatly preferred, despite any potential authorship questions.

Consider the following low-tech scenario. Sandy is locked-in, with just a single eye-blink serving to provide binary yes/no feedback. Sandy's communication partner, Kim, initiates communication by verbally stepping through an imagined row/column grid, first by number (to identify the row); then by letter. In such a way, Sandy can indicate the first desired symbol. Communication can continue in this way until Kim has a good idea of the word that Sandy intends and proposes the word. If Sandy says yes, the word has been completed, much as automatic word completion may occur within an AAC device. But Kim doesn't necessarily stop with word completion; subsequent word prediction, phrase prediction, in fact whole utterance prediction can follow, driven by Kim's intuitions derived from knowledge of Sandy, true sensitivity to context, topic, social protocol, etc. It is no wonder that such methods are often chosen over high-tech alternatives.

In this paper, we present some preliminary ideas and experiments on an approach to providing technology support to this sort of co-construction during typing. The core idea is to provide an enhanced interface to the communication partner (Kim in the example above), which does not allow them to *directly* contribute to the message construction, but rather to *indirectly* contribute, by predicting what they believe the individual will type next. Because most text generation AAC devices typically already rely upon symbol, word and phrase prediction from statistical language models to speed text input, the predictions of the conversation partner could be used to influence (or adapt) the language model. Such adaptation could be as simple as assigning high probability to words or symbols explicitly predicted by the communication partner, or as complex as deriving the topic or context from the partner's predictions and using that context to improve the model.

Statistical language models in AAC devices can capture regularities in language, e.g., frequent word collocations or phrases and names commonly used by an individual. People, however, have access to much more information than computational models, including rich knowledge of language, any relevant contextual factors that may skew prediction, familiarity with the AAC user, and extensive world knowledge – none of which can be easily included in the kinds of simple statistical models that constitute the current state of the art. People are typically quite good at predicting what might come next in a sentence, particularly if it is part of a larger discourse or dialogue. Indeed, some of the earliest work looking at statistical models of language established the entropy of English by asking subjects to play a simple language guessing game (Shannon, 1950). The so-called "Shannon game" starts with the subject guessing the first letter of the text. Once they have guessed correctly, it is uncovered, and the subject guesses the next letter, and so on. A similar game could be played with words instead of letters. The number of guesses required is a measure of entropy in the language. People are understandably very good at this game, often correctly predicting symbols on the first try for very long stretches of text. No purely computational model can hope to match the contextual sensitivity, partner familiarity, or world knowledge that a human being brings to such a task.

A co-construction scenario differs from a Shannon game in terms of the time constraints under which it operates. The communication partner in such a scenario must offer completions and predictions to the user in a way that actually speeds communication relative to independent text generation. Given an arbitrary amount of time, it is clear that people have greater information at their disposal for predicting subsequent content; what happens under time constraints is less clear. Indeed, in this paper we demonstrate that the time constraints put human subjects at a strong disadvantage relative to language models in the scenarios we simulated. While it is far from clear that this disadvantage will also apply in scenarios closer to the motivating example given above, it is certainly the case that providing useful input is a challenging task.

The principal benefit of technology-assisted co-construction with communication partners is making use of the partner's knowledge of language and context, as well as their familiarity with the AAC user and the world, to yield better predictions of likely continuations than are currently made by the kinds of relatively uninformed (albeit state of the art) computational language models. A secondary benefit is that such an approach engages the conversation partner in a high utility collaboration during the AAC user's turn, rather than simply sitting and waiting for the reply to be produced. Lack of engagement is a serious obstacle to successful conversation in AAC (Hoag et al., 2004). The slow speed of AAC input is itself a contributing factor to AAC user dissatisfaction with face-to-face conversation, one of the most critical modes of human social interaction, and the one least served by current technology. Because of the slow turnaround, the conversation partner tends to lose focus and interest in the conversation, leading to shorter and less satisfying exchanges than those enjoyed by those using spoken language. A system which leverages communication partner predictions will more fully engage the conversation partner in the process, rather than forcing them to wait for a response with nothing to do.

Importantly, an enhanced interface such as that proposed here provides predictive input from the communication partner, but not direct compositional input. The responsibility of selecting symbols and words during text entry remains with the AAC user, as the sole author of the text. In the preliminary experiments presented later in the paper, we simulate a direct selection typing system with word prediction, and measure the utility of human generated word completions and predictions relative to n-gram models. In such a scenario, n-gram predictions can be replaced or augmented by human predictions. This illustrates how easily technology assisted co-construction with communication partners could potentially be integrated into a user's interface.

Despite the lack of speedup achieved versus n-gram models in the results reported below, the potential for capturing communication partner intuitions about AAC user intended utterances seems a compelling topic for future research.

2 Background and Related Work

Over the past forty years, there has been a vast array of technological solutions to aid AAC users who present with severe speech and physical impairments, from methods for generating possible responses, to techniques for selecting among responses. The simplest methods to generate language involve the use of pre-stored phrases, such as "hello", "thank you", "I love you", etc., which are available on many AAC devices. Some studies have indicated that use of such phrases improves the perception of fluid communication (McCoy et al., 2007; Hoag et al., 2008).

Prediction options vary in AAC devices, ranging from letter-by-letter prediction – see Higginbotham (1992) and Lesher et al. (1998) for some reviews – to word-based prediction. Some systems can be quite sophisticated, for example incorporating latent semantic analysis to aid in the better modeling of discourse-level information (Wandmacher and Antoine, 2007). The WebCrawler project in Jeffrey Higginbotham's lab uses topic-related wordlists mined from the Web to populate a user's AAC device with terminology that is likely to be of utility to the current topic of conversation.

Going beyond word prediction, there has been an increased interest in *utterance-based* approaches (Todman et al., 2008), which extend prediction from the character or word level to the level of whole sentences. For example, systems like FrameTalker/Contact (Higginbotham and Wilkins, 1999; Wilkins and Higginbotham, 2006) populate the AAC device with pre-stored phrases that can be organized in various ways. In a similar vein, recent work reported in Wisenburn and Higginbotham (2008; 2009) proposed a novel method that uses automatic speech recognition (ASR) on the speech of the communication partner, extracts noun phrases from the speech, and presents those noun phrases on the AAC device, with frame sentences that the AAC user can select. Thus if the communication partner says "Paris", the AAC user will be able to select from phrases like "Tell me more about Paris" or "I want to talk about Paris". This can speed up the conversation by providing topically-relevant responses. Perhaps the most elaborate system of this kind is the *How Was School Today* system (Reiter et al., 2009). This system, which is geared towards children with severe communication disabilities, uses data from sensors, the Web, and other sources as input for a natural language generation system. The system acquires information about the child's day in school: which classes he or she attended, what activities there were, information about visitors, food choices at the cafeteria, and so forth. The data are then used to generate natural language sentences, which are converted to speech via a speech synthesizer. At the end of the day, the child uses a menu to select sentences that he or she wants the system to utter, and thereby puts together a narrative that describes what he/she did. The system allows for vastly more rapid output than a system where the child constructs each sentence from scratch.

Perhaps the closest work to what we are proposing is the study of non-disabled adults in Cornish and Higginbotham (No Date), where one of the adults played the role of an AAC user, and the other a non-disabled communication partner. The participants completed a narrative, a map and a puzzle task. Of interest was the relative amount of co-construction of the other's utterances by each partner, and in particular its relation to which of the partners was the one initiating the attempt to achieve a common ground with the other speaker — the "grounded contribution owner". In all tasks both the communication partner and the AAC user co-constructed each other's contributions, but there was the greatest asymmetry between the two users in the puzzle task.

In what follows, we will first describe a preliminary experiment of word completion for a simulated AAC user, using sentences from the Enron email corpus and the New York Times. We then will present results for word completion and prediction within the context of dialogs in the Switchboard corpus. While we ultimately believe that the potential for co-construction goes far beyond simple word completion/prediction, these experiments serve as a first indication of the challenges to an enhanced technology-assisted interface for co-construction with communication partners during novel text generation.

3 Preliminary experiment

In this section, we present a preliminary experiment to evaluate the potential utility of our technology-assisted co-construction scenario. The experiment is akin to a Shannon Game (Shannon, 1950), but with a time limit for guesses imposed by the speed of typing. For the current experiment we chose 5 seconds per keystroke as the simulated typing speed: target sentences appeared one character at a time, every five seconds. The subjects' task was to provide a completion for the current word. If the correct word is provided by the subject, it is selected by the simulated AAC user as the next keystroke.

```
with^the^nat
        nation
        national
        nation's
        natural

▯
```

Figure 1: Preliminary experimental interface in terminal window, with 4 predicted completions and cursor below

For this preliminary experiment, we used a simple program running in the terminal window of a Mac laptop. Figure 1 shows a screenshot from this program in operation. The target string is displayed at the top of the terminal window, one character at a time, with the carat symbol showing white space word boundaries. Predicted word completions are made by typing with a standard qwerty keyboard; and when the enter key is pressed, the word that has been typed is aligned with the current incomplete word. If it is consistent with the prefix of the word that has been typed, it remains as a candidate for completion. When the current five second interval has passed, the set of accumulated predictions are filtered to just those which are consistent with the new letter that the user would have typed (e.g., 'i' in Figure 1). If the correct word completion for the target string is present, it is selected with the following keystroke. Otherwise the following letter will be typed (with the typical 5-second delay) and the interface proceeds as before.

Three able-bodied, adult, literate subjects were recruited for this initial experiment, and all three completed trials with both Enron email and New York Times target strings. The Enron data comes from the Enron email dataset (http://www-2.cs.cmu.edu/~enron/) and the NY Times data from the English Gigaword corpus (LDC2007T07). Both corpora were pre-processed to remove duplicate data (e.g., spam or multiple recipient emails), tabular data and other material that does not represent written sentences. Details on this normalization can be found in Roark (2009). Both corpora consist of written sentences, one heavily edited (newspaper), the other less formal (email); and both are large enough to allow for robust statistical language modeling.

Task	Ngram training sents	words	Testing sents	words	chars
NYT	1.9M	35.6M	10	201	1199
Enron	0.6M	6.1M	10	102	528

Table 1: Statistics for each task of n-gram training corpus size and test set size in terms of sentences, words and characters (baseline keystrokes)

Task	N-gram 1g	2g	3g	Subject 1	2	3
NYT	47.4	54.5	56.0	36.5	32.0	32.9
Enron	54.4	61.4	64.4	34.5	32.0	34.1

Table 2: Keystroke savings percentage for test set across models and subjects

The two corpora were split into training and testing sets, to allow for training of n-gram language models to compare word completion performance. To ensure fair comparison between n-gram and human word completion performance, no sentences in the test sets were seen in the training data. From each test corpus, we extracted sets of 10 contiguous sentences at periodic intervals, to use as test or practice sets. Each subject used a 10 sentence practice set from the NY Times to become familiar with the task and interface; then performed the word completion task on one 10 sentence set from the NY Times and one 10 sentence set from the Enron corpus. Statistics of the training and test sets are given in Table 1.

Language models were n-gram word-based models trained from the given corpora using Kneser-Ney smoothing (Kneser and Ney, 1995). We performed no pruning on the models.

We evaluate in terms of keystroke savings percentage. Let k be the baseline number of keystrokes without word completion, which is the number of characters in the sample, i.e., 1 keystroke per character. With a given word completion method, let c be the number of keystrokes required to enter the text, i.e., if the word completion method provides correct words for selection, those will reduce the number of keystrokes required[1]. Then keystroke savings percentage is $100 * (k - c)/k$, the percentage of original keystrokes that were saved with word completion. Table 2 shows the keystroke savings percentage on our two tasks for three n-gram language models (unigram, bigram and trigram) and our three subjects.

It is clear from this table that the n-gram language models are achieving much higher keystroke savings than our three human subjects. Further, our three subjects performed quite similarly, not only in comparison with each other, but across the two tasks. On the face of it, the relatively poor performance of the human predictors might be surprising, given that the original Shannon game was intended to establish a lower bound on the entropy of English. The assumption has always been that people have better language models than we can hope to learn automatically. However, in contrast to the original Shannon game, our predictions are carried out with a fairly tight time limit, i.e., predictions need to be made within a fairly short period in order to be made available to individuals for word completion. The time limit within the current scenario is one factor that seems to be putting the subjects at a disadvantage compared to automated n-gram models on this task.

There are a couple of additional reasons why n-gram models are performing better on these tasks. First, they are specific domains with quite ample training data for the language models. As the amount of training data decreases – which would certainly be the case for individual AAC users – the efficacy of the n-gram models decrease. Second, there is a 1-character advantage of n-gram models relative to human predictions in this approach. To see this point clearly, consider the position at the start of the string. N-gram models can (for practical purposes) instantaneously provide predictions for that word. But our subjects must begin typing the words that they are predicting for this position at the same time the individual is making their first keystroke. Those predictions do not become operative until after that keystroke. Hence the time overhead of prediction places a lag relative to what is possible for the n-gram model. We will return to this point in the discussion section at the end of the paper.

There are some scenarios, however, where the subjects did provide word completions prior to the trigram language model in both domains. Interestingly, a fairly large fraction of these words were faster than n-gram for more than one of the three

[1]Each word completion requires a selection keystroke, but saves the keystrokes associated with the remaining characters in the selected word.

NY Times			Enron
company	**cranbury**	creditor	**hearing**
creditors	denied	facility	suggestions
foothill	**jamesway**	**jamesways**	**stairs**
plan	proposal	sandler	**savings**
stock	stockholders	warrants	

Table 3: Words completed using subject suggestions with fewer keystrokes than trigram model. Bold indicates more than one subject was faster for that word.

subjects. Table 3 shows the list of these words for our trials. These tended to be longer, open-class words with high topical importance. In addition, they tended to be words with common word prefixes, which lead to higher confusability in the n-gram model. Of course, common prefixes also lead to higher confusability in our subjects, yet they appear to be able to leverage their superior context sensitivity to yield effective disambiguation earlier than the n-gram model in these cases.

Based on these results, we designed a second experiment, with a few key changes from this preliminary experiment, including an improved interface, the ability to predict as well as complete, and a domain that is closer to a proposed model for this co-construction task.

4 Switchboard experiment

Based on the preliminary experiment, we created a new protocol and ran seven able-bodied, adult, literate subjects. We changed the interface and domain in ways that we believed would make a difference in the ability of subjects to compete with n-gram models in keystroke savings. What remained the same was the timing of the interface: characters for target strings were displayed every five seconds. Word completions were then evaluated for consistency with what had been typed, and if the correct word was present, the word was completed and revealed, and typing continued.

Data Our primary motivating case for technology-assisted co-construction comes from face-to-face dialog, yet the corpora from which target strings were extracted in the preliminary experiments were from large corpora of text produced under very different conditions. One corpus that does represent a varied-topic, conversational dialog scenario is the Switchboard corpus (Godfrey et al., 1992), which contains transcripts of both sides of telephone conversations. The idea in using this data was to provide some number of utterances of dialog context (from the 10 previous dialog turns), and then ask subjects to provide word completions for some number of subsequent utterances.

While the Switchboard corpus does represent the kind of conversational dialog we are interested in, it is a spoken language corpus, yet we are modeling written (typed) language. The difference between written and spoken language does present something of an issue for our task. To mitigate this mismatch somewhat, we made use of the Switchboard section of the Penn Treebank (Marcus et al., 1993), which contains syntactic annotations of the Switchboard transcripts, including explicit marking of disfluencies ("EDITED" non-terminals in the treebank), interjections or parentheticals such as "I mean" or "you know". Using these syntactic annotations, we produced edited transcripts that omit much of the spoken language specific phenomena, thus providing a closer approximation to the kind of written dialogs we would like to simulate. In addition, we decased the corpus and removed all characters except the following: the 26 letters of the English alphabet, the apostrophe, the space, and the dash.

Interface Figure 2 shows the graphical user interface that was created for these trials. In the upper box, ten utterances from the context of the dialog are presented, with an indication of which speaker (A or B) took the turn. Participants are asked to first read this context and then press enter to begin the session. Below this box, the current utterance is displayed, along with which of the two participants is currently producing the utterance. As in the previous experiment, the string is displayed one character at a time in this region. Below this is a text box where word completions and predictions are entered. Finally, at the bottom of the interface, Figure 2 shows two of the five rows of current word completions (left column) and next word predictions (right column).

Perhaps the largest departure from the preliminary experiment is the ability to not only complete the current word but also to provide predictions about the subsequent word. The subject uses a space delimiter to indicate whether predictions are for the current word or for the subsequent word. Words preceding a space are taken as current word completions; the first word after a space is taken as a

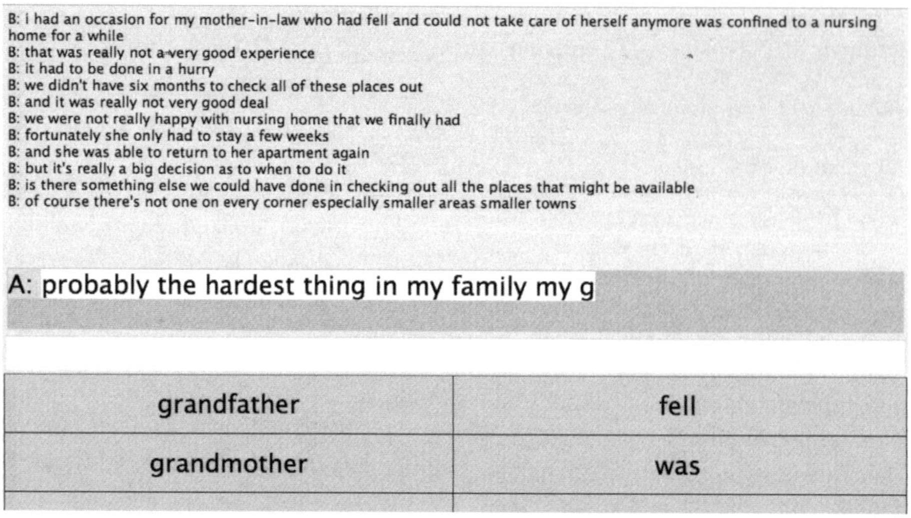

Figure 2: Experimental graphical user interface

subsequent word prediction. To just predict the subsequent word, one can lead with a space, which results in no current word completion and whatever comes after the space as next word prediction. Once the current word is complete, any words on the subsequent word prediction list are immediately shifted to the word completion list. We limited current and next word predictions to five.

We selected ten test dialogs, and subjects produced word completions and predictions for three utterances per dialog, for a total of thirty utterances. We selected the test dialogs to conform to the following characteristics:

1. Each group of three utterances was consecutive and spoken by the same person.
2. Each utterance contained more than 15 characters of text.
3. Each group of three utterances began turn-initially; the first of the three utterances was always immediately after the other speaker in the corpus had spoken at least two consecutive utterances of 15 characters or more.
4. Each group of three utterances was far enough into its respective conversation that there was enough text to provide the ten lines of context required above.

Language models used to contrast with human performance on this task were trained separately for every conversation in the test set. For each conversation, Kneser-Ney smoothed n-gram models were built using all other conversations in the normalized Switchboard corpus. Thus no conversation is in its own training data. Table 4 shows statistics of training and test sets.

Table 5 shows the results for n-gram models and our seven subjects on this test. Despite the differences in the testing scenario from the preliminary experiment, we can see that the results are very similar to what was found in that experiment. Also similar to the previous trial was the fact that a large percentage of tokens for which subjects provided faster word completion than the trigram model were faster for multiple subjects. Table 6 shows the nine words that were completed faster by more than half of the subjects than the trigram model. Thus, while there is some individual variation in task performance, subjects were fairly consistent in their ability to predict.

5 Discussion

In this paper we presented two experiments that evaluated a new kind of technology-assisted co-construction interface for communication partners during time-constrained text generation. Results

	Ngram training		Testing		
Task	sents	words	sents	words	chars
SWBD	0.66M	3.7M	30	299	1501

Table 4: Statistics for the Switchboard task of n-gram training corpus size and test set size in terms of utterances, words and characters (baseline keystrokes)

	N-gram			Subject						
Task	1g	2g	3g	1	2	3	4	5	6	7
Switchboard	51.0	59.0	60.0	28.7	33.1	28.4	28.6	34.1	31.8	32.5

Table 5: Keystroke savings percentage for Switchboard test set across models and subjects

applied	can't	comes
every	failure	named
physics	should	supervisor

Table 6: Words completed in more than half of the Switchboard trials using subject suggestions with fewer keystrokes than trigram model.

from both experiments are negative, in terms of the ability of our human subjects to speed up communication via word prediction under time constraints beyond what is achievable with n-gram language models. These results are somewhat surprising given conventional wisdom about the superiority of human language models versus their simplified computational counterparts. One key reason driving the divergence from conventional wisdom is the time constraint on production of predictions. Another is the artificiality of the task and relative unfamiliarity of the subjects with the individuals communicating.

While these results are negative, there are reasons why they should not be taken as an indictment of the approach as a whole, rather an indication of the challenges faced by this task. First, we would stress the fact that we have not yet tested the approach in a situation where the user knows the speaker well, and therefore can be presumed to have knowledge well beyond general knowledge of English and general topical knowledge. In future work we are planning experiments based on interactions between people who have a close relationship with each other. In such a scenario, we can expect that humans would have an advantage over statistical language models, for which appropriate training data would not, in any case, be available.

None of the domains that we evaluated were a perfect match to the application: the text data was not dialog, and the dialogs were spoken rather than written language. Further, the tasks that we evaluated in this paper are quite rigid compared to what might be considered acceptable in real use. For example, our task required the prediction of a particular word type, whereas in actual use synonyms or other ways of phrasing the same information will likely be quite acceptable to most AAC users. In such an application, the task is not to facilitate production of a specific word string, rather production of an idea which might be realized variously. We were interested in the tasks reported here as a first step towards understanding the problem, and among the lessons learned are the shortcomings of these very tasks.

Another take-away message relates to the utility of the new interface itself. The subjects in these trials had the difficult task of quickly predicting intended words; this is also a communication task that may be assisted. Providing access to what n-gram models are predicting may allow the communication partner to quickly select or winnow down the options. Further, it is apparent that single word completions or predictions is not where communication partners are going to achieve order-of-magnitude speedups in communication; rather such speedups may be realized in facilitation of larger phrase or whole utterance production, particularly when the communication is between familiar partners on known topics.

In summary, this paper presented preliminary results on the ability of human subjects to provide word completion and prediction information to users of AAC systems, through simulation of such a new interface concept. While the subjects were not able to match n-gram language models in terms of keystroke reduction, we did see consistent performance across many subjects and across several domains, yielding real keystroke reductions on the stimulus strings. Ultimately, the tasks were not as representative of real co-construction scenarios a we would have liked, but they serve to illustrate the challenges of such an application.

Acknowledgments

This research was supported in part by NIH Grant #1R01DC009834-01. Any opinions, findings, conclusions or recommendations expressed in this publication are those of the authors and do not necessarily reflect the views of the NIH.

References

D.R. Beukelman, S. Fager, L. Ball, and A. Dietz. 2007. AAC for adults with acquired neurological conditions: A review. *Augmentative and Alternative Communication*, 23(3):230–242.

Jennifer Cornish and Jeffrey Higginbotham. No Date. Assessing AAC interaction III: Effect of task type on co-construction & message repair. AAC-RERC, available from `http:aac-rerc.psu.edu/_userfiles/asha3.pdf`.

J.J. Darragh, I.H. Witten, and M.L. James. 1990. The reactive keyboard: A predictive typing aid. *Computer*, 23(11):41–49.

J.J. Godfrey, E.C. Holliman, and J. McDaniel. 1992. Switchboard: A telephone speech corpus for research and develpment. In *Proceedings of ICASSP, volume I*, pages 517–520.

D. Jeffery Higginbotham and David Wilkins. 1999. Frametalker: A system and method for utilizing communication frames in augmented communication technologies. US Patent No. 5,956,667.

D. Jeffery Higginbotham. 1992. Evaluation of keystroke savings across five assistive communication technologies. *Augmentative and Alternative Communication*, 8:258–272.

Linda A. Hoag, Jan L. Bedrosian, Kathleen F. McCoy, and Dallas Johnson. 2004. Informativeness and speed of message delivery trade-offs in augmentative and alternative communication. *Journal of Speech, Language, and Hearing Research*, 47:1270–1285.

Linda A. Hoag, Jan L. Bedrosian, Kathleen F. McCoy, and Dallas Johnson. 2008. Hierarchy of conversational rule violations involving utterance-based augmentative and alternative communication systems. *Augmentative and Alternative Communication*, 24(2):149–161.

R. Kneser and H. Ney. 1995. Improved backing-off for m-gram language modeling. In *Proceedings of the IEEE International Conference on Acoustics, Speech, and Signal Processing (ICASSP)*, pages 181–184.

Heidi H. Koester and Simon Levine. 1996. Effect of a word prediction feature on user performance. *Augmentative and Alternative Communication*, 12(3):155–168.

Heidi H. Koester and Simon Levine. 1997. Keystroke-level models for user performance with word prediction. *Augmentative and Alternative Communication*, 13(4):239257.

Heidi H. Koester and Simon Levine. 1998. Model simulations of user performance with word prediction. *Augmentative and Alternative Communication*, 14(1):25–36.

G.W. Lesher, B.J. Moulton, and D.J. Higginbotham. 1998. Techniques for augmenting scanning communication. *Augmentative and Alternative Communication*, 14:81–101.

J. Li and G. Hirst. 2005. Semantic knowledge in word completion. In *Proceedings of the 7th International ACM Conference on Computers and Accessibility*.

Mitchell P. Marcus, Beatrice Santorini, and Mary Ann Marcinkiewicz. 1993. Building a large annotated corpus of English: The Penn Treebank. *Computational Linguistics*, 19(2):313–330.

Kathleen F. McCoy, Jan L. Bedrosian, Linda A. Hoag, and Dallas E. Johnson. 2007. Brevity and speed of message delivery trade-offs in augmentative and alternative communication. *Augmentative and Alternative Communication*, 23(1):76–88.

Ehud Reiter, Ross Turner, Norman Alm, Rolf Black, Martin Dempster, and Annalu Waller. 2009. Using NLG to help language-impaired users tell stories and participate in social dialogues. In *12th European Workshop on Natural Language Generation*, pages 1–8. Association for Computational Linguistics.

B. Roark. 2009. Open vocabulary language modeling for binary response typing interfaces. Technical Report #CSLU-09-001, Center for Spoken Language Processing, Oregon Health & Science University. `cslu.ogi.edu/publications/ps/roark09.pdf`.

C.E. Shannon. 1950. Prediction and entropy of printed English. *Bell System Technical Journal*, 30:50–64.

John Todman, Norman Alm, D. Jeffery Higginbotham, and Portia File. 2008. Whole utterance approaches in AAC. *Augmentative and Alternative Communication*, 24(3):235–254.

K. Trnka, D. Yarrington, K.F. McCoy, and C. Pennington. 2006. Topic modeling in fringe word prediction for AAC. In *Proceedings of the International Conference on Intelligent User Interfaces*, pages 276–278.

K. Trnka, D. Yarrington, J. McCaw, K.F. McCoy, and C. Pennington. 2007. The effects of word prediction on communication rate for AAC. In *Proceedings of HLT-NAACL; Companion Volume, Short Papers*, pages 173–176.

H. Trost, J. Matiasek, and M. Baroni. 2005. The language component of the FASTY text prediction system. *Applied Artificial Intelligence*, 19(8):743–781.

T. Wandmacher and J.Y. Antoine. 2007. Methods to integrate a language model with semantic information for a word prediction component. In *Proceedings of the Conference on Empirical Methods in Natural Language Processing (EMNLP)*, pages 506–513.

David Wilkins and D. Jeffery Higginbotham. 2006. The short story of Frametalker: An interactive AAC device. *Perspectives on Augmentative and Alternative Communication*, 15(1):18–21.

Bruce Wisenburn and D. Jeffery Higginbotham. 2008. An AAC application using speaking partner speech recognition to automatically produce contextually relevant utterances: Objective results. *Augmentative and Alternative Communication*, 24(2):100–109.

Bruce Wisenburn and D. Jeffery Higginbotham. 2009. Participant evaluations of rate and communication efficacy of an AAC application using natural language processing. *Augmentative and Alternative Communication*, 25(2):78–89.

Trap Hunting: Finding Personal Data Management Issues in Next Generation AAC Devices

Joseph Reddington
Royal Holloway College
Egham, UK
j.reddington@rhul.ac.uk

Lizzie Coles-Kemp
Royal Holloway College
Egham, UK
lizzie.coles-kemp@rhul.ac.uk

Abstract

Advances in natural language generation and speech processing techniques, combined with changes in the commercial landscape, have brought within reach dramatic improvements in Augmentative Alternative Communication (AAC). These improvements, though overwhelmingly positive, amplify a family of personal data use problems. This paper argues that the AAC design and implementation process needs to identify and address personal data use problems. Accordingly, this paper explores personal data management problems and proposes responses. This paper is situated in the context of AAC technology but the responses could be generalised for other communities affected by low digital literacy, low literacy levels and cognitive challenges.

1 Introduction

Electronic Augmentative and Alternative Communication (AAC) systems enable individuals with severe speech impairment to verbally communicate their needs, often using Text-to-Speech technology. Such devices are designed to give communication impaired people greater independence and improved opportunities of social integration. The devices enable users to construct utterances, many of which describe themselves or aspects of their lives, including their actions with others and, as such, can be considered 'personal data'. Recent work by Patel and Radhakrishnan (2007), Black et al. (2010), Reiter et al. (2009), and Reddington and Tintarev (2011) makes explicit use of personal data (about both the user and other parties) to improve the functionality of AAC devices. Depending on context, the use of these utterances, in an institutional setting, may be controlled under data protection legislation, or (e.g. domestically) their use may be influenced more by social norms within the context. A key factor in personal data management is the highly contextual nature of privacy related issues; privacy concerns and practices are situated in their context (Nissenbaum, 2009) and influenced by cultural issues (Milberg et al., 2000).

The diversity of technology in the AAC sector is set to increase dramatically. Apple's iPad[1] has caused a huge investment in tablet technology. Multiple, third party applications (e.g. proloque2go[2], myVoice[3], and verbally[4]) already exist that allow this new range of tablets to function as AAC devices.

The effect of this research movement maturing at a time when many new devices and producers are entering the market foreshadows probable major changes and innovations in coming years. This includes a risk of the "panoply of different privacy problems" that privacy theorist Solove (2008) foresaw as a result of diversifying and enhancing technologies.

The authors' position is that it is very timely to explore personal data management problems in this new AAC landscape and in so doing identify traps that AAC design might stumble into as this technology change gathers pace. This perspective can con-

[1] http://www.apple.com/ipad/, retrieved May 2011
[2] http://www.proloquo2go.com, retrieved May 2011
[3] http://new.myvoiceaac.com, retrieved May 2011
[4] http://verballyapp.com/index.html,retrieved May 2011

Proceedings of the 2nd Workshop on Speech and Language Processing for Assistive Technologies, pages 32–42,
Edinburgh, Scotland, UK, July 30, 2011. ©2011 Association for Computational Linguistics

tribute to the design of technologies and governance structures that are able to both identify and respond to such traps.

As AAC devices are designed to be used in all areas of the AAC user's life, there are a broad range of personal data management problems, which are highly context sensitive and incorporate legal, social, and technical issues. This complex problem space centres on informational privacy issues that contribute to a wider family of personal data management problems that can be found in contexts of AAC use.

This paper situates the personal data management problems in the use of natural language generation and speech processing techniques in AAC. It considers all of the following as personal data: utterances constructed by the system, communication logs and re-communication of stored utterances. Following an overview of state-of-the-art AAC and discussion of how functionality development in next-generation AAC devices maps to the use of personal data, Section 2 identifies and explores personal data use problems in three AAC-specific examples. Section 3 presents possible responses to problems introduced by the examples and Section 4 considers a governance framework that enables emergent personal data management problems with future AAC devices to be identified and considers its applicability for other communities.

1.1 Personal data generated, and used, by AAC devices

Today, AAC devices may excel at needs-based communication (e.g. *"I am hungry"*, *"I'm cold"*, *"get the phone"*) but they are limited for real conversation (Soto et al., 2006). So, in the current generation of AAC devices, the implications for both personal data generation and its use are relatively small because the linguistic capabilities are small. Typical AAC devices tend towards a hierarchical structure of pages, each of which typically focuses on a context (e.g. shopping) or a category (e.g. clothes, sports), rather than observations or recent personal stories (Beukelman and Mirenda, 2005). However, Higginbotham et al. (2007) report that spontaneous conversation with typical devices is slow and difficult (new utterances are typically constructed at a rate of between 8 and 10 words per minute, slightly more if e.g. word prediction is used). Todman et al. (2008) propose utterance-based devices in which devices focus on prepared phrases to facilitate social communication rather than needs-based communication; however, in general, new utterances must be prepared in advance either by the user or a carer, with a large time and energy cost. It is this implementation of functionality designed to speed up utterance production that restricts the production of personal data rather than the underlying technology. A study by Rackensperger et al. (2005) shows that using pre-programmed phrases can reduce the ability for self-expression; as a result, the range of personal data produced is likely to be limited. As an example, there is a particular difficulty in communicating recent or single use events such as talking about one's day or talking about yesterday's television: such utterances are expensive to prepare in advance due to the potential for limited and low-probability use. Thus, AAC users tend to be passive, responding to questions with single words or short sentences, and personal stories tend to be told as a monologue or a sequence of pre-stored utterances (Soto et al., 2006).

To develop the potential for interaction, and therefore increase the degree to which AAC devices can support increased independence, recent research has examined the potential for location-aware devices to offer different content to the user under different conditions (Dominowska et al., 2002; Patel and Radhakrishnan, 2007), and for devices that generate new phrases automatically. In the later case: Black et al. (2010) use external data to populate a communication device, and Reiter et al. (2009) use a NLG engine to generate text from a database of personal facts. These innovations could allow users to increase social interaction and reduce the device maintenance, complementing the growing range of AAC systems with internet connectivity.

1.1.1 Impact on personal data

As the capability for interaction increases, the potential for increased personal data also increases. For example:

- utterances generated from geo-location enabled devices can potentially include information about people (data subjects) other than the

AAC user, as well as increased information about the device users themselves;

- utterances generated from input by teachers, care staff and parents can again potentially contain information about other data subjects, as well as increase the range of information about device users themselves;

- internet access as a medium brings a range of issues for personal data use in terms of the methods used to broadcast and replay utterances and it greatly increases the possibilities for data input (potentially including information about third parties) into the utterances;

- the general browsing facility of internet access increases the ability of users to communicate with the wider world, carrying with it a set of personal data management and privacy issues, much of which is the subject of on-going research (Kani-Zabihi and Coles-Kemp, 2010; Kumaraguru and Cranor, 2005; Spiekermann and Cranor, 2009).

Increasing the potential for interaction and giving more control to the AAC user will increase the range of personal data generated and hence the range of potential personal data use problems. Moreover, the increased creation of novel utterances and wider opportunity to relay such utterances potentially increase intellectual property issues.

AAC devices are designed to increase social interaction in all settings and therefore the devices, and their supporting approaches, must be equally effective in all situations. This is a challenge for any type of personal data management that includes aspects of privacy. Also, AAC users themselves develop their uses and desires for communication (Rackensperger et al., 2005). Therefore, any approach to personal data management has to be highly context sensitive and capable of responding to changing requirements.

1.2 Related work in AAC literature

Although ethics in the context of complex disabilities is well studied, there is little direct research into privacy and personal data management issues in AAC: much of the work is in small accompanying sections to other research contributions and focuses directly on personal data dissemination. For example, Smith (2005) notes that externally displayed lexicons (such as a communications board) violate some aspects of privacy and proposes finding ways to ensure that vocabulary can be delivered discreetly without affecting access. Similarly, Black et al. (2010) address privacy as part of a discussion of security. Additionally, there is some meta-work that looks at the ethics of research into AAC rather than AAC itself: Pennington et al. (2007) notes that the data collected by AAC devices makes identification of the individual trivial, especially when considering the relatively small pool of users, a theme that is also examined in work by Lesher et al. (2000) on logging output of AAC devices.

Privacy has also been raised explicitly in the AAC community by researchers considering design frameworks for next generation devices, e.g., Rackensperger et al. (2005) and DeRuyter et al. (2007). There is also a growing body of AAC research that, in discussing next generation AAC technology, raises a wide range of implicit issues related to privacy and ICT mediated communication. These issues include: anonymity; personalisation of services; identity management; autonomy; and the changing of relationship boundaries through mediation. These are topics that feature in traditional privacy research, but with added complexity.

Therefore, work on the future of AAC and internet connectivity (in particular key features highlighted in DeRuyter et al. (2007)) have great bearing on personal data management, although privacy and personal data management are not directly discussed. DeRuyter et al. (2007) discuss simplified usability, including 'embeddedness' functionality: making AAC devices unobtrusive in their environment. When simplifying usability, there is a tension between requiring user intervention and decision making automation. For example, where should consent mechanisms related to personal information disclosure be placed?

Discussions on future AAC functionality also emphasise adaptive technology that personalises AAC use so that AAC devices are able to recognise a user and adjust functionality accordingly (DeRuyter et al., 2007). However, adaptation algorithms designed to anticipate or assess user capabilities will make adjustments to functionality based on logs of personal data and usage patterns and thus implicitly process personal data. The ability to adjust such algorithms would give users and their carers increased control over the use of this personal data. In addition, adjusting the capabilities of Internet-enabled AAC devices is likely to also result in changes to the disclosure of a user's personal data. This disclosure would be determined using a logic internal to the adaptation algorithms. Making the logic explicit to users and their carers would make both the personal data disclosure implications of adjustment visible and give greater control over disclosure.

2 Examples

Given the situated nature of informational privacy, in order to explore personal data management issues meaningfully, it is vital to situate the evaluation policy and its related personal data management issues into a particular context. We have selected three AAC-specific examples through which to explore the issues in particular contexts.

This section describes three illustrative scenarios for potential personal data use problems. They are broadly based on the categories of generated content in Reddington and Tintarev (2011) and are constructed with input from legal experts, youth work practitioners, and disability officers. The examples situate the personal data management problems before analysis in Section 3.

2.1 Example 1 - Creating Novel Utterances

The simplest, and least intrusive level of automatically generated content contains inferred utterances that can be deduced from logs of previous utterances. Thus, if a device logged the phrase "Hello Mary" and later "Thanks Mary" the phrase "Today I spent time with Mary" could be added to the list of available phrases. It is trivial to imagine other possible situations where this is applicable - "My communications unit has been away for repair", "I was up very late last night", and "I like to talk about football", are all deducible from previous utterances.

We consider an AAC user Alice, who is solely reliant on her AAC device for communication and is non-literate. Alice is able to generate novel utterances using utterance segments programmed by care staff and by taking advantage of inferred utterances that her device has been designed to provide. Alice has the right to delete certain utterances but care staff and family members are able to restore the deleted utterances. The digest of Alice's activities are backed up every day and could be placed in a catalogue of utterances that the care provider uses at promotional events or on the provider's website.

This scenario raises issues related to intellectual property rights, ownership, and the management of personal data. The management issues centre on control of data, and rights to recover deleted items.

2.2 Example 2 - Implicit and Explicit Personal Data Exchange Rules

The second and third levels of automatically generated content involve receiving data from network portals (such as the internet) and local sensors. For example: "It's very warm today", and "It rained on Friday!". Also included is media data: "On YouTube I watched the 'Star Wars Kid' video ", or "New series of Doctor Who!".

A useful context here is the "How was School Today...?" (HWST) project (Black et al., 2010; Reddington and Tintarev, 2011), which generates stories for students with complex communication needs at a special needs school. The project logs interactions with people, objects and location changes. This sensor data is supplemented with timetable information (to infer classes based on time and location) and voice recordings, before new content is generated.

Consider that Alice is in a class and that her AAC device reads information from sensors to generate novel content in a similar way to the HWST system. Also in class is Charlie, a typically developing child. Charlie's actions are also recorded by the sensors and he takes part in activities with Alice. Alice is able to report Charlie's behaviour to her parents and to other class members. Unlike when her classmate Charlie verbally communicates about his school day, Alice's utterances take a permanent form and can be replayed and reused. Charlie is not really aware of this capability and what this means. Charlie's parents are aware that Alice has some kind of communication device and that sensors are used at school but are not clear on the details. Alice's Mum puts some of Alice's stories, including the one about

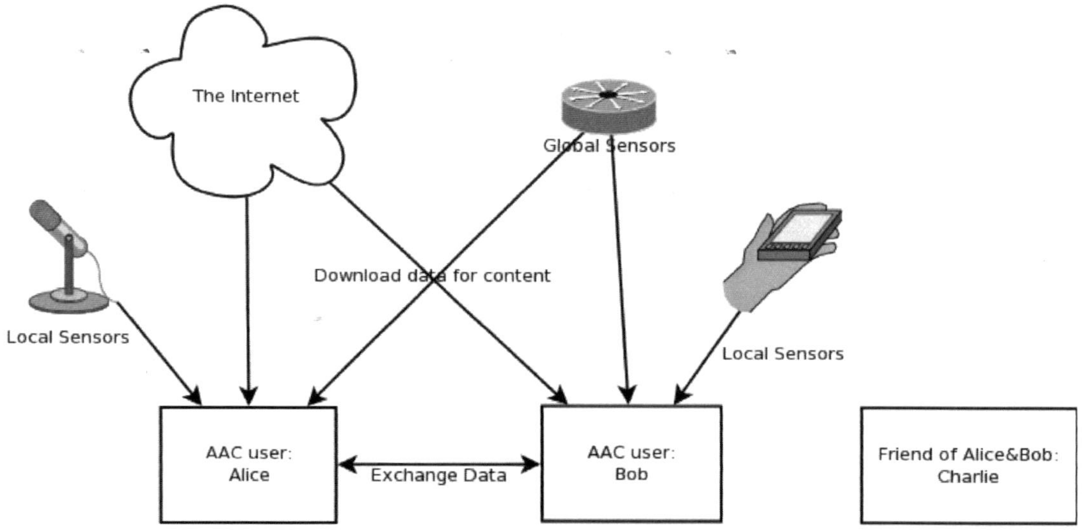

Figure 1: An example information flow

Charlie and the water fight, up on their family blog.

This scenario raises issues of consent to obtain data from sensor sources and of processing the sensor data. It also raises questions related to the dissemination of personal data - about the user and other data subjects. In this scenario, personal data is processed in two contexts: school and Alice's home. This shows the complex array of stakeholders involved in managing personal data. Moreover, there are questions of how non-AAC users are informed of the implications of AAC use in the school or in any other setting. Implicitly there is a problem of ensuring that AAC and non-AAC users are treated equally in terms of the personal data rights, which in turn raises issues of how verbal and AAC generated utterances are valued in the social context.

2.3 Example 3 - Control over Data Sharing

An additional level of complexity is the creation of narrative flow. Narratives are groups of messages that together relate an experience or tell a story. This adds the problem of creating a narrative structure and consistent style to the data-mining exercise (for NLG work on the importance of narrative information exchange see e.g. (Reiter et al., 2008)). An example might be:

> I had my breakfast quickly because I was excited to go to the arcade. I got on the bus, I went to the arcade, I played in the arcade and won a cuddly bear.

Now consider that Alice and Charlie are joined by Bob, who is also an AAC user on the same system as Alice. Alice and Bob's devices are capable of sharing data at all levels. At the device level, Alice and Bob share raw data to confirm, for example, that their system clocks are in sync and that they have the same records of people who are in the same room. It is also possible at the social episode level that Alice's system can import utterances from Bob's system so that Alice could say 'Bob liked the swimming'. It is important to note that in this scenario, if Alice deletes an utterance from her machine 'The teacher gave me a bad mark on my work', Bob could still use the deleted story because Alice is unable to delete the disseminations. However, data sharing is not only between device users. Data sharing could also take place between the agencies involved in Alice and Bob's care and support. Figure 1 shows this data sharing taking place on three levels: device, individual AAC user, and institutional.

This scenario raises the issues of personal data flow control and indicates that controls for the flow of personal data have to be set at all three levels. Importantly, when personal data flows are managed at these levels responses will always be sociotechnical in nature; therefore they include technical responses, governance responses and technology practice responses. This is a familiar combination of responses in privacy management (Paine et al., 2007)

3 Finding traps and responding to them

Section 2 demonstrated a family of personal data use problems. These problems address various aspects of using personal data in the context of AAC devices. Our family of problems partly relate to the oft used definition of privacy from Westin (1967): "the claim of individuals, groups, or institutions to determine for themselves when, how, and to what extent information about them is communicated to others". This is not a hierarchy with a root problem and a tree structure of related problems but a family of problems with complex relations and which are enmeshed rather than conceptually linear. Analytically, the family has four members: IPR; compliance responsibility; institutional personal data access and disclosure rights; and individual personal data access and disclosure rights. Each family member is addressed in this section. Whitley points out that Whitley (2009) "Wittgenstein (1956) tells us that language is a social activity and hence that specialised terms like privacy are arrived at socially.". The social construction of concepts related to personal data mean that personal data issues will be enmeshed in particular contexts and, as a result, the significance of these issues will vary from context to context.

Discussions with legal experts and practitioners (see Acknowledgements) revealed that responses to these problems occur at the institutional, individual, and technical levels, and an individual interpretation of personal data management issues underpins all responses. This is true of all personal data management issues; however, in the case of AAC users, the individual level will be a unique combination of AAC user, family, and care workers. At the next level is the sociocultural system in place within each institutional context, which contains the personal data management policies, procedures, practices and institutional values. This sociocultural system is supported by technological controls used to control personal data information flow.

Unlike spoken conversation, AAC devices create embodiments of conversations that can be permanently stored or logged. Then conversations become data that largely focuses on living individuals, either the users themselves or their family and friends. Under certain conditions processing this data will be regulated by data protection legislation. In other settings the processing will be governed more by social norms. Furthermore, the permanent nature of these embodiments means that they can carry copyright. Then there is a natural question of information flow control, the need for rights management and traditional information security issues such as confidentiality and access control. However, privacy is also an elastic concept (Allen, 1988) and is often considered wider than the Westin definition, including aspects of identity and relationship management. As the work of Smith (2005) and Rackensperger et al. (2005) shows, use of AAC devices is related to notions of self and relationship to others. The notions of self and relationship to others are a central aspect of privacy (Kani-Zabihi and Coles-Kemp, 2010) (Barnard-Wills and Ashenden, 2010) and the link between personal data use and privacy and identity issues should not be ignored when considering these personal data management problems.

3.1 A Family of Personal Data Use Problems

Practically, any technical, regulatory, or social response to personal data use issues in AAC must be able to operate in a range of contexts and support a user as they blend and adjust contexts. For example, an AAC user may use their device at home, in formal education, in youth group activities, and in social settings. These different contexts may include many of the same people, but the personal data control requirements and the regulatory and personal data management frameworks are likely to differ from context to context. A further level of complexity in the case of AAC users is that capabilities and backgrounds differ widely within the AAC community (DeRuyter et al., 2007) and any personal data management approach has to adjust to these varying capabilities and different perspectives.

Technical responses would primarily be formed by meshing the AAC functionality into the underlying technical architecture of each device. Technical responses include personal information flow control over the network; encryption of sensitive utterances, e.g. health or financial information (such as credit card numbers), stored on the AAC device; access control to location databases and so on.

3.1.1 Management of IPR

Automatically generated text in AAC devices can be coupled or merged with input from other sources, increasing the ability of users to develop additional novel utterances. Given the digital nature of the utterances, there is potentially a close comparison with music copyright, which has three sets of rights: mechanical, rights related to the creation of the lyrics and performing. Using music copyright as the parallel, consider the situation where an AAC user, Alice say, imports text from a novel under copyright (mechanical rights) and adapts it by adding other text and other copyright material in order to create her own monologue (intellectual property rights). Another AAC user, Bob say, then downloads Alice's monologue and performs it through his AAC device at a concert for a school (performing rights). Clearly the majority of instances carry an implicit rights clearance, particularly in the content and performing rights elements of this example. However, if the monologue was posted on YouTube and then became sampled by a recording artist or made into a digital novel, rights clearance may not apply. Communicating the rules relating to copyright and ensuring understanding can be problematic.

Social and institutional responses to IPR problems are largely related to awareness training and the agreement of 'ground rules' or social contracts in communities such as schools and youth clubs where the legal issues and social expectations are made clear. The traditional methods for negotiating and agreeing ground rules is heavily based on the use of informational literature, one-to-one and group discussion (Barnard-Wills and Ashenden, 2010). These methods do not translate well into an environment where users may have cognitive development issues, or may be non-literate. It could be envisaged that guardians and parents would be used to negotiate and agree the ground rules and then left with the task of communicating the ground rules to their dependents. The difficulty in this is that at the same time, AAC users can become very skilled in the use of technology and may well develop practices that involve copyright material, in a way that their guardians have not been able to communicate effectively. In order to respond to this mismatch of capabilities, methods of engagement need to be sought that ensure AAC users are as integral as possible to the establishment of such rules.

3.1.2 Management of compliance responsibility

Due to the digital nature of AAC utterances, personal data output by a device is regulated by data protection legislation when being processed in the context of institutions such as schools, health, or social service. In the UK, this legislation is the Data Protection Act 1998. Under the Act there are eight principles of personal data management and the requirement that there must be a *data controller* who is responsible for compliance with the legislation. The term 'data subject' denotes individuals to whom the personal data relates. If Alice and Bob were young adults with sufficient cognitive abilities they would likely be the data controllers. However, as speech, language and communication disabilities are regularly a pan-disability, Alice and Bob may also be cognitively impaired and a parent or guardian is likely to be regarded as the data controller.

Typically, the mechanism for specifying compliance requirements is via the creation of a compliance schedule. In the case of AAC use, a compliance schedule for AAC devices is likely to be between the institution (school or health services) and the parents. The compliance schedule would establish the responsibility for data processing and agree the relationship between parents and institutions. Note that the AAC user's capabilities for technology can potentially exceed that of their guardians and parents. The relationship the AAC user has to the technology is quite possibly very different from that of the parent or guardian. If effective compliance management is to be achieved, new engagement methods need to be sought to ensure that AAC users are actively engaged in the establishment of compliance schedules. The connection between the individual, the institution (school) and privacy legislation is illustrated in Figure 2.

3.1.3 Management of institutional personal data access and disclosure rights

A set of rights must be agreed as part of the compliance schedule when AAC devices are used in school and healthcare settings. Many AAC devices have their data backed up to a central database. An

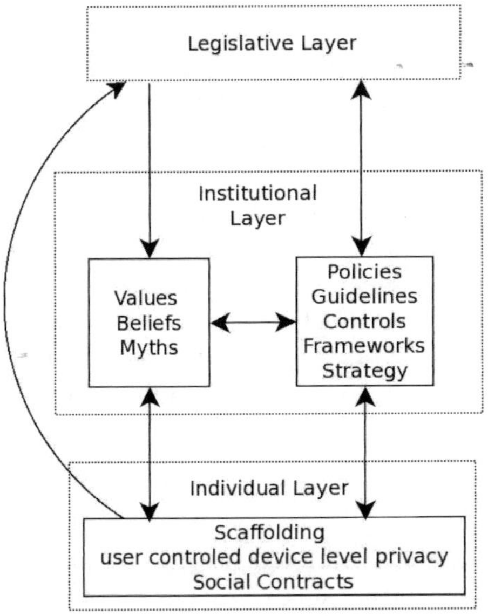

Figure 2: This diagram adapts the characterisation of institutional culture found in (Allaire and Firsirotu, 1984)

issue arises as to who has the right to back up or access the AAC data. AAC devices that can restore data that a user has deleted raise particular problems, which relate to who has the right to restore the data and the subsequent disclosure rights that this individual would have. Problems also occur as to whether other AAC users have the right to download content from another AAC device and the subsequent disclosure rights that this would afford.

AAC users will typically have considerable intervention from education and health support workers. Unlike spoken forms of conversations in other care situations, AAC utterances have a digital embodiment. This allows different teams in the care, education and support of the user to easily share utterances, and it may be deemed to make care more effective to do so. From an institutional perspective, data sharing policies should be set up to state which aspects of AAC utterances can be shared, the people that such utterances can be shared with, and a need for transparency in the logic used to interpret the utterances. In addition, the compliance schedule could specify which data transfers are permitted.

3.1.4 Management of individual personal data access and disclosure rights

Whilst many institutional issues are related to personal data use, importantly, AAC users are likely to use devices for personal data disclosure outside of the institutional context as part of family and social life. In this instance processing is controlled by social norms and practices that could be considered a social contract (Milne and Gordon, 1993).

From a social perspective, developing social contracts or norms organically responds to problems related to publishing of data about other data subjects, misuse of the AAC user's personal data by friends and family, and unintentional copyright infringements. In the scenario of AAC use, these social contracts and norms are re-enforced with education and awareness briefings (Bogdanovic et al., 2009) that are typically driven by the education and health institutions. As part of these ground rules, the degree of anonymity in any disclosures and the rights of non-AAC users to have their personal data removed from an AAC device are agreed or follow a socially accepted path. From a technical perspective, the device interface could be developed to include utterances about information disclosure and feelings of privacy. The log files could also include information disclosure and processing comments that practitioners and family members might wish to discuss or consider. Role play games could also be considered as a way of re-enforcing and encouraging ground rules.

4 AAC personal data management framework

As illustrated in Figure 2, personal data management within the AAC context is complex and any response to a personal data management problem has both technical, governance and cultural aspects. These responses have to be adaptive to differing levels of capabilities and different contextual requirements. Any technical response has to be scalable to enable users with different privacy and technical requirements to have access to their personal data controlled accordingly so that, where practical, users are able to have some control over their personal data. This scaleability can, in part, be addressed by the design and implementation of the personal data management framework.

4.1 Extending the existing framework

The personal data management problems related to AAC use have links with work in the mainstream privacy and consent research communities. Section 2 illustrates that AAC use adds additional layers of complexity to privacy and consent issues and, as a result, adds additional requirements to any personal data management framework. Due to space constraints the factors are merely highlighted to note that each is a large piece of research in its own right.

The required extensions fall into three areas:

4.1.1 Technical capability

Technical capability, in addition to education, is a factor in assessing ability to manage privacy (Coles-Kemp et al., 2010; Kumaraguru and Cranor, 2005; Buchanan et al., 2007) because a relatively sophisticated level of technical capability is required to implement the privacy controls. Technical capability and education levels are likely to be lower, on average, in AAC users.

4.1.2 Family roles

AAC users typically remain 'scaffolded' by family and the family will therefore remain involved in decisions about personal data disclosure. Whilst, family plays an important role at the start of an individual's internet journey[5], typically this intervention recedes over time and the design of privacy controls does not traditionally cater for varying levels of user independence in decision making. This needs to be addressed by the management framework.

4.1.3 Governance system design

Responses to personal data management issues use a governance system composed of policy, regulation, and practices to support the use of privacy enhancing technologies. Engagement with such a system is notoriously inconsistent because of language and conceptual complexities (Kani-Zabihi and Coles-Kemp, 2010; Bogdanovic et al., 2009; Bonnici and Coles-Kemp, 2010; McDonald and Cranor, 2008; McDonald and Cranor, 2009). It is reasonable to assume that such a governance system would require specific modifications for the AAC community to make policies more understandable, to allow for adaptations in privacy and internet safety education and to enable the role of family in decision support. However, it should also be kept in mind that similar modifications could be made for other communities with lower levels of digital literacy, literacy and cognitive challenges. Whilst the problems themselves are AAC-specific and the problems are brought about, in part, by the direction of development of AAC technology, the governance responses respond to underlying problems found in a range of communities.

5 Conclusions

Advances in text-to-speech technology and mobile computing have made a range of AAC devices available to the public. Advances in natural language generation and speech processing techniques have co-incided with changes to the commercial landscape to bring dramatic advances in AAC capabilities within reach. These advances in AAC design, though overwhelmingly positive, do result in a family of personal data use problems that were not encountered with previous generations of the devices. This paper argued that AAC devices can only significantly support users with communication difficulties to achieve greater independence and social inclusion if their design and implementation both addresses and identifies personal data problems.

Acknowledgments

The authors wish to thank the staff of the HWST project, the Natural Language Generation Group at Aberdeen and the Sociotechnical Group, within the Information Security Group at Royal Holloway. The work was developed with input from legal experts, youth work practitioners, and disability officers: in particular Robert Carolina, Amanda Gerry, and Karen Wood are gratefully acknowledged. Similarly, the insights of Nava Tintarev, Sarah Moffat, and Margaret Mitchell made this work possible. This paper was produced in collaboration with the Visualisation and Other Methods of Expression (VOME) project, which is supported by the Technology Strategy Board; the Engineering and Physical Sciences Research Council and the Economic and Social Research Council [grant number EP/G00255X/1].

[5]UK online Centres (2010) "Digital engagement understanding customers", a study (available for download at www.ukonlinecentres.com/research/research/centres-research)

References

Y. Allaire and M.E. Firsirotu. 1984. Theories of organizational culture. *Organization studies*, 5(3):193.

A.L. Allen. 1988. *Uneasy access: Privacy for women in a free society*. Rowman & Littlefield Pub Inc.

S. Balandin, N. Berg, and A. Waller. 2006. Assessing the loneliness of older people with cerebral palsy. *Disability & Rehabilitation*, 28(8):469–479.

D. Barnard-Wills and D. Ashenden. 2010. Public sector engagement with online identity management. *Identity in the Information Society*, pages 1–18.

DR Beukelman and P. Mirenda. 2005. *Augmentative and alternative communication: Supporting children and adults with complex communication needs3rd ed.* Paul H. Brookes, Baltimore, MD.

R. Black, J. Reddington, E. Reiter, N. Tintarev, and A. Waller. 2010. Using NLG and sensors to support personal narrative for children with complex communication needs. In *Proceedings of the NAACL HLT 2010 Workshop on Speech and Language Processing for Assistive Technologies*, pages 1–9, Los Angeles, California, June. Association for Computational Linguistics.

D. Bogdanovic, C. Crawford, and L. Coles-Kemp. 2009. The need for enhanced privacy and consent dialogues. *Information Security Technical Report*, 14(3):167–172.

C.J. Bonnici and L. Coles-Kemp. 2010. Principled Electronic Consent Management: A Preliminary Research Framework. In *2010 International Conference on Emerging Security Technologies*, pages 119–123. IEEE.

T. Buchanan, C. Paine, A.N. Joinson, and U.D. Reips. 2007. Development of measures of online privacy concern and protection for use on the internet. *Journal of the American Society for Information Science and Technology*, 58(2):157–165.

L. Coles-Kemp and E. Kani-Zabihi. 2010. On-line privacy and consent: a dialogue, not a monologue. In *Proceedings of the 2010 workshop on New security paradigms*, pages 95–106. ACM.

L. Coles-Kemp, Y.L. Lai, M. Ford, and C. Hyperion. 2010. Privacy on the Internet: Attitudes and Behaviours.

J. Cornwell, I. Fette, G. Hsieh, M. Prabaker, J. Rao, K. Tang, K. Vaniea, L. Bauer, L. Cranor, J. Hong, et al. 2007. User-controllable security and privacy for pervasive computing. In *Mobile Computing Systems and Applications, 2007. HotMobile 2007. Eighth IEEE Workshop on*, pages 14–19. IEEE.

F. DeRuyter, D. McNaughton, K. Caves, D.N. Bryen, and M.B. Williams. 2007. Enhancing AAC connections with the world. *Augmentative and Alternative Communication*, 23(3):258–270.

E. Dominowska, D. Roy, and R. Patel. 2002. An adaptive context-sensitive communication aid. In *Proceedings of the 17th Annual International Conference Technology and Persons with Disabilities.*

P. Golle, F. McSherry, and I. Mironov. 2008. Data collection with self-enforcing privacy. *ACM Transactions on Information and System Security (TISSEC)*, 12(2):1–24.

D. J. Higginbotham, H.Shane, S. Russell, and K.Caves. 2007. Access to AAC: Present, past, and future. *Augmentative and Alternative Communication*, 23(3):243–257.

M.A. Kamp, P. Slotty, S. Sarikaya-Seiwert, H.J. Steiger, and D. Hanggi. Traumatic brain injuries in illustrated literature: experience from a series of over 700 head injuries in the asterix comic books. *Acta Neurochirurgica*, pages 1–5.

E. Kani-Zabihi and L. Coles-Kemp. 2010. Service Users Requirements for Tools to Support Effective On-line Privacy and Consent Practices. In *Procedings of the 15th Conference on Secure IT Systems, Nordic 2010.*

C.M. Karat, C. Brodie, and J. Karat. 2006. Usable privacy and security for personal information management. *Communications of the ACM*, 49(1):56–57.

P. Kumaraguru and L.F. Cranor. 2005. Privacy indexes: A survey of westins studies. *Institute for Software Research International.*

G.W. Lesher, G.J. Rinkus, B.J. Moulton, and D.J. Higginbotham. 2000. Logging and analysis of augmentative communication. In *Proceedings of the RESNA Annual Conference*. Citeseer.

A.M. McDonald and L.F. Cranor. 2008. The cost of reading privacy policies. *ACM Transactions on Computer-Human Interaction*, 4(3):1–22.

A. McDonald and L. Cranor. 2009. An empirical study of how people perceive online behavioral advertising.

S.J. Milberg, H.J. Smith, and S.J. Burke. 2000. Information privacy: Corporate management and national regulation. *Organization Science*, pages 35–57.

G.R. Milne and M.E. Gordon. 1993. Direct mail privacy-efficiency trade-offs within an implied social contract framework. *Journal of Public Policy & Marketing*, 12(2):206–215.

H. Nissenbaum. 2009. *Privacy in context: Technology, policy, and the integrity of social life*. Stanford Law Books.

C. Paine, U.D. Reips, S. Stieger, A. Joinson, and T. Buchanan. 2007. Internet users' perceptions of privacy concerns' and privacy actions'. *International Journal of Human-Computer Studies*, 65(6):526–536.

R. Patel and R. Radhakrishnan. 2007. Enhancing Access to Situational Vocabulary by Leveraging Geographic Context. *Assistive Technology Outcomes and Benefits*, page 99.

L. Pennington, J. Marshall, and J. Goldbart. 2007. Describing participants in AAC research and their communicative environments: Guidelines for research and practice. *Disability & Rehabilitation*, 29(7):521–535.

T. Rackensperger, C. Krezman, D. Mcnaughton, M.B. Williams, and K. D'silva. 2005. When I first got it, I wanted to throw it off a cliff: The challenges and benefits of learning AAC technologies as described by adults who use AAC. *Augmentative and Alternative Communication*, 21(3):165–186.

J. Reddington and N. Tintarev. 2011. Automatically generating stories from sensor data. In *Proceedings of the 15th international conference on Intelligent user interfaces*, pages 407–410. ACM.

S. Reilly, J. Douglas, and J. Oates. 2004. *Evidence-based practice in speech pathology*. Whurr, London.

E. Reiter, F. Portet A. Gatt, and M. van der Meulen. 2008. The importance of narrative and other lessons from an evaluation of an NLG system that summarises clinical data. In *International Natural Language Generation Conference (INLG)*, pages 147–156.

E. Reiter, R. Turner, N. Alm, R. Black, M. Dempster, and A. Waller. 2009. Using NLG to help language-impaired users tell stories and participate in social dialogues. In *European Workshop on Natural Language Generation (ENLG-09)*.

M.M. Smith. 2005. The dual challenges of aided communication and adolescence. *Augmentative and Alternative Communication*, 21(1):67–79.

D.J. Solove. 2008. *Understanding privacy*. Harvard university press.

G. Soto, E. Hartmann, and D. Wilkins. 2006. Exploring the elements of narrative that emerge in the interactions between an 8-year-old child who uses an AAC device and her teacher. *Augmentative and Alternative Communication*, 22(4):231–241.

S. Spiekermann and L.F. Cranor. 2009. Engineering privacy. *Software Engineering, IEEE Transactions on*, 35(1):67–82.

J. Todman, N. Alm, J. Higginbotham, and P. File. 2008. Whole utterance approaches in AAC. *Augmentative and Alternative Communication*, 24(3):235–254.

A.F. Westin. 1967. *Privacy and freedom*, volume 97. London.

E.A. Whitley. 2009. Informational privacy, consent and the. *Information security technical report*, 14(3):154–159.

L. Wittgenstein. 1956. Philosophical investigations.(trans. GEM Anscombe) Basil Blackwell.

Asynchronous fixed-grid scanning with dynamic codes

Russ Beckley and Brian Roark
Center for Spoken Language Understanding, Oregon Health & Science University
{beckleyr,roark}@cslu.ogi.edu

Abstract

In this paper, we examine several methods for including dynamic, contextually-sensitive binary codes within indirect selection typing methods using a grid with fixed symbol positions. Using Huffman codes derived from a character n-gram model, we investigate both synchronous (fixed latency highlighting) and asynchronous (self-paced using long versus short press) scanning. Additionally, we look at methods that allow for scanning past a target and returning to it versus methods that remove unselected items from consideration. Finally, we investigate a novel method for displaying the binary codes for each symbol to the user, rather than using cell highlighting, as the means for identifying the required input sequence for the target symbol. We demonstrate that dynamic coding methods for fixed position grids can be tailored for very diverse user requirements.

1 Introduction

For many years, a key focus in Augmentative and Alternative Communication (AAC) has been providing text processing capabilities to those for whom direct selection of symbols on a keyboard (virtual or otherwise) is not a viable option. In lieu of direct selection, a binary (yes/no) response can be given through any number of switches, including buttons or pads that are pressed with hand, head, or foot, eyeblink detectors, or other switches that can leverage whatever reliable movement is available. These indirect selection methods typically involve systematically scanning through options and eliciting the binary yes/no response at each step of scanning. For example, row/column scanning is a very common approach for indirect selection. Auto row/column scanning on a square grid, such as that shown in Figure 1, will highlight each row in turn for some fixed duration (dwell time); if the binary switch is triggered before the dwell time expires, the row is selected; otherwise the next row is highlighted. Once a row is selected, cells in this row are then individually highlighted in turn, until one is selected, which identifies the intended character.

This sort of indirect selection method amounts to assigning a binary code to every symbol in the grid. If triggering the switch (e.g., pressing a button or blinking) is taken as a 'yes' or 1, then its absence is taken as a 'no' or 0. In such a way, every letter in the grid has a binary code based on the scanning strategy. For example, in Figure 1, the letter 'n' is in the third row and fourth column; if row scanning starts at the top, it takes two 'no's and a 'yes' to select the correct row; and then three 'no's and a 'yes' to select the correct column. This translates to a binary code of '0010001'.

In the preceding example, the codes for all symbols are determined by their position in the alpha-ordered grid. However, faster input can be achieved by assigning shorter codes to likely symbols. For example, imagine a user has just typed 'perso' and is ready to type the next letter. In this context, the letter 'n' is quite likely in English, hence if a very short code is assigned to that letter (e.g., '01'), then the user requires only two actions (a 'no' and a 'yes') to produce the letter, rather than the 7 actions re-

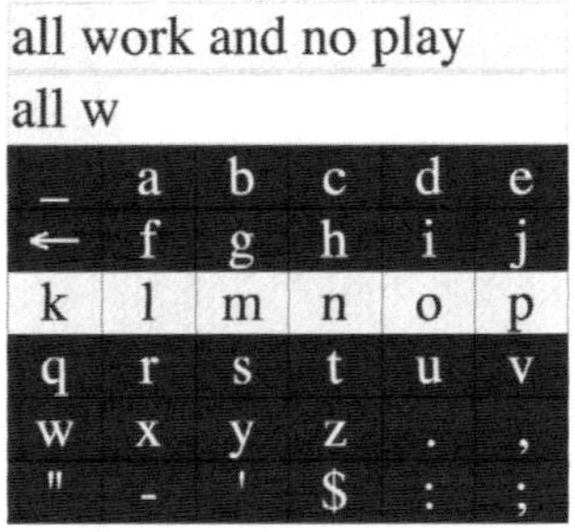

Figure 1: Spelling grid in rough alpha order.

Proceedings of the 2nd Workshop on Speech and Language Processing for Assistive Technologies, pages 43–51,
Edinburgh, Scotland, UK, July 30, 2011. ©2011 Association for Computational Linguistics

quired by the row/column code given above. There are methods for assigning codes that minimize the expected code length for a given probability model (Huffman, 1952). The quality of the probability model used for deriving codes can make a large difference in the code length and hence in the efficiency of the input method. When the model can accurately assign probabilities to symbols, the shortest binary codes can be assigned to the likeliest symbols, which thus require the fewest inputs (either yes or no) from the user. The best probabilistic models will take into account what has already been typed to assign probability to each symbol. The probabilities are contextually dependent, and therefore so are the optimal binary code assignments. This was illustrated in the 'person' example provided earlier. To provide another example, the probability of the letter 'u' is not particularly high overall in English (less than 0.02), but if the previously typed symbol is 'q', its probability is very high. Thus, in many contexts, there are other letters that should get the shortest code, but in that particular context, following 'q', 'u' is very likely, hence it should receive the shortest code.

Common scanning methods, however, present a problem when trying to leverage contextually sensitive language models for efficient scanning. In particular, methods of scanning that rely on highlighting contiguous regions – such as widely used row/column scanning – define their codes in terms of location in the grid, e.g., upper left-hand corner requires fewer keystrokes to select than lower right-hand corner using row/column scanning. To improve the coding in such an approach requires moving characters to short-code regions of the grid. In other words, with row/column scanning methods, the symbol needing the shortest code must move into the upper left-hand corner of the grid. Yet the cognitive overhead of dealing with frequent grid reorganization is typically thought to outweigh any speedup that is achieved through more efficient coding (Baletsa et al., 1976; Lesher et al., 1998). If one assumes a fixed grid, i.e., no dynamic reorganization of the symbols, then row/column scanning can gain efficiency by placing frequent characters in the upper left-hand corner, but cannot use contextually informed models. This is akin to Morse code, which assigns fixed codes to symbols based on overall frequency, without considering context.

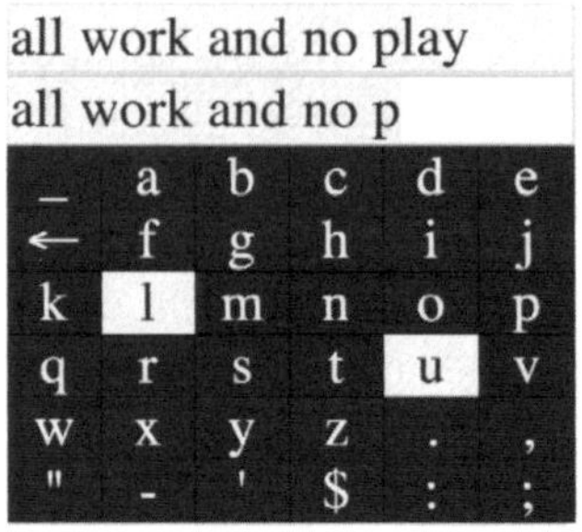

Figure 2: Scanning of non-contiguous sets of cells

Roark et al. (2010) presented a new approach which dropped the requirement of contiguous highlighting, thus allowing the use of variable codes on a fixed grid. For example, consider the grid in Figure 2, where two symbols in different rows and columns are jointly highlighted. This approach, which we will term "Huffman scanning", allowed the binary codes to be optimized using Huffman coding methods (see Section 2.2) with respect to contextually sensitive language models without dynamic reorganization of the grid. The method resulted in typing speedups over conventional row/column scanning.

One downside to the variable scanning that results from Huffman scanning is that users cannot anticipate their target symbol's binary code in any given context. In row/column scanning, the binary code of each symbol is immediately obvious from its location in the grid, hence users can anticipate when they will need to trigger the switch. In Huffman scanning, users must continuously monitor and react when their target cells light up. The time required to allow for this motor reaction means that scan rates are typically slower than in row/column scanning; and stress levels – due to the demands of immediate response to highlighting – higher.

Huffman scanning is not the only way to allow variable coding on a fixed grid. In this paper, we investigate alternatives to Huffman scanning that also allow for efficient coding on a fixed grid. The three alternative methods that we investigate are *asynchronous* methods, i.e., all of the scanning is self-paced; there is no scan rate that must be matched by the user. Rather than 'yes' being a button press and 'no' a timeout, these approaches, like Morse code, differentiate between short and long presses[1]. There are several benefits of this sort of asynchronous ap-

[1]Alternatively, two switches can be used.

proach: individuals who struggle with the timing requirements of auto, step or directed scanning can proceed without having to synchronize their movements to the interface; individuals can interrupt their communication – e.g., for side talk – for an arbitrary amount of time and come back to it in exactly the same state; and it reduces the stress of constantly monitoring the scanning sequence and reacting to it within the time limits of the interface.

The last of our alternative methods is a novel approach that displays the code for each symbol at once as a series of dots and dashes underneath the symbol – as used in Morse code – rather than using cell highlighting to prompt the user as in the other conditions. Unlike Morse code, these codes are derived using Huffman coding based on n-gram language models, thus change with every context. Since they are displayed for the user, no code memorization is required. This novel interface differs from Huffman scanning in several ways, so we also present intermediate methods that differ in only one or another dimension, so that we can assess the impact of each characteristic.

Our results show that displaying entire codes at once for asynchronous scanning was a popular and effective method for indirect selection, despite the fact that it shared certain dis-preferred characteristics with the least popular of our methods. This points the way to future work investigating methods to combine the preferred characteristics from our set of alternatives into a yet more effective interface.

2 Background and Related Work

2.1 Indirect selection

Some of the key issues influencing the work in this paper have already been mentioned above, such as the tradeoffs between fixed versus dynamic grids. For a full presentation of the range of indirect selection methods commonly in use, we refer the readers to Beukelman and Mirenda (1998). But in this section we will highlight several key distinctions of particular relevance to this work.

As mentioned in the previous section, indirect selection strategies allow users to select target symbols through a sequence of simpler operations, typically a yes/no indication. This is achieved by scanning through options displayed in the user interface. Beukelman and Mirenda (1998) mention circular scanning (around a circular interface), linear scanning (one at a time), and group-item scanning (e.g., row/column scanning to find the desired cell). Another variable in scanning is the speed of scanning – e.g., how long does the highlighting linger on the options before advancing. Finally, there are differences in selection control strategy. Beukelman and Mirenda (1998) mention automatic scanning, where highlighted options are selected by activating a switch, and advance automatically if the switch is not activated within the specified dwell time; step scanning, where highlighted options are selected when the switch is *not* activated within the specified dwell time, and advance only if the switch is activated; and directed scanning, where the highlighting moves while the switch is activated and selection occurs when the switch is *released*. In all of these methods, synchrony with the scan rate of the interface is paramount.

Speech and language pathologists working with AAC users must assess the specific capabilities of the individual to determine their best interface option. For example, an individual who has difficulty precisely timing short duration switch activation but can hold a switch more easily might do better with directed scanning.

Morse code, with its dots and dashes, is also an indirect selection method that has been used in AAC, but it is far less common than the above mentioned approaches due to the overhead of memorizing the codes. Once learned, however, this approach can be an effective communication strategy, as discussed with specific examples in Beukelman and Mirenda (1998). Often the codes are entered with switches that allow for easy entry of both dots and dashes, e.g., using two switches, one for dot and one for dash. In this study, we have one condition that is similar to Morse code in using dots and dashes, but without requiring code memorization[2]. The interface used for the experiments identifies dots and dashes with short and long keypresses.

[2]Thanks to a reviewer for pointing out that DynaVox Series 5 displays dynamically-assigned codes for non-letter buttons in their Morse code interface, much as we do for the entire symbol set. In contrast to our approach, their codes are not assigned using probabilistic models, rather to contrast with the standard Morse codes, which are used for the letters. Further, the cursor that we use to identify position within the code (see Section 3.5) is not used in the Dynavox interface.

2.2 Binary codes

In indirect selection, the series of actions required to select a given character is determined by the binary code. As mentioned in Section 1, row/column scanning assigns binary codes based on location within the grid. Ordering the symbols so that frequent characters are located in the upper left-hand corner of the grid will provide those frequent characters with short codes with a row/column scanning approach, though not the minimal possible binary codes. Given a probability distribution over symbols, there are known algorithms for building a binary code that has the minimum expected bits according to the distribution, i.e., codes will be optimally short (Huffman, 1952). The quality of the codes, however, depends on the quality of the probability model, i.e., whether the model fits the actual distribution in that context.

Roark et al. (2010) presented a scanning approach for a fixed grid that used Huffman codes derived from n-gram language models (see Section 2.3). The approach leveraged better probability models to achieve shorter code lengths, and achieved an overall speedup over row/column scanning for the 10 subjects in the trial, despite the method being closely tied to reaction time. The method requires monitoring of the target cell in the grid and reaction when it is highlighted, since the pattern of highlighting is not predictable from symbol position in the grid, unlike row/column scanning.

2.3 Language modeling

Language models assign probabilities to strings in the language being modeled, which has broad utility for many tasks in speech and language processing. The most common language modeling approach is the n-gram model, which estimates probabilities of strings as the product of the conditional probability of each symbol given previous symbols in the string, under a Markov assumption. That is, for a string $S = s_1 \ldots s_n$ of n symbols, a k+1-gram model is defined as

$$\begin{aligned} \mathrm{P}(S) &= \mathrm{P}(s_1)\prod_{i=2}^{n}\mathrm{P}(s_i \mid s_1 \ldots s_{i-1}) \\ &\approx \mathrm{P}(s_1)\prod_{i=2}^{n}\mathrm{P}(s_i \mid s_{i-k} \ldots s_{i-1}) \end{aligned}$$

where the approximation is made by imposing the Markov assumption. Note that the probability of the first symbol s_1 is typically conditioned on the fact that it is first in the string. Each of the conditional probabilities in such a model is a multinomial distribution over the symbols in a vocabulary Σ, and the models are typically regularized (or smoothed) to avoid assigning zero probability to strings in Σ^*. See Chen and Goodman (1998) for an excellent overview of modeling and regularization methods.

For the current application, the conditional probability $\mathrm{P}(s_i \mid s_{i-k} \ldots s_{i-1})$ can be used to assign probabilities to all possible next symbols, and these probabilities can be used to assign Huffman codes. For example, if the user has typed 'the perso' and is preparing to type the next letter, we estimate $\mathrm{P}(\text{n} \mid \text{t h e \_ p e r s o})$ as well as $\mathrm{P}(\text{m} \mid \text{t h e \_ p e r s o})$ and every other possible next symbol, from a large corpus. Note that smoothing methods mentioned above ensure that every symbol receives non-zero probability mass. Also note that the space character (represented above as '_') is a symbol in the model, hence the models take into account context across word boundaries. Given these estimated probabilities, known algorithms for assigning Huffman codes are used to assign short codes to the most likely next symbols, in a way that minimizes expected code length.

3 Methods

Since this paper aims to compare new methods with Huffman scanning presented in Roark et al. (2010), we follow that paper in many key respects, including training data, test protocol, and evaluation measures. For all trials we use a 6×6 grid, as shown in Figures 1 and 2, which includes the 26 characters in the English alphabet, 8 punctuation characters (comma, period, double quote, single quote, dash, dollar sign, colon and semi-colon), a white space delimiter (denoted with underscore) and a delete symbol (denoted with ←). Unlike Roark et al. (2010), our grid is in rough alphabetic order rather than in frequency order. In that paper, they compared Huffman scanning with row/column scanning, which would have been put at a disadvantage with alphabetic order, since frequent characters would have received longer codes than they do in a frequency ordered grid. In this paper, however, all of the approaches are using Huffman codes and scanning of possibly non-contiguous subsets of characters, so the code efficiency does not depend on location in the grid. Thus for ease of visual scanning, we chose in this study to use alphabetic ordering.

3.1 Language models and binary codes

We follow Roark et al. (2010) and build character-based smoothed 8-gram language models from a normalized 42M character subset of the English gigaword corpus and the CMU pronunciation dictionary. This latter lexicon is used to increase coverage of words that are unobserved in the corpus, and is included in training as one observation per word in the lexicon. Smoothing is performed with a generalized version of Witten-Bell smoothing (Witten and Bell, 1991) as presented in Carpenter (2005). Text normalization and smoothing parameterizations were as presented in Roark et al. (2010). Probability of the delete symbol $\leftarrow$ was taken to be 0.05 in all trials (the same as the probability of an error, see Section 3.2), and all other probabilities derived from the trained n-gram language model.

3.2 Huffman scanning

Our first scanning condition replicates the Huffman scanning from Roark et al. (2010), with two differences. First, as stated above, we use an alphabetic ordering of the grid as shown in Figure 2, in place of their frequency ordered grid. Second, rather than calibrating the scan rate of each individual, we fixed the scan rate at 600 ms across all subjects.

One key aspect of their method is dealing with errors of omission and commission, i.e., what happens when a subject misses their target symbol. In standard row/column scanning, rows are highlighted starting from the top of the grid, incrementing downwards one row at a time. If no row has been selected after iterating through all rows, the scanning begins again at the top. In such a way, if the subject mistakenly neglects to select their intended row, they can just wait until it is highlighted again. Similarly, if the wrong row is selected, there is usually a mechanism whereby the columns are scanned for some number of iterations, at which point row scanning resumes. The upshot of this is that users can make an error and still manage to select their intended symbol after the scanning system returns to it.

Roark et al. (2010) present a method for allowing the same kind of robustness to error in Huffman scanning, by recomputing the Huffman code after every bit. If the probability that the bit was correct is p, then the probability that it was incorrect is $1-p$. In Huffman scanning, a subset is highlighted and the user indicates yes or no – yes, the target symbol is in the set; or no, the target symbol is not in the set. If the answer is 'yes' and the set includes exactly one symbol, it is typed. Otherwise, for all symbols in the selected set (highlighted symbols if 'yes'; non-highlighted if 'no'), their probabilities are multiplied by p (the probability of being correct), while the probabilities of the other set of symbols are multiplied by $1-p$. The probabilities are then re-normalized and a new Huffman code is generated, the first bit of which drives which symbols are highlighted at the next step. In such a way, even if the target symbol is in the highlighted set when it is not selected (or vice versa), it is not eliminated from consideration; rather its probability is diminished (by multiplying by $1-p$, which in this paper is set to 0.05) and scanning continues. Eventually the symbol will be highlighted again, much as is the case in row/column scanning. We also use this method within the Huffman scanning condition reported in this paper.

3.3 Asynchronous scanning

Our second condition replaces the scan rate of 600 ms from the Huffman scanning approach outlined in Section 3.2 with an asynchronous approach that does not rely upon a scan rate. The grid and scanning method remain identical, but instead of switch versus no switch, we use short switch (rapid release) versus long switch (slower release). This is similar to the dot/dash distinction in Morse code. For this paper, we used a threshold of 200 ms to distinguish a short versus a long switch, i.e., if the button press is released within 200 ms it is short; otherwise long. Since Huffman scanning already has switch activation as 'yes', this could be thought of as having the long press replace no-press in the interface.

With this change, the scanning does not automatically advance to the next set, but waits indefinitely for the user to enter the next bit of the code. The same method for dealing with errors as with Huffman scanning is employed in this condition, i.e., re-

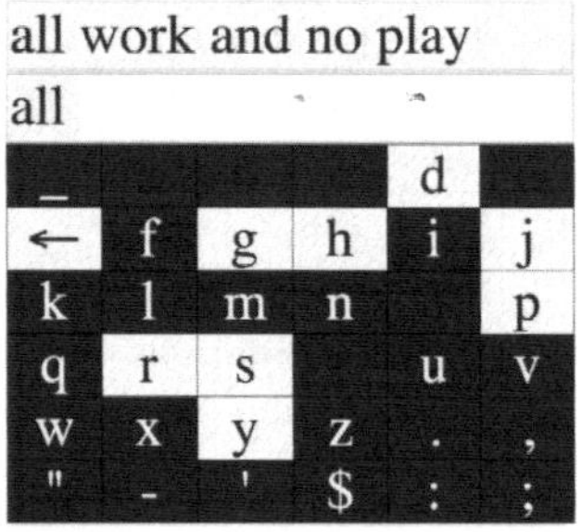

Figure 3: Scanning of non-contiguous sets of cells, with symbols that have been eliminated from consideration deemphasized (a, b, c, e, o, t)

computing the Huffman code after every bit and taking into account the probability of the bit being in error. One might see this as a self-paced version of Huffman scanning.

One benefit of this approach is that it does not require the user to synchronize their movements to a particular scan rate of the interface. One potential downside for some users is that it does require more active keypresses than auto scanning. In auto scanning, only the '1' bits of the code require switch activation; the '0' bits are produced passively by waiting for the dwell time to expire. In contrast, all bits in the asynchronous approaches require one of two kinds of switch activation.

3.4 Not returning to non-selected symbols

Our third condition is just like the second except it does not recompute the Huffman codes after every bit, changing the way in which user errors are handled. At the start of the string or immediately after a letter has been typed, the Huffman codes are calculated in exactly the same way as the previous two conditions, based on the n-gram language model given the history of what has been typed so far. However, after each bit is entered for the current symbol, rather than multiplying by p and $1-p$ as detailed in Section 3.2, symbols that have not been selected are eliminated from consideration and will not be highlighted again, i.e., will not be returned to for subsequent selection. For example, in Figure 3 we see that there is a set of highlighted characters, but also a set of characters that have been eliminated from consideration and are deemphasized in the interface to indicate that they can no longer be selected (specifically: a, b, c, e, o and t). Those are symbols that were not selected in previous steps of the scanning, and are no longer available to be typed in this position. If the user makes a mistake in the input, eliminating the actual target symbol, the only way to fix it is to type another symbol, delete it, and retype the intended symbol.

This condition is included in the study because recalculation of codes after every bit becomes problematic when the codes are explicitly displayed (the next condition). By including these results, we can tease apart the impact of not recalculating codes after every bit versus the impact of displaying codes in the next condition. Later, in the discussion, we will return to this characteristic of the interface and discuss some alternatives that may allow for different error recovery strategies.

This change to the interface has a couple of implications. First, the optimal codes are slightly shorter than with the previous Huffman scanning methods, since no probability mass is reserved for errors. In other words, the perfect user that never makes a mistake would be able to type somewhat faster with this method, which is not surprising, since reserving probability for returning to something that was rejected is of no utility if no mistakes are ever made. The experimental results presented later in the paper will show explicitly how much shorter the codes are for our particular test set. Second, it is possible to type a symbol without ever actively selecting it, if all other symbols in the grid have been eliminated. For example, if there are two symbols left and the system highlights one symbol, which is rejected, then the other symbol is typed. This contrasts with the previous methods that only type when a single character set is actively selected.

3.5 Displaying codes

Our final condition also does not recompute codes after every bit, but in addition does away with highlighting of cells as the mechanism for scanning, and instead displays dots and dashes directly beneath each letter in the fixed grid. For example, Figure 4 shows the dots and dashes required for each letter directly below that letter in the grid, and Figure 5 shows a portion of that grid magnified for easier detailed viewing. Each code includes the dots and dashes required to input that symbol, plus a cursor '|' that indicates how much of the code has already

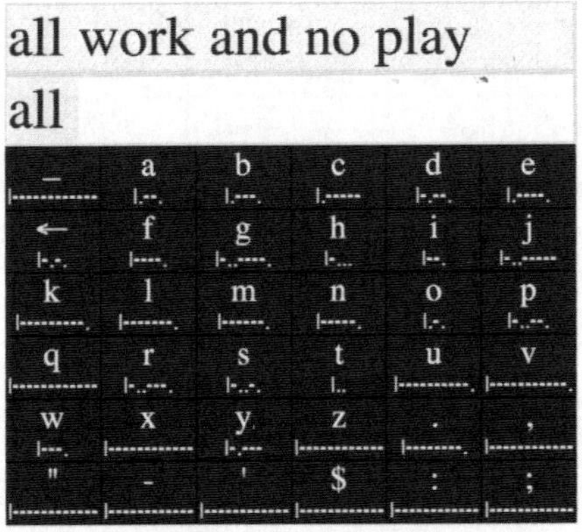

Figure 4: Scanning of non-contiguous sets of cells, displaying dots and dashes rather than highlighting

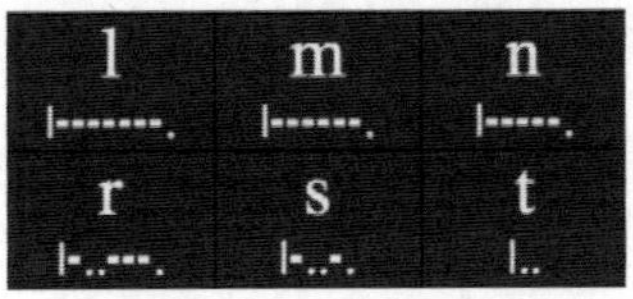

Figure 5: A magnification of part of the above grid

been entered. For example, to type the letter 's' using the code in Figure 5 , one must input: long, short, short, long, short.

Since these codes are displayed, there is no memorization required to input the target symbol. Like row/column scanning, once the target symbol has been found in the grid, the input sequence is known in entirety by the user, which can facilitate planning of sequences of actions rather than simply reacting to updates in the interface. The cursor helps the user know where they are in the code, which can be helpful for long codes. Figure 6 shows a magnification of the interface when there are only two options remaining – a dot selects 'l' and a dash selects 'u'.

4 Experiments

We recruited 10 native English speaking subjects between the ages of 26 and 50 years, who are not users

Figure 6: Cursor shows how much of code has been entered

of scanning interfaces for typing and have typical motor function. Following Roark et al. (2010), we use the phrase set from MacKenzie and Soukoreff (2003) to measure typing performance, and the same five strings from that set were used as evaluation strings in this study as in Roark et al. (2010). Practice strings were randomly selected from the rest of the phrase set. Subjects used an Ablenet Jellybean® button as the binary switch. The error rate parameter was fixed at 5% error rate.

The task in all conditions was to type the presented phrase exactly as it is presented. Symbols that are typed in error – as shown in Figure 7 – must be repaired by selecting the delete symbol (←) to delete the incorrect symbol, followed by the correct symbol. The reported times and bits take into account the extra work required to repair errors.

We tested subjects under four conditions. All four conditions made use of 8-gram character language models and Huffman coding, as described in Section 3.1, and an alpha-ordered grid. The first condition is a replication of the Huffman scanning condition from Roark et al. (2010), with the difference in scan rate (600ms versus mean 475ms in their paper) and the grid layout. This is an auto scan approach, where the highlighting advances at the end of the dwell time, as described in Section 3.2. The second condition is asynchronous scanning, i.e., replacing the dwell time with a long button press as described in Section 3.3, but otherwise identical to condition 1. The third condition was also asynchronous, but did not recompute the binary code after every bit, so that there is no return to characters eliminated from consideration, as described in Section 3.4, but otherwise identical to condition 2. Finally, the fourth condition

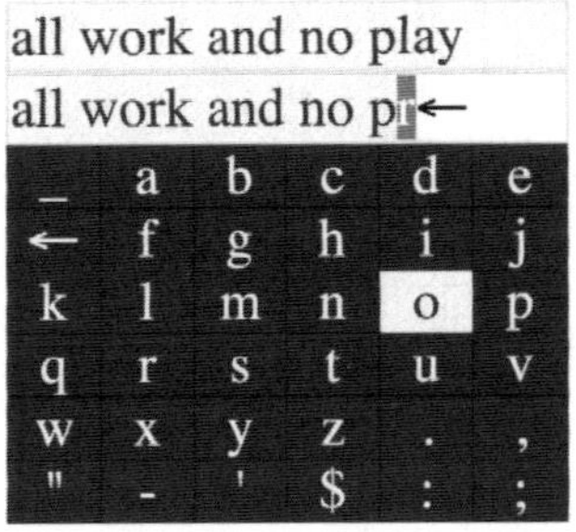

Figure 7: After an incorrect symbol is typed, it must be deleted and the correct symbol typed in its place

Scanning condition		Speed (cpm) mean (std)	Bits per character mean (std)	opt.	Error rate mean (std)	Long code rate mean (std)
1.Huffman synchronous	Roark et al. (2010)	23.4 (3.7)	4.3 (1.1)	2.6	4.1 (2.2)	19.3 (14.2)
	This paper	25.5 (3.2)	3.3 (0.4)	2.6	1.8 (1.1)	7.3 (4.1)
2. Huffman asynchronous		20.0 (3.7)	3.1 (0.2)	2.6	3.1 (2.5)	3.8 (1.2)
3. Huffman asynch, no return		17.2 (3.2)	3.1 (0.3)	2.4	7.7 (2.7)	0 (0)
4. Huffman asynch, display codes		18.7 (3.9)	3.0 (0.3)	2.4	6.9 (2.5)	0 (0)

Table 1: Typing results for 10 users on 5 test strings (total 31 words, 145 characters) under 4 conditions.

displays the codes for each character as described in Section 3.5, without highlighting, but is otherwise identical to condition 3.

Subjects were given a brief demo of the four conditions by an author, then proceeded to a practice phase. Practice phrases were given in each of the four conditions, until subjects reached sufficient proficiency in the method to type a phrase with fewer than 10% errors. After the practice phases in all four conditions were completed, the test phases commenced. The ordering of the conditions in the test phase was random. Subjects again practiced in a condition until they typed a phrase with fewer than 10% errors, and then were presented with the five test strings in that condition. After completion of the test phase for a condition, they were prompted to fill out a short survey about the condition.

Table 1 presents means and standard deviations across our subjects for characters per minute, bits per character, error rate and what Roark et al. (2010) termed "long code rate", i.e., percentage of symbols that were correctly selected after being scanned past. For condition 1, we also present the result for the same condition reported in Roark et al. (2010). Comparing the first two rows of that table, we can see that our subjects typed slightly faster than those reported in Roark et al. (2010) in condition 1, with fewer bits per character, mainly due to lower error rates and less scanning past targets. This can be attributed to either the slower scanning speed or the alphabetic ordering of the grid (or both). In any case, even with the slower scan rate, the overall speed is faster in this condition than what was reported in that paper.

The other three conditions are novel to this paper. Moving from synchronous to asynchronous (with long press) but leaving everything else the same

Survey Question	Huffman synch	Huffman asynch	No return	Display codes
Fatigued	2.1	3.2	3.4	2.5
Stressed	1.9	2.2	2.9	2.0
Liked it	3.8	3.0	2.3	3.5
Frustrated	1.9	2.8	4.0	2.4

Table 2: Mean Likert scores to survey questions (5 = a lot; 1 = not at all)

(condition 2) leads to slower typing speed but fewer bits per character. The error rate is higher than in the synchronous condition 1, but there is less scanning past the target symbol. In discussion with subjects, the higher error rate might be attributed to losing track of which button press (short or long) goes with highlighting, or also to intended short presses being registered by the system as long.

The final two conditions allow no return to characters once they have been scanned past, hence the "long code rates" go to zero, and the error rates increase. Note that the optimal bits per character are slightly better than in the other trials, as mentioned in Section 3.4, yet the subject bits per character stay mostly the same as with condition 2. Typing speed is slower in these two conditions, though slightly higher when the codes are displayed versus the use of highlighting.

In Table 2 we present the mean Likert scores from the survey. The four statements that subjects assessed were:

1. I was fatigued by the end of the trial
2. I was stressed by the end of the trial
3. I liked this trial
4. I was frustrated by this trial

The scores were: 1 (not at all); 2 (a little); 3 (not sure); 4 (somewhat) and 5 (a lot).

The results in Table 2 show high frustration and stress with condition 3, and much lower fatigue, stress and frustration (hence higher 'liking') for condition 4, where the codes are displayed. Overall, there seemed to be a preference for Huffman synchronous, followed by displaying the codes.

5 Discussion

There are several take-away lessons from this experiment. First, the frustration and slowdown that result from the increased error rates in condition 3 make this a dispreferred solution, even though disallowing returning to symbols that have been ruled out in scanning reduced the bits per character (optimal and in practice). Yet in order to display a stable code in condition 4 (which was popular), recalculation of codes after every bit (as is done in the first two conditions) is not an option. To make condition 4 more effective, some effective means for allowing scanning to return to symbols that have been scanned past must be devised.

Second, asynchronous scanning does seem to be a viable alternative to auto scanning, which may be of utility for certain AAC users. Such an approach may be well suited to individuals using two switches for asynchronous row/column scanning. Other users may find the increased level of switch activation required for scanning in these conditions too demanding. One statistic not shown in Table 1 is number of keypresses required. In condition 1, some of the "bits" required to type the character are produced by *not* pressing the button. In the other three conditions, all "bits" result from either a short or long press, so the button is pressed for every bit. In condition 1, the mean number of key presses per character was 1.5, which is approximately half of the total button presses required per character in the other methods.

Future directions include investigations into methods that combine some of the strengths of the various approaches. In particular, we are interested in methods that allow for the direct display of codes for either synchronous or asynchronous scanning, but which also allow for scanning past and return to target characters that were mistakenly not selected. The benefit of displaying codes – allowing for anticipation and planning in scanning – are quite high, and this paper has not exhausted the exploration of such approaches. Among the alternatives being considered are: requiring all codes to have a short press (confirmation) bit as the last bit of the code; having a "reset" symbol or gesture; and recalculating codes after some number of bits, greater than one. Each of these methods would somewhat increase the optimal bits per character, but may result in superior user performance. Finally, we intend to include active AAC users in subsequent studies of these methods.

References

G. Baletsa, R. Foulds, and W. Crochetiere. 1976. Design parameters of an intelligent communication device. In *Proceedings of the 29th Annual Conference on Engineering in Medicine and Biology*, page 371.

D. Beukelman and P. Mirenda. 1998. *Augmentative and Alternative Communication: Management of Severe Communication Disorders in Children and Adults*. Paul H. Brookes, Baltimore, MD, second edition.

B. Carpenter. 2005. Scaling high-order character language models to gigabytes. In *Proceedings of the ACL Workshop on Software*, pages 86–99.

Stanley Chen and Joshua Goodman. 1998. An empirical study of smoothing techniques for language modeling. Technical Report, TR-10-98, Harvard University.

D.A. Huffman. 1952. A method for the construction of minimum redundancy codes. In *Proceedings of the IRE*, volume 40(9), pages 1098–1101.

G.W. Lesher, B.J. Moulton, and D.J. Higginbotham. 1998. Techniques for augmenting scanning communication. *Augmentative and Alternative Communication*, 14:81–101.

I.S. MacKenzie and R.W. Soukoreff. 2003. Phrase sets for evaluating text entry techniques. In *Proceedings of the ACM Conference on Human Factors in Computing Systems (CHI)*, pages 754–755.

B. Roark, J. de Villiers, C. Gibbons, and M. Fried-Oken. 2010. Scanning methods and language modeling for binary switch typing. In *Proceedings of the NAACL-HLT Workshop on Speech and Language Processing for Assistive Technologies (SLPAT)*, pages 28–36.

I.H. Witten and T.C. Bell. 1991. The zero-frequency problem: Estimating the probabilities of novel events in adaptive text compression. *IEEE Transactions on Information Theory*, 37(4):1085–1094.

Improving the Accessibility of Line Graphs in Multimodal Documents

Charles F. Greenbacker **Peng Wu** **Sandra Carberry** **Kathleen F. McCoy**
Stephanie Elzer* **David D. McDonald†** **Daniel Chester** **Seniz Demir‡**
Dept. of Computer & Information Sciences, University of Delaware, USA
[charlieg|pwu|carberry|mccoy|chester]@cis.udel.edu
*Dept. of Computer Science, Millersville University, USA elzer@cs.millersville.edu
†SIFT LLC., Boston, Massachusetts, USA dmcdonald@sift.info
‡TÜBİTAK BİLGEM, Gebze, Kocaeli, Turkey senizd@uekae.tubitak.gov.tr

Abstract

This paper describes our work on improving access to the content of multimodal documents containing line graphs in popular media for people with visual impairments. We provide an overview of our implemented system, including our method for recognizing and conveying the intended message of a line graph. The textual description of the graphic generated by our system is presented at the most relevant point in the document. We also describe ongoing work into obtaining additional propositions that elaborate on the intended message, and examine the potential benefits of analyzing the text and graphical content together in order to extend our system to produce summaries of entire multimodal documents.

1 Introduction

Individuals with visual impairments have difficulty accessing the information contained in multimodal documents. Although screen-reading software can render the text of the document as speech, the graphical content is largely inaccessible. Here we consider information graphics (e.g., bar charts, line graphs) often found in popular media sources such as *Time* magazine, *Businessweek*, and *USA Today*. These graphics are typically intended to convey a message that is an important part of the overall story, yet this message is generally not repeated in the article text (Carberry et al., 2006). People who are unable to see and assimilate the graphical material will be left with only partial information.

While some work has addressed the accessibility of scientific graphics through alternative means like touch or sound (see Section 7), such graphs are designed for an audience of experts trained to use them for data visualization. In contrast, graphs in popular media are constructed to make a point which should be obvious without complicated scientific reasoning. We are thus interested in generating a textual presentation of the content of graphs in popular media. Other research has focused on textual descriptions (e.g., Ferres et al. (2007)); however in that work the same information is included in the textual summary for each instance of a graph type (i.e., all summaries of line graphs contain the same sorts of information), and the summary does not attempt to present the overall intended message of the graph.

SIGHT (Demir et al., 2008; Elzer et al., 2011) is a natural language system whose overall goal is providing blind users with interactive access to multimodal documents from electronically-available popular media sources. To date, the SIGHT project has concentrated on simple bar charts. Its user interface is implemented as a browser helper object within Internet Explorer that works with the JAWS screen reader. When the system detects a bar chart in a document being read by the user, it prompts the user to use keystrokes to request a brief summary of the graphic capturing its primary contribution to the overall communicative goal of the document. The summary text can either be read to the user with JAWS or read by the user with a screen magnifier tool. The interface also enables the user to request further information about the graphic, if desired.

However, SIGHT is limited to bar charts only. In this work, we follow the methodology put forth by SIGHT, but investigate producing a summary of

Proceedings of the 2nd Workshop on Speech and Language Processing for Assistive Technologies, pages 52–62,
Edinburgh, Scotland, UK, July 30, 2011. ©2011 Association for Computational Linguistics

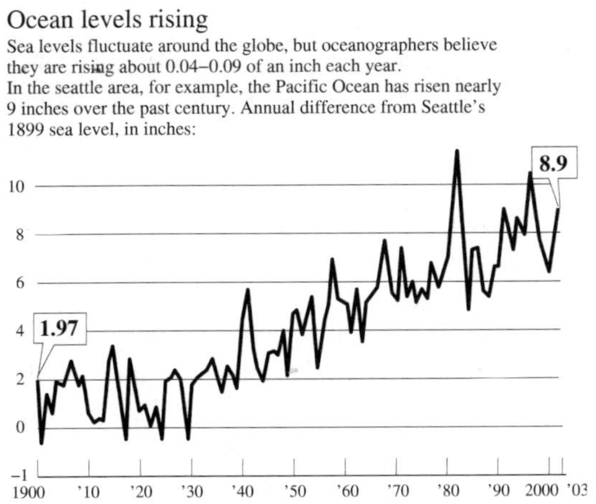

Figure 1: From "Worry flows from Arctic ice to tropical waters" in USA Today, May 31, 2006.

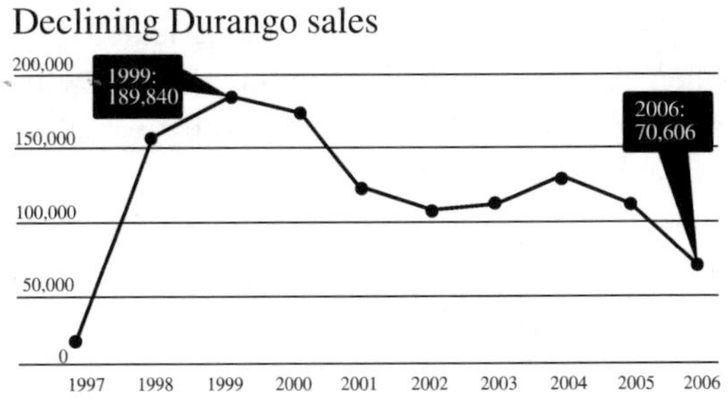

Figure 2: From "Chrysler: Plant had $800 million impact" in The (Wilmington) News Journal, Feb 15, 2007.

line graphs. Line graphs have different discourse goals and communicative signals than bar charts,[1] and thus require significantly different processing. In addition, our work addresses the issue of coherent placement of a graphic's summary when reading the text to the user and considers the summarization of entire documents — not just their graphics.

2 Message Recognition for Line Graphs

This section provides an overview of our implemented method for identifying the intended message of a line graph. In processing a line graph, a visual extraction module first analyzes the image file and produces an XML representation which fully specifies the graphic (including the beginning and ending points of each segment, any annotations on points, axis labels, the caption, etc.). To identify the intended message of a line graph consisting of many short, jagged segments, we must generalize it into a sequence of visually-distinguishable trends. This is performed by a graph segmentation module which uses a support vector machine and a variety of attributes (including statistical tests) to produce a model that transforms the graphic into a sequence of straight lines representing visually-distinguishable trends. For example, the line graph in Figure 1 is divided into a stable trend from 1900 to 1930 and a rising trend from 1930 to 2003. Similarly, the line graph in Figure 2 is divided into a rising trend from 1997 to 1999 and a falling trend from 1999 to 2006.

In analyzing a corpus of around 100 line graphs collected from several popular media sources, we identified 10 intended message categories (including *rising-trend*, *change-trend*, *change-trend-return*, and *big-jump*, etc.), that seem to capture the kinds of high-level messages conveyed by line graphs. A suggestion generation module uses the sequence of trends identified in the line graph to construct all of its possible candidate messages in these message categories. For example, if a graph contains three trends, several candidate messages are constructed, including two change-trend messages (one for each adjacent pair of trends), a change-trend-return message if the first and third trends are of the same type (rising, falling, or stable), as well as a rising, falling, or stable trend message for each individual trend.

Next, various communicative signals are extracted from the graphic, including visual features (such as a point annotated with its value) that draw attention to a particular part of the line graph, and linguistic clues (such as the presence of certain words in the caption) that suggest a particular intended message category. Figure 2 contains several such signals, including two annotated points and the word *declining* in its caption. Next, a Bayesian network is built to estimate the probability of the candidate messages; the extracted communicative signals serve as evidence for or against each candidate message. For Figure 2, our system produces change-trend(1997, rise, 1999, fall, 2006) as the logical representation of the most probable intended message. Since the dependent axis is often not explicitly labeled, a series of heuristics are used to identify an appropriate referent, which we term the *measurement axis descriptor*. In Figure 2, the measurement axis descriptor is identified as *durango sales*. The

[1] Bar charts present data as discrete bars and are often used to compare entities, while line graphs contain continuous data series and are designed to portray longer trend relationships.

intended message and measurement axis descriptor are then passed to a realization component which uses FUF/SURGE (Elhadad and Robin, 1996) to generate the following initial description:

> *This graphic conveys a changing trend in durango sales, rising from 1997 to 1999 and then falling to 2006.*

3 Identifying a Relevant Paragraph

In presenting a multimodal document to a user via a screen reader, if the author does not specify a reading order in the accessibility preferences, it is not entirely clear where the description of the graphical content should be given. The text of scientific articles normally makes explicit references to any graphs contained in the document; in this case, it makes sense to insert the graphical description alongside the first such reference. However, popular media articles rarely contain explicit references to graphics. We hypothesize that describing the graphical content together with the most relevant portion of the article text will result in a more coherent presentation. Results of an experiment described in Section 3.3 suggest the paragraph which is geographically closest to the graphic is very often not relevant. Thus, our task becomes identifying the portion of the text that is most relevant to the graph.

We have developed a method for identifying the most relevant paragraph by measuring the similarity between the graphic's textual components and the content of each individual paragraph in the document. An information graphic's textual components may consist of a title, caption, and any additional descriptions it contains (e.g., the five lines of text in Figure 1 beneath the caption *Ocean levels rising*). An initial method (P-KL) based on KL divergence measures the similarity between a paragraph and the graphic's textual component; a second method (P-KLA) is an extension of the first that incorporates an augmented version of the textual component.

3.1 Method P-KL: KL Divergence

Kullback-Leibler (KL) divergence (Kullback, 1968) is widely used to measure the similarity between two language models. It can be expressed as:

$$D_{KL}(p||q) = \sum_{i \in V} p(i) log \frac{p(i)}{q(i)}$$

where i is the index of a word in vocabulary V, and p and q are two distributions of words. Liu et al. (Liu and Croft, 2002) applied KL divergence to text passages in order to improve the accuracy of document retrieval. For our task, p is a smoothed word distribution built from the line graph's textual component, and q is another smoothed word distribution built from a paragraph in the article text. Smoothing addresses the problem of zero occurrences of a word in the distributions. We rank the paragraphs by their KL divergence scores from lowest to highest, since lower scores indicate a higher similarity.

3.2 Method P-KLA: Using Augmented Text

In analyzing paragraphs relevant to the graphics, we realized that they included words that were germane to describing information graphics in general, but not related to the domains of individual graphs. This led us to build a set of "expansion words" that tend to appear in paragraphs relevant to information graphics. If we could identify domain-independent terms that were correlated with information graphics in general, these expansion words could then be added to the textual component of a graphic when measuring its similarity to a paragraph in the article text.

We constructed the expansion word set using an iterative process. The first step is to use P-KL to identify m pseudo-relevant paragraphs in the corresponding document for each graphic in the training set (the current implementation uses $m = 3$). This is similar to pseudo-relevance feedback used in IR (Zhai, 2008), except only a single query is used in the IR application, whereas we consider many pairs of graphics and documents to obtain an expansion set applicable to any subsequent information graphic. Given n graphics in the training set, we identify (up to) $m * n$ relevant paragraphs.

The second step is to extract a set of words related to information graphics from these $m * n$ paragraphs. We assume the collection of pseudo-relevant paragraphs was generated by two models, one producing words relevant to the information graphics and another producing words relevant to the topics of the individual documents. Let W_g represent the word frequency vector yielding words relevant to the graphics, W_a represent the word frequency vector yielding words relevant to the document topics, and W_p represent the word frequency vector of the pseudo-relevant paragraphs. We compute W_p from the pseudo-relevant paragraphs themselves, and we estimate W_a using the word frequencies from the article text in the documents. Finally, we compute W_g by filtering-out the components of W_a from W_p. This process is related to the work by Widdows (2003) on orthogonal negation of vector spaces.

The task can be formulated as follows:

1. $W_p = \alpha W_a + \beta W_g$ where $\alpha > 0$ and $\beta > 0$, which means the word frequency vector for the pseudo-relevant paragraphs is a linear combination of the background (topic) word frequency vector and the graphic word vector.
2. $< W_a, W_g >= 0$ which means the background word vector is orthogonal to the graph description word vector, under the assumption that the graph description word vector is independent of the background word vector and that these two share minimal information.
3. W_g is assumed to be a unit vector, since we are only interested in the relative rank of the word frequencies, not their actual values.

Solving the above equations, we obtain:

$$\alpha = \frac{< W_p, W_a >}{< W_a, W_a >}$$

$$W_g = \text{normalized}\left(W_p - \frac{< W_p, W_a >}{< W_a, W_a >} \cdot W_a \right)$$

After computing W_g, we use WordNet to filter-out words having a predominant sense other than *verb* or *adjective*, under the assumption that nouns will be mainly relevant to the domains or topics of the graphs (and are thus "noise") whereas we want a general set of words (e.g., *"increasing"*) that are typically used when describing the data in any graph. As a rough estimate of whether a word is predominantly a verb or adjective, we determine whether there are more verb and adjective senses of the word in WordNet than there are noun senses.

Next, we rank the words in the filtered W_g according to frequency and select the k most frequent as our expansion word list (we used $k = 25$ in our experiments). The two steps (identifying $m*n$ pseudo-relevant paragraphs and then extracting a word list of size k to expand the graphics' textual components) are applied iteratively until convergence occurs or minimal changes are observed between iterations.

In addition, parameters of the intended message that represent points on the x-axis capture domain-specific content of the graphic's communicative goal. For example, the intended message of the line graph in Figure 1 conveys a changing trend from 1900 to 2003 with the change occurring in 1930. To help identify relevant paragraphs mentioning these years, we also add these parameters of the intended message to the augmented word list.

The result of this process is the final expansion word list used in method P-KLA. Because the textual component may be even shorter than the expansion word list, we do not add a word from the expansion word list to the textual component unless the paragraph being compared also contains this word.

3.3 Results of P-KL and P-KLA

334 training graphs with their accompanying articles were used to build the expansion word set. A separate set of 66 test graphs and articles was analyzed by two human annotators who identified the paragraphs in each document that were most relevant to its associated information graphic, ranking them in terms of relevance. On average, annotator 1 selected 2.00 paragraphs and annotator 2 selected 1.71 paragraphs. The annotators agreed on the top ranked paragraph for only 63.6% of the graphs. Considering the agreement by chance, we can calculate the kappa statistic as 0.594. This fact shows that the most relevant paragraph is not necessarily obvious and multiple plausible options may exist.

We applied both P-KL and P-KLA to the test set, with each method producing a list of the paragraphs ranked by relevance. Since our goal is to provide the summary of the graphic at a suitable point in the article text, two evaluation criteria are appropriate:

1. TOP: the method's success rate in selecting *the most relevant paragraph*, measured as how often it chooses the paragraph ranked highest by either of the annotators
2. COVERED: the method's success rate in selecting *a relevant paragraph*, measured as how often it chooses one of the relevant paragraphs identified by the annotators

Table 1 provides the success rates of both of our methods for the TOP and COVERED criteria, along with a simple baseline that selected the paragraph geographically-closest to the graphic. These results show that both methods outperform the baseline, and that P-KLA further improves on P-KL. P-KLA selects the best paragraph in 60.6% of test cases, and selects a relevant paragraph in 71.2% of the cases. For both TOP and COVERED, P-KLA nearly doubles the baseline success rate. The improvement of P-KLA over P-KL suggests that our expansion set successfully adds salient words to the textual component. A one-sided Z-test for proportion based on binomial distribution is shown in Table 1 and indicates that the improvements of P-KL over the baseline and P-KLA over P-KL are statistically-significant at the 0.05 level across both criteria. The Z-test is calculated as:

$$\frac{p - p_0}{\sqrt{\frac{p_0(1-p_0)}{n}}}$$

where p_0 is the lower result and p is the improved result. The null hypothesis is $H_0 : p = p_0$ and the alternative hypothesis is $H_1 : p > p_0$.

3.4 Using relevant paragraph identification to improve the accessibility of line graphs

Our system improves on SIGHT by using method P-KLA to identify the paragraph that is most relevant to an information graphic. When this paragraph is encountered, the user is asked whether he or she would like to access the content of the graphic. For example, our system identifies the following paragraph as most relevant to Figure 2:

> *Doing so likely would require the company to bring in a new model. Sales of the Durango and other gas-guzzling SUVs have slumped in recent years as prices at the pump spiked.*

In contrast, the geographically-closest paragraph has little relevance to the graphic:

> *"We have three years to prove to them we need to stay open," said Sam Latham, president of the AFL-CIO in Delaware, who retired from Chrysler after 39 years.*

4 Identifying Additional Propositions

After the intended message has been identified, the system next looks to identify elaborative informational propositions that are salient in the graphic. These additional propositions expand on the initial description of the graph by filling-in details about the knowledge being conveyed (e.g., noteworthy points, properties of trends, visual features) in order to round-out a summary of the graphic.

We collected a corpus of 965 human-written summaries for 23 different line graphs to discover which propositions were deemed most salient under varied conditions.[2] Subjects received an initial description of the graph's intended message, and were asked to write additional sentences capturing the most important information conveyed by the graph. The propositions appearing in each summary were manually coded by an annotator to determine which were most prevalent. From this data, we developed rules to identify important propositions in new graphs. The rules assign weights to propositions indicating their importance, and the weights can be compared to decide which propositions to include in a summary.

Three types of rules were built. Type-1 (message category-only) rules were created when a plurality of summaries for all graphs having a given intended message contained the same proposition (e.g., *provide the final value for all rising-trend and falling-trend graphs*). Weights for type-1 rules were based on the frequency with which the proposition appeared in summaries for graphs in this category.

Type-2 (visual feature-only) rules were built when there was a correlation between a visual feature and the use of a proposition describing that feature, regardless of the graph's message category (e.g., *mention whether the graph is highly volatile*). Type-2 rule weights are a function of the covariance between the magnitude of the visual feature (e.g., degree of volatility) and the proportion of summaries mentioning this proposition for each graph.

For propositions associated with visual features linked to a particular message category (e.g., *describe the trend immediately following a big-jump or big-fall when it terminates prior to the end of the graph*), we constructed Type-3 (message category + visual feature) rules. Type-3 weights were calculated just like Type-2 weights, except the graphs were limited to the given category.

As an example of identifying additional proposi-

[2]This corpus is described in greater detail by Greenbacker et al. (2011) and is available at www.cis.udel.edu/~mccoy/corpora

	closest	P-KL	significance level over closest	P-KLA	significance level over P-KL
TOP	0.272	0.469	$(z = 3.5966, p < 0.01)$	0.606	$(z = 2.2303, p < 0.025)$
COVERED	0.378	0.606	$(z = 3.8200, p < 0.01)$	0.712	$(z = 1.7624, p < 0.05)$

Table 1: Success rates for baseline method ("closest"), P-KL, and P-KLA using the TOP and COVERED criteria.

tions, consider Figures 1 and 2. Both line graphs belong to the same intended message category: change-trend. However, the graph in Figure 1 is far more volatile than Figure 2, and thus it is likely that we would want to mention this proposition (i.e., "*the graph shows a high degree of volatility...*") in a summary of Figure 1. By finding the covariance between the visual feature (i.e., volatility) and the frequency with which a corresponding proposition was annotated in the corpus summaries, a Type-2 rule assigns a weight to this proposition based on the magnitude of the visual feature. Thus, the volatility proposition will be weighted strongly for Figure 1, and will likely be selected to appear in the initial summary, while the weight for Figure 2 will be very low.

5 Integrating Text and Graphics

Until now, our system has only produced summaries for the graphical content of multimodal documents. However, a user might prefer a summary of the entire document. Possible use cases include examining this summary to decide whether to invest the time required to read a lengthy article with a screen reader, or simply addressing the common problem of having too much material to review in too little time (i.e., *information overload*). We are developing a system extension that will allow users to request summaries of arbitrary length that cover both the text and graphical content of a multimodal document.

Graphics in popular media convey a message that is generally not repeated in the article text. For example, the March 3, 2003 issue of *Newsweek* contained an article entitled, "The Black Gender Gap," which described the professional achievements of black women. It included a line graph (Figure 3) showing that the historical gap in income equality between white women and black women had been closed, yet this important message appears nowhere in the article text. Other work in multimodal document summarization has relied on image captions and direct references to the graphic in the text (Bhatia et al., 2009); however, these textual elements do not necessarily capture the message conveyed by information graphics in popular media. Thus, the user may miss out on an essential component of the overall communicative goal of the document if the summary covers only material presented in the text.

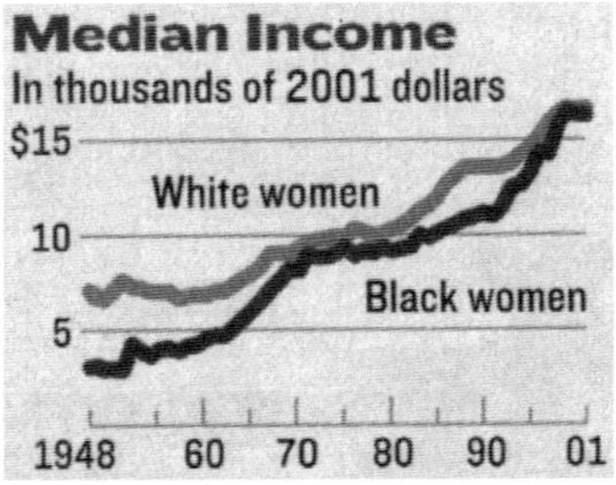

Figure 3: From "The Black Gender Gap" in Newsweek, Mar 3, 2003.

One approach to producing a summary of the entire multimodal document might be to "concatenate" a traditional extraction-based summary of the text (Kupiec et al., 1995; Witbrock and Mittal, 1999) with the description generated for the graphics by our existing system. The summary of the graphical content could be simply inserted wherever it is deemed most relevant in the text summary. However, such an approach would overlook the relationships and interactions between the text and graphical content. The information graphics may make certain concepts mentioned in the text more salient, and vice versa. Unless we consider the contributions of both the text and graphics together during the content selection phase, the most important information might not appear in the summary of the document.

Instead, we must produce a summary that *integrates* the content conveyed by the text and graphics. We contend that this integration must occur at the *semantic* level if it is to take into account the influence of the graphic's content on the salience of concepts in the text and vice versa. Our tack is to first build a single semantic model of the concepts expressed in both the article text and information graphics, and then use this model as the basis for generating an abstractive summary of the multimodal document.

Drawing from a model of the semantic content of the document, we select as many or as few concepts as we wish, at any level of detail, to produce summaries of arbitrary length. This will permit the user to request a quick overview in order to decide whether to read the original document, or a more comprehensive synopsis to obtain the most important content without having to read the entire article.

5.1 Semantic Modeling of Multimodal Documents

Content gathered from the article text by a semantic parser and from the information graphics by our graph understanding system is combined into a single semantic model based on typed, structured objects organized under a foundational ontology (McDonald, 2000a). For the semantic parsing of text, we use Sparser (McDonald, 1992), a bottom-up, phrase-structure-based chart parser, optimized for semantic grammars and partial parsing.[3] Using a built-in model of core English grammar plus domain-specific grammars, Sparser extracts information from the text and produces categorized objects as a semantic representation (McDonald, 2000b). The intended message and salient additional propositions identified by our system for the information graphics are decomposed and added to the model constructed by Sparser.[4]

Model entries contain slots for attributes in the concept category's ontology definition (fillable by other concepts or symbols), the original phrasings mentioning this concept in the text (represented as parameterized synchronous TAG derivation trees), and markers recording document structure (i.e., where in the text [including title, headings, etc.] or graphic the concept appeared). Figure 4 shows some of the information contained in a small portion of the semantic model built for an article entitled "Will Medtronic's Pulse Quicken?" from the May 29, 2006 edition of *Businessweek* magazine[5], which included a line graph. Nodes correspond to concepts and edges denote relationships between concepts; dashed lines indicate links to concepts not shown in this figure. Nodes are labelled with the name of the conceptual category they instantiate, and a number to distinguish between individuals. The middle of each box displays the attributes of the concept, while the bottom portion shows some of the original text phrasings. Angle brackets ($<>$) note references to other concepts, and hash marks (#) indicate a symbol that has not been instantiated as a concept.

Figure 4: Detail of model for *Businessweek* article.

5.2 Rating Content in Semantic Models

The model is then rated to determine which items are most salient. The concepts conveying the most information and having the most connections to other important concepts in the model are the ones that should be chosen for the summary. The importance of each concept is rated according to a measure of *information density* (ID) involving several factors:[6]

Saturation Level Completeness of attributes in model entry: a concept's filled-in slots (f) vs. its total slots (s), and the importance of the concepts (c_i) filling those slots: $\frac{f}{s} * log(s) * \sum_{i=1}^{f} ID(c_i)$

Connectedness Number of connections (n) with other concepts (c_j), and the importance of these connected concepts: $\sum_{j=1}^{n} ID(c_j)$

Frequency Number of observed phrasings (e) realizing the concept in text of the current document

Prominence in Text Prominence based on document structure (W_D) and rhetorical devices (W_R)

Graph Salience Salience assessed by the graph understanding system (W_G) – only applies to concepts appearing in the graphics

[3]https://github.com/charlieg/Sparser

[4]Although the framework is general enough to accommodate any modality (e.g., images, video) given suitable semantic analysis tools, our prototype implementation focuses on bar charts and line graphs analyzed by SIGHT.

[5]http://www.businessweek.com/magazine/content/06_22/b3986120.htm

[6]The first three factors are similar to the dominant slot fillers, connectivity patterns, and frequency criteria described by Reimer and Hahn (1988).

Saturation corresponds to the completeness of the concept in the model. The more attribute slots that are filled, the more we know about a particular concept instance. However, this measure is highly sensitive to the degree of detail provided in the semantic grammar and ontology class definition (whether created by hand or automatically). A concept having two slots, both of which are filled-out, is not necessarily more important than a concept with only 12 of its 15 slots filled. The more important a concept category is in a given domain, the more detailed its ontology class definition will likely be. Thus, we can assume that a concept definition having a dozen or more slots is, broadly speaking, more important in the domain than a less well-defined concept having only one or two slots. This insight is the basis of a normalization factor ($log(s)$) used in ID.

Saturation differs somewhat from repetition in that it attempts to measure the amount of information associated with a concept, rather than simply the number of times a concept is mentioned in the text. For example, a news article about a proposed law might mention "Washington" several times, but the fact that the debate took place in Washington, D.C. is unlikely to be an important part of the article. However, the key provisions of the bill, which may individually be mentioned only once, are likely more important as a greater amount of detail is provided concerning them. Simple repetition is not *necessarily* indicative of the importance of a concept, but if a large amount of information is provided for a given concept, it is safe to assume the concept is important in the context of that document.

Document structure (W_D) is another important clue in determining which elements of a text are important enough to include in a summary (Marcu, 1997). If a concept is featured prominently in the title, or appears in the first or final paragraphs, it is likely more important than a concept buried in the middle of the document. Importance is also affected by certain rhetorical devices (W_R) which serve to highlight particular concepts. Being used in an idiom, or compared to another concept by means of juxtaposition suggests that a given concept may hold special significance. Finally, the weights assigned by our graph understanding system for the additional propositions identified in the graphics are incorporated into the ID of the concepts involved as W_G.

5.3 Selecting Content for a Summary

To select concepts for inclusion in the summary, the model will then be passed to a discourse-aware graph-based content selection framework (Demir et al., 2010), which selects concepts one at a time and iteratively re-weights the remaining items so as to include related concepts and avoid redundancy. This algorithm incorporates PageRank (Page et al., 1999), but with several modifications. In addition to centrality assessment based on relationships between concepts, it includes apriori importance nodes enabling us to incorporate concept completeness, number of expressions, document structure, and rhetorical devices. More importantly from a summary generation perspective, the algorithm iteratively picks concepts one at a time, and re-ranks the remaining entries by increasing the weight of related items and discounting redundant ones. This allows us to select concepts that complement each other while simultaneously avoiding redundancy.

6 Generating an Abstractive Summary of a Multimodal Document

Figure 4 shows the two most important concepts (Company1 & Person1) selected from the Medtronic article in Section 5.1. Following McDonald and Greenbacker (2010), we use the phrasings observed by the parser as the "raw material" for expressing these selected concepts. Reusing the original phrasings reduces the reliance on built-in or "canned" constructions, and allows the summary to reflect the style of the original text. The derivation trees stored in the model to realize a particular concept may use different syntactic constituents (e.g., noun phrases, verb phrases). Multiple trees are often available for each concept, and we must select particular trees that fit together to form a complete sentence.

The semantic model also contains concepts representing propositions extracted from the graphics, as well as relationships connecting these graphical concepts with those derived from the text, and there are no existing phrasings in the original document that can be reused to convey this graphical content. However, the set of proposition types that can be extracted from the graphics is finite. To ensure that we have realizations for every concept in our model, we create TAG derivation trees for each type of graphical proposition. As long as realizations are supplied for every proposition that can be decomposed in the model, our system will never be stuck with a concept without the means to express it.

The set of expressions is augmented by many built-in realizations for common semantic relationships (e.g., "is-a," "has-a"), as well as expressions inherited from other conceptual categories in the hierarchy. If the observed expressions are retained as the system analyzes multiple documents over time, making these realizations available for later use by concepts in the same category, the variety of utterances we can generate is increased greatly.

By using synchronous TAG trees, we know that the syntactic realizations of two semantically-related concepts will fit together syntactically (via substitution or adjunction). However, the concepts selected for the summary of the Medtronic article (Company1 & Person1), are not directly connected in the model. To produce a single summary sentence for these two concepts, we must find a way of expressing them together with the available phrasings. This can be accomplished by using an intermediary concept that connects both of the selected items in the semantic model, in order to "bridge the gap" between them. In this example, a reasonable option would be TargetStockPrice1, one of the many concepts linking Company1 and Person1. Combining original phrasings from all three concepts (via substitution and adjunction operations on the underlying TAG trees), along with a "built-in" realization inherited by the TargetStockPrice category (a subtype of Expectation), yields this surface form:

> *Wuensch expects a 12-month target of 62 for medical device giant Medtronic.*

7 Related Work

Research into providing alternative access to graphics has taken both verbal and non-verbal approaches. Kurze (1995) presented a verbal description of the properties (e.g., diagram style, number of data sets, range and labels of axes) of business graphics. Ferres et al. (2007) produced short descriptions of the information in graphs using template-driven generation based on the graph type. The SIGHT project (Demir et al., 2008; Elzer et al., 2011) generated summaries of the high-level message content conveyed by simple bar charts. Other modalities, like sound (Meijer, 1992; Alty and Rigas, 1998; Choi and Walker, 2010) and touch (Ina, 1996; Krufka et al., 2007), have been used to impart graphics via a substitute medium. Yu et al. (2002) and Abu Doush et al. (2010) combined haptic and aural feedback, enabling users to navigate and explore a chart.

8 Discussion

This paper presented our system for providing access to the full content of multimodal documents with line graphs in popular media. Such graphics generally have a high-level communicative goal which should constitute the core of a graphic's summary. Rather than providing this summary at the point where the graphic is first encountered, our system identifies the most relevant paragraph in the article and relays the graphic's summary at this point, thus increasing the presentation's coherence. System extensions currently in development will provide a more integrative and accessible way for visually-impaired readers to experience multimodal documents. By producing abstractive summaries of the entire document, we reduce the amount of time and effort required to assimiliate the information conveyed by such documents in popular media.

Several tasks remain as future work. The intended message descriptions generated by our system need to be evaluated by both sighted and non-sighted human subjects for clarity and accuracy. We intend to test our hypothesis that graphics ought to be described alongside the most relevant part of the text by performing an experiment designed to determine the presentation order preferred by people who are blind. The rules developed to identify elaborative propositions also must be validated by a corpus or user study. Finally, once the system is fully implemented, the abstractive summaries generated for entire multimodal documents will need to be evaluated by both sighted and sight-impaired judges.

Acknowledgments

This work was supported in part by the by the National Institute on Disability and Rehabilitation Research under grant H133G080047 and by the National Science Foundation under grant IIS-0534948.

References

Iyad Abu Doush, Enrico Pontelli, Tran Cao Son, Dominic Simon, and Ou Ma. 2010. Multimodal presentation of two-dimensional charts: An investigation using Open Office XML and Microsoft Excel. *ACM Transactions on Accessible Computing (TACCESS)*, 3:8:1–8:50, November.

James L. Alty and Dimitrios I. Rigas. 1998. Communicating graphical information to blind users using music: the role of context. In *Proceedings of the SIGCHI Conference on Human Factors in Computing Systems*, CHI '98, pages 574–581, Los Angeles, April. ACM.

Sumit Bhatia, Shibamouli Lahiri, and Prasenjit Mitra. 2009. Generating synopses for document-element search. In *Proceeding of the 18th ACM Conference on Information and Knowledge Management*, CIKM '09, pages 2003–2006, Hong Kong, November. ACM.

Sandra Carberry, Stephanie Elzer, and Seniz Demir. 2006. Information graphics: an untapped resource for digital libraries. In *Proceedings of the 29th Annual International ACM SIGIR Conference on Research and Development in Information Retrieval*, SIGIR '06, pages 581–588, Seattle, August. ACM.

Stephen H. Choi and Bruce N. Walker. 2010. Digitizer auditory graph: making graphs accessible to the visually impaired. In *Proceedings of the 28th International Conference on Human Factors in Computing Systems*, CHI '10, pages 3445–3450, Atlanta, April. ACM.

Seniz Demir, Sandra Carberry, and Kathleen F. McCoy. 2008. Generating textual summaries of bar charts. In *Proceedings of the 5th International Natural Language Generation Conference*, INLG 2008, pages 7–15, Salt Fork, Ohio, June. ACL.

Seniz Demir, Sandra Carberry, and Kathleen F. McCoy. 2010. A discourse-aware graph-based content-selection framework. In *Proceedings of the 6th International Natural Language Generation Conference*, INLG 2010, pages 17–26, Trim, Ireland, July. ACL.

Michael Elhadad and Jacques Robin. 1996. An overview of SURGE: a re-usable comprehensive syntactic realization component. In *Proceedings of the 8th International Natural Language Generation Workshop (Posters and Demonstrations)*, Sussex, UK, June. ACL.

Stephanie Elzer, Sandra Carberry, and Ingrid Zukerman. 2011. The automated understanding of simple bar charts. *Artificial Intelligence*, 175:526–555, February.

Leo Ferres, Petro Verkhogliad, Gitte Lindgaard, Louis Boucher, Antoine Chretien, and Martin Lachance. 2007. Improving accessibility to statistical graphs: the iGraph-Lite system. In *Proceedings of the 9th International ACM SIGACCESS Conference on Computers and Accessibility*, ASSETS '07, pages 67–74, Tempe, October. ACM.

Charles F. Greenbacker, Sandra Carberry, and Kathleen F. McCoy. 2011. A corpus of human-written summaries of line graphs. In *Proceedings of the EMNLP 2011 Workshop on Language Generation and Evaluation*, UCNLG+Eval, Edinburgh, July. ACL. (to appear).

Satoshi Ina. 1996. Computer graphics for the blind. *SIGCAPH Newsletter on Computers and the Physically Handicapped*, pages 16–23, June. Issue 55.

Stephen E. Krufka, Kenneth E. Barner, and Tuncer Can Aysal. 2007. Visual to tactile conversion of vector graphics. *IEEE Transactions on Neural Systems and Rehabilitation Engineering*, 15(2):310–321, June.

Solomon Kullback. 1968. *Information Theory and Statistics*. Dover, revised 2nd edition.

Julian Kupiec, Jan Pedersen, and Francine Chen. 1995. A trainable document summarizer. In *Proceedings of the 18th Annual International ACM SIGIR Conference on Research and Development in Information Retrieval*, SIGIR '95, pages 68–73, Seattle, July. ACM.

Martin Kurze. 1995. Giving blind people access to graphics (example: Business graphics). In *Proceedings of the Software-Ergonomie '95 Workshop on Nicht-visuelle graphische Benutzungsoberflächen (Non-visual Graphical User Interfaces)*, Darmstadt, Germany, February.

Xiaoyong Liu and W. Bruce Croft. 2002. Passage retrieval based on language models. In *Proceedings of the eleventh international conference on Information and knowledge management*, CIKM '02, pages 375–382.

Daniel C. Marcu. 1997. *The Rhetorical Parsing, Summarization, and Generation of Natural Language Texts*. Ph.D. thesis, University of Toronto, December.

David D. McDonald and Charles F. Greenbacker. 2010. 'If you've heard it, you can say it' - towards an account of expressibility. In *Proceedings of the 6th International Natural Language Generation Conference*, INLG 2010, pages 185–190, Trim, Ireland, July. ACL.

David D. McDonald. 1992. An efficient chart-based algorithm for partial-parsing of unrestricted texts. In *Proceedings of the 3rd Conference on Applied Natural Language Processing*, pages 193–200, Trento, March. ACL.

David D. McDonald. 2000a. Issues in the representation of real texts: the design of KRISP. In Lucja M. Iwańska and Stuart C. Shapiro, editors, *Natural Language Processing and Knowledge Representation*, pages 77–110. MIT Press, Cambridge, MA.

David D. McDonald. 2000b. Partially saturated referents as a source of complexity in semantic interpretation. In *Proceedings of the NAACL-ANLP 2000 Workshop on Syntactic and Semantic Complexity in Natural*

Language Processing Systems, pages 51–58, Seattle, April. ACL.

Peter B.L. Meijer. 1992. An experimental system for auditory image representations. *IEEE Transactions on Biomedical Engineering*, 39(2):112–121, February.

Lawrence Page, Sergey Brin, Rajeev Motwani, and Terry Winograd. 1999. The pagerank citation ranking: Bringing order to the web. Technical Report 1999-66, Stanford InfoLab, November. Previous number: SIDL-WP-1999-0120.

Ulrich Reimer and Udo Hahn. 1988. Text condensation as knowledge base abstraction. In *Proceedings of the 4th Conference on Artificial Intelligence Applications*, CAIA '88, pages 338–344, San Diego, March. IEEE.

Dominic Widdows. 2003. Orthogonal negation in vector spaces for modelling word-meanings and document retrieval. In *Proceedings of the 41st Annual Meeting on Association for Computational Linguistics - Volume 1*, ACL '03, pages 136–143, Stroudsburg, PA, USA. Association for Computational Linguistics.

Michael J. Witbrock and Vibhu O. Mittal. 1999. Ultra-summarization: a statistical approach to generating highly condensed non-extractive summaries. In *Proceedings of the 22nd Annual International ACM SIGIR Conference on Research and Development in Information Retrieval*, SIGIR '99, pages 315–316, Berkeley, August. ACM.

Wai Yu, Douglas Reid, and Stephen Brewster. 2002. Web-based multimodal graphs for visually impaired people. In *Proceedings of the 1st Cambridge Workshop on Universal Access and Assistive Technology*, CWUAAT '02, pages 97–108, Cambridge, March.

Chengxiang Zhai. 2008. *Statistical Language Models for Information Retrieval*. Morgan and Claypool Publishers, December.

Indian Language Screen Readers and Syllable Based Festival Text-to-Speech Synthesis System

Anila Susan Kurian, Badri Narayan, Nagarajan Madasamy, Ashwin Bellur, Raghava Krishnan, Kasthuri G., Vinodh M.V., Hema A. Murthy
IIT-Madras, India
{anila,badri,nagarajan,ashwin,raghav,kasthuri,vinodh}@lantana.tenet.res.in
hema@cse.iitm.ac.in

Kishore Prahallad
IIIT-Hyderabad, India
kishore@iiit.ac.in

Abstract

This paper describes the integration of commonly used screen readers, namely, NVDA [NVDA 2011] and ORCA [ORCA 2011] with Text to Speech (TTS) systems for Indian languages. A participatory design approach was followed in the development of the integrated system to ensure that the expectations of visually challenged people are met. Given that India is a multilingual country (22 official languages), a uniform framework for an integrated text-to-speech synthesis systems with screen readers across six Indian languages are developed, which can be easily extended to other languages as well. Since Indian languages are syllable centred, syllable-based concatenative speech synthesizers are built.

This paper describes the development and evaluation of syllable-based Indian language Text-To-Speech (TTS) synthesis system (around festival TTS) with ORCA and NVDA, for Linux and Windows environments respectively. TTS systems for six Indian Languages, namely, Hindi, Tamil, Marathi, Bengali, Malayalam and Telugu were built. Usability studies of the screen readers were performed. The system usability was evaluated by a group of visually challenged people based on a questionnaire provided to them. And a Mean Opinion Score(MoS) of 62.27% was achieved.

1 Introduction

India is home to the world's largest number of visually challenged (VC) population [Chetna India 2010]. No longer do VC persons need to depend on others to access common information that others take for granted, such as newspapers, bank statements, and scholastic transcripts. Assistive technologies (AT), enable physically challenged persons to become part of the mainstream in the society. A screen reader is an assistive technology potentially useful to people who are visually challenged, visually impaired, illiterate or learning disabled, to use/access standard computer software, such as Word Processors, Spreadsheets, Email and the Internet.

Over the last three years, Indian Institute of Technology, Madras (IIT Madras) [Training for VC, IITM 2008], has been conducting a training programme for visually challenged people, to enable them to use the computer using a screen reader. The screen reader used was JAWS [JAWS 2011], with English as the language. Although, the VC persons have benefited from this programme, most of them felt that:

- The English accent was difficult to understand.
- Most students would have preferred a reader in their native language.
- They would prefer English spoken in Indian accent.
- The price for the individual purchase of JAWS was very high.

Although some Indian languages have been incorporated with screen readers like JAWS and NVDA, no concerted effort has been made to test the efficacy

Proceedings of the 2nd Workshop on Speech and Language Processing for Assistive Technologies, pages 63–72,
Edinburgh, Scotland, UK, July 30, 2011. ©2011 Association for Computational Linguistics

of the screen readers. Some screen readers, read Indian languages using a non native phone set [acharya 2007]. The candidates were forced to learn by-heart the sounds and their correspondence to Indian languages. It has therefore been a dream for VC people to have screen readers that read using the native tongue using a keyboard of their choice.

Given this feedback and the large VC population ($\approx$ 15%) (amongst 6% physically challenged) in India, a consortium consisting of five institutions were formed to work on building TTS for six Indian languages namely Hindi, Telugu, Tamil, Bengali, Marathi and Malayalam. This led to the development of screen readers that support Indian languages, one that can be made freely available to the community.

This paper is organized as follows. Section 2 explains the selection of a speech engine, details of speech corpus, selection of screen readers and the typing tools for Indian languages. Section 3 discusses the integration of screen readers with Indian language festival TTS voices. Although the integration is quite easy, a number of issues had to be addressed to make the screen reader user-friendly. To do this, a *participatory design* [Participatory Design Conference 2011], approach was followed in the development of the system. Section 4 summarises the participation of the user community in the design of the system. To evaluate the TTS system, different tests over and above the conventional MOS [ITU-T Rec, P.85 1994], [ITU-T Rec, P.800 1996] were performed. Section 4 also describes different quality attributes that were used in the design of the tests. Section 5 provides the results of the System Usability Test. Section 6 provides details of the MOS evaluation conducted for the visually challenged community. Section 7 describes the future work and Section 8 concludes the paper.

2 Primary components in the proposed TTS framework

2.1 Selection of Speech Engine

One of the most widely used speech engine is *eSpeak* [espeak speech synthesis2011]. *eSpeak* uses "formant synthesis" method, which allows many languages to be provided with a small footprint. The speech synthesized is intelligible, and provides quick responses, but lacks naturalness. As discussed in Section 1 the demand is for a high quality natural sounding TTS system.

We have used festival speech synthesis system developed at The Centre for Speech Technology Research, University of Edinburgh, which provides a framework for building speech synthesis systems and offers full text to speech support through a number of APIs [Festival 1998]. A large corpus based unit selection paradigm has been employed. This paradigm is known to produce [Kishore and Black 2003], [Rao et al. 2005] intelligible natural sounding speech output, but has a larger foot print.

2.2 Details of Speech Corpus

As part of the consortium project, we recorded a speech corpus of about 10 hours per language, which was used to develop TTS systems for the selected six Indian languages. The speech corpus was recorded in a noise free studio environment, rendered by a professional speaker. The sentences and words that were used for recording were optimized to achieve maximal syllable coverage. Table 1 shows the syllable coverage attained by the recorded speech corpus for different languages. The syllable level database units that will be used for concatenative synthesis, are stored in the form of indexed files, under the festival framework.

Language	Hours	No.Syll Covered
Malayalam	13	6543
Marathi	14	8136
Hindi	9	7963
Tamil	9	6807
Telugu	34	2770
Bengali	14	4374

Table 1: Syllable coverage for six languages.

2.3 Selection of Screen Readers

The role of a screen reader is to identify and interpret what is being displayed on the screen and transfer it to the speech engine for synthesis. JAWS is the most popular screen reader used worldwide for Microsoft Windows based systems. But the main drawback of this software is its high cost, approximately 1300 USD, whereas the average per capita income in India is 1045 USD [per capita Income of India 2011]

Different open source screen readers are freely available. We chose ORCA for Linux based systems and NVDA for Windows based systems. ORCA is a flexible screen reader that provides access to the graphical desktop via user-customizable combinations of speech, braille and magnification. ORCA supports the Festival GNOME speech synthesizer and comes bundled with popular Linux distibutions like Ubuntu and Fedora.

NVDA is a free screen reader which enables vision impaired people to access computers running Windows. NVDA is popular among the members of the AccessIndia community. AccessIndia is a mailing list which provides an opportunity for visually impaired computer users in India to exchange information as well as conduct discussions related to assistive technology and other accessibility issues [Access India 2011]. NVDA has already been intergated with Festival speech Engine by Olga Yakovleva [NVDA 2011]

2.4 Selection of typing tool for Indian Languages

The typing tools map the qwerty keyboard to Indian language characters. Widely used tools to input data in Indian languages are Smart Common Input Method(SCIM) [SCIM Input method 2009] and inbuilt InScript keyboard, for Linux and Windows systems respectively. Same has been used for our TTS systems, as well.

3 Integration of Festival TTS with Screen readers

ORCA and NVDA were integrated with six Indian language Festival TTS systems. Preliminary adaptations to the system for Indian languages are as follows.

- Though syllable based systems produce good quality speech output for syllabic Indian languages, syllables being larger units, require a large speech corpus to maximize syllable coverage. This means a larger footprint.

- In the paradigm being used, text processing modules are required to provide the syllable or phoneme sequence for the word to be synthesized. With input text for Indian languages being UTF-8 encoded, Indian language festival TTS systems have to be modified to accept UTF-8 input. A module was included in festival to parse the input text and give the appropriate syllable sequence. With grapheme to phoneme conversion being non-trivial, a set of grapheme to phoneme rules were included as part of the module.

- Indian languages have a special representation for vowel modifiers, which do not have a sound unit as opposed to that in Latin script languages. Hence, to deal with such characters while typing, they were mapped to sound units of their corresponding full vowels. An example in Hindi is shown in Figure 1.

ही = ह + ी
he = h + e

ी => ई
The vowel modifier ी is
mapped to corresponding full
vowel ई

Figure 1: Mapping of vowel modifiers

To enable the newly built voice to be listed in the list of festival voices under ORCA preferences menu, it has to be proclaimed as UTF-8 encoding in the lexicon scheme file of the voice [Nepali TTS 2008].

To integrate festival UTF-8 voice with NVDA, the existing driver, Festival synthDriver for NVDA by Olga Yakovleva was used [NVDA festival driver 2008]. To implement the rules for syllabifying Indian language text, a new C module was added to festival. Hence, festival [Festival compilation in Windows 2011] and synthDriver had to be recompiled [Compilation of NVDA Synthdriver 2011], for the new voice to be completely integrated with festival and usable under NVDA.

4 Participatory design

The design of the TTS system was arrived at, by active participation of visually challenged people, who

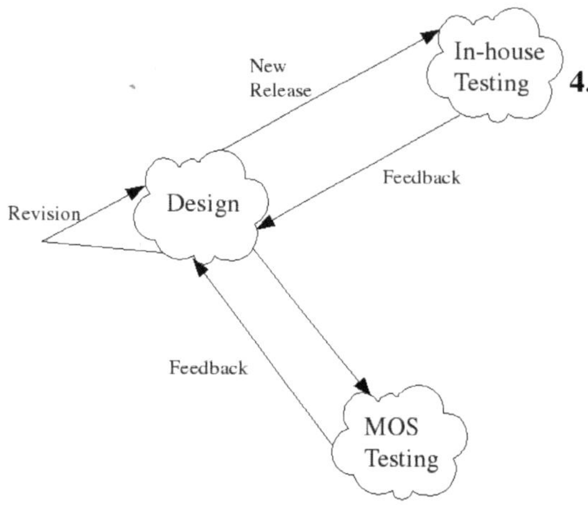

Figure 2: Flow of Development process

are the end users of the system. An educationally qualified visually challenged person was employed to test the integrated TTS system. The person is well versed in using JAWS screen reader on Windows. The quality attributes tested, were irrespective of languages. Hence, as a study, these tests were exclusively conducted on Tamil festival voice for both NVDA and ORCA.

When a new version of the system was released, it was provided to the in-house tester for evaluation. The suggestions and issues reported were then incorporated in the next release of the system. This process was done on an iterative basis. This helped in enhancing the system to meet the expectations of visually challenged people. Finally, the overall system performance was evaluated by conducting a Mean Opinion Score(MOS) test by visually challenged people, which is explained in detail in Sections 6. Figure 2 describes this development process.

The various quality attributes tested for, are :

- Usability of the TTS system
  - Adaptability of users to the new system
  - Navigation through desktop and web pages
- Availability of the TTS system
- Performance of the TTS system
  - Loading of voices
  - Response time for typing and reading

4.1 Usability of the TTS system

- **Adaptability of users to the new system**

  As the common screenreader used among the visually challenged community is JAWS, a study was conducted to find out the ease of adaptability for the user to the new system. Since the front end for the system are screen readers, the parameter used in this testing was primarily the learning involved in switching from JAWS to ORCA or NVDA. As JAWS and NVDA are Windows based screen readers, all the keystokes and shortcut keys are the same. A computer literate who has used JAWS, will learn NVDA quicker than others. As ORCA is a Linux based screen reader, the shortcut keys, key strokes and navigation through the system are different compared to that of JAWS. It takes more time for a JAWS user to familiarize with the Linux operating system, ORCA settings and keystokes.

- **Navigation of desktop and web pages using the screen reader**

  When default *English locale* is selected for Windows and Linux systems, all the program menus and navigational keys are in English. The initial version of the TTS system was not able to parse these English words. As a solution, *switching of voices* between English and the selected Indian language was tried. The system was made to switch between Festival's English *Kal diphone* voice and one of the Indian language voices. When an English word is given as input, the English voice would be loaded and when an Indian language word is given as input, it switches to the respective Indian language, loads the voice and speaks the word. This frequent switching of voices degraded the performance of the system and hearing two different voices, without continuity was annoying to the listener. This led to the development of a bilingual voice.

Bilingual Voice: Each Indian language voice is provided with an English pronunciation dictionary, so that when an English word is provided to the system, speech is synthesized using the Indian language voice itself. Following are the enhancements made to better the TTS system.

- **Pronunciation Dictionary for English words in native sound units**
  The English dictionary from Carnegie Mellon University(CMU) with phone pronunciation was used to create English to Native language pronounciation dictionary. An entry in the CMU dictionary :
  ("abolish" ax b aa l ih sh). These English phones were mapped to phones in native language. An example mapping from English to Hindi language :
  ax=अ , b=ब् , aa=आ, l=ल् , ih=इ , sh=श्.
  For all the English words in the dictionary, the native language representation was created, abolish = अबाल्शि्. The pronunciation dictionary was then created by breaking these words down into syllables and phone sequences present in the database.
  ("abolish" अ बा ल्शि्)
  All such English words that are required to navigate through a desktop(including special keys) and web, were collected and added to the pronunciation dictionary. The drawback of this method is that if an English word which is not present in the pronunciation dictionary, is provided as input, the TTS system cannot synthesize it. In order to overcome this, English Letter To Sound (LTS) rules were implemented.

- **Implementation of English LTS Rules**
  Inputs can be in English or the native language. In the case of a word being absent in the pronunciation dictionary, LTS rules should supplement. LTS rules have been developed for English in festival using a pronunciation dictionary of around 100000 words as the training set [Black et al. 1998]. These LTS rules generate a sequence of phones for the English word. By mapping the English phones to phones in the native language, one can provide a phone sequence in terms of the Indian language, for an English word. For example, a part of the Classification and Regression Tree(CART) for letter 'd' in a word, by looking at the context in which it is occuring is shown in Figure 3. The first part of the figure is a partial tree in English. The second part of the figure is the corresponding entry for the Indian language. If 'd' is followed by another 'd', no sound('epsilon;) is assigned. If it is followed by 'i' and 'r' 'phone d' is assigned for English, whereas 'phone d' is mapped to ड for Hindi language.

```
(d
 ((n.name is d)
  (((_epsilon_ 0.993658) (d 0.00634249) _epsilon_))
  ((n.name is i)
   ((n.n.name is r)
    (((_epsilon_ 0.0909091) (d 0.909091) d))

to

(d
 ((n.name is d)
  (((_epsilon_ 0.993658) (d 0.00634249) _epsilon_))
  ((n.name is i)
   ((n.n.name is r)
    (((_epsilon_ 0.0909091) (d 0.909091) ड ))

n = next, p = previous _epsilon_ = silent
```

Figure 3: CART for letter d

- **Recording of Common English words**
  Most of the English words when spoken in the Indian language voice did not sound intelligible enough. This is because, many English sounds were not available in Indian languages. Hence frequently seen English words while navigating a Windows/Linux desktop were recorded. Instead of concatenating Indian phones to synthesize the English word, the naturally uttered English word is spoken. This increased the usability of the system.

4.2 Availability of the TTS system

The system was tested to check if it responded to each and every input provided to it. Words, sentences and paragraphs were provided as input to the system using commonly used applications like notepad, word processor and browser. The system was able to read the words whose syllables were present in the database. The testing was done extensively for each language which resulted in some words not being spoken, which helped in the identification of those syllables which need to be included in the database. Some of the major issues identified during this test were:

- **Issues during typing**

  The evaluator tested the system by typing using SCIM in Linux systems and the inbuilt InScript keyboard in Windows systems. As it is unit selection based synthesis, the sound units for the corresponding characters that are picked up from the database may not be clear or audible. Also, the prosody of these individual characters, when taken from different contexts will vary. While typing, flat and prosodically neutral sounds are preffered. This led to recording of all *aksharas* (alphabets) in all six languages, in a prosodically neutral flat tone. It was also observed that the system was not reading vowel modifiers. This issue was solved by adding entries for vowel modifiers in the pronunciation dictionary. The vowel modifiers were mapped to the corresponding vowel pronunciation.

- **Issues during reading web pages**

  The system was tested for reading content from web pages. It was found that when a line with any special character(for example <,>,') is given as input, the system would fail to read the entire line. This led to the handling of special characters in the Indian language voice. If anything outside the unicode range of the language is provided to the system, it is ignored. In this way, even if some special or junk characters are present in a line, the system will read the whole line ignoring these characters.

4.3 Performance of the TTS system

The evaluator noted the response time of the system while loading the voice, typing, navigation through desktop and web pages.

- **Loading of voices**

  In the unit selection paradigm, we have a large repository of multiple realizations of a unit (syllables) in different contexts. The text to be spoken is broken down into these units. Syllable speech units are then indexed with their linguistic and phonetic features using clustering techniques (CART) to capture the context in which they are uttered. With many realizations of the same syllable being present, CART are used to select a smaller set of candidate units for the syllable to be spoken. These CART built as part of the voice building process, attempt to predict the acoustic properties of the unit using its phonetic and linguistic features at the time of synthesis [Black and Taylor 1997].

  When the festival engine loads a voice, although the speech waveforms are saved on the hard disk, the CART gets loaded into the heap memory. As the size of this tree file exceeds the default heap size set in the festival framework, the initial version of the Indian language TTS voices failed to load. Hence, a larger heap size was provided as a runtime argument for the festival synthesizer.

- **Response time for typing and reading**

  The user expects the system to respond in a reasonable amount of time (approx 125 milliseconds). For the initial system, the response time for a sentence with 5 to 10 words was 1 to 2 seconds. To improve the response time of the system, the voice(s) had to be pruned. In the case of unit selection paradigm, a large database with multiple realizations is used to produce natural speech. Around 300000 units with multiple realizations of syllables including the 'silence' unit are present in the database. In the cluster unit framework [Black and Taylor 1997], these syllables are clustered into similar sounding groups and form the leaves of the CART built. This resulted in a large CART file which in turn slowed down the system.

  With around 300000 realizations of syllables being present, it is seen that there are far too many realizations of frequently occuring syllables. So it was vital to prune the CART built. To effectively capture prosody for syllables, after experimenting heuristically with various cluster sizes, a leaf size of eight was used, i.e syllables are clustered into groups of eight. To prune the tree using the tools available within festival [Black and Lenzo 2000], within each cluster only two units closest to the centroid were retained and the rest were removed, hence reducing the tree size. Even after pruning the voice, it was seen that there were still a very large number (around 20000) of silence units, which are used to annotate phrase and sentence boundaries, in the speech corpus. It was seen that the silence units could be quantized into two units, one to denote end of phrase and another for end of sentence, without affecting the performance. Hence silence trees were removed from the CART retaining just the two quantized units, further pruning the tree and improving the speed. After pruning, the size of the tree for Tamil language was reduced from an 8 MB file to 1.7 MB file. The response time for sentences having word rate between 5 to 10 for the pruned system was 200milliseconds to 900 milliseconds. On an average there was 61% improvement in the response time.

5 System Usability Rating

For comparing the overall usability of the TTS system, before and after carrying out all the modifications listed in Section 4, a Usability test was conducted using screen readers by a group of visually challenged people. The System Usability Scale developed by John Brooke [Brooke 1996], which uses the Likert scale for providing a global view of subjective assessments of usability was used. The evaluators were provided with a questionnaire for which they have to provide Likert scale ratings. Table 2 shows the Likert scale used for the evaluation.

Scores	Scales
5	Strongly agree
4	Agree
3	Neither agree nor disagree
2	Disagree
1	Strongly disagree

Table 2: Likert Scales.

Questionnaire used for evaluation.

1. I found the system easy to use.
2. I need the support of a technical/non visually challenged person to be able to use the system.
3. I am able to navigate through Desktop and internet using the system without any help.
4. System is not able to clearly read each and every character I type.
5. Availability of the system is more than 90%. i.e. the system provides appropriate response to more than 90% of the input given to it.
6. Response time of the system is good and is within my tolerable limits.
7. I feel that most of the visually challenged people, having basic knowledge on computers, can learn this system quickly.
8. The system is not natural sounding.
9. The overall understanding/comprehensibility of the content read out by the system is high.
10. The system is very useful for the VC community.

The rating of the system was calculated as follows [Brooke 1996]. First, the score contributions from each item were summed up. Each item's score contribution will range from 0 to 4. The score contribution for positive questions 1,3,5,6,7,9 and 10 is the scale position minus 1. The score contribution for negative questions 2,4 and 8 is 5 minus the scale position. Multiply the sum of the scores by 2.5 to obtain the overall value of System Usability out of 100. A group of visually challenged people evaluated the initial and final system based on the questionnaire. The average System Usability score for the initial system was 35.63 and that of the final system was 89.38. Thus an improvement of around 50% in System Usability scores were seen due to the changes made in Section 4.

6 MOS Evaluation

MOS([ITU-T Rec, P.85 1994], [ITU-T Rec, P.800 1996]) and Degradation MOS (DMOS) tests were conducted for six Indian languages, across various centers in India. Synthesized speech files were played to the evaluators. Sentences belonging to different domains were chosen for quality evaluation, in order to test the performance of TTS system(s) upon receiving input text from varied domains.

The various factors that were considered, while administering the quality evaluation tests were:

- The MOS evaluators were chosen, such that they should not have participated in any listening quality test for synthetic speech, at least for the last 6 months and are well versed with the language.
- The tests were done up to a maximum of 30-40 minutes, in order to avoid listener fatigue.
- A reasonable number of MOS evaluators (a minimum of 20) were involved for evaluating the quality.
- The tests were conducted in a quiet room and the content to be evaluated was played through a good quality speaker.
- For MOS tests, the sentences belonging to various domains were grouped into various sets and the order of these sets were randomized in order to avoid any learning effects.
- Randomized sentences were played one after the other, with a brief pause for listeners to provide the quality score, based on the scales provided in Table 3.
- In the case of DMOS tests, a natural sentence followed by its synthesized counterpart is played after a brief pause and the listeners have to rate the amount of degradation in the synthesized sentence, relative to the natural sentence. This rating is based on the scales provided in Table 3.
- DMOS tests were conducted first, so that the participants get a feeling of how natural and synthesized sentences sound.

Figure 4: Active discussion among Visually Challenged candidates, during a training session

- 40 sentences were used to conduct the MOS test and 10 sentences for DMOS test.

The MOS and DMOS scores for the six Indian languages are provided in Table 4. Overall comprehension was also considered important, as the primary goal or aim of the TTS system was to be able to communicate information to the user. Thus, a preliminary comprehension based MOS test was conducted, which involved playing out a paragraph to the MOS evaluators and testing their level of comprehension.

Scores	Quality scales	
	MOS	**DMOS**
5	Excellent	Imperceptible
4	Good	Perceptible but not annoying
3	Fair	Slightly annoying
2	Poor	Annoying
1	Bad	Very annoying

Table 3: MOS and DMOS Scales.

7 Future Work

As a second phase of the project, we plan to carry out the following tasks

- To improve the prosody of synthetic speech.
- Enable the system to synthesize emotional speech.

Language	No. of Mos evaluators	News	Natural	Sports	InDomain	Science	DMOS	Overall MOS
Hindi	40	2.64	4.48	-	2.63	2.99	2.9	2.75
Bengali	8	3.31	-	2.91	3.18	2.85	3.14	3.06
Marathi	26	-	4.73	3.25	3.03	3.03	3.06	3.1
Telugu	23	-	4.66	2.46	2.89	2.83	3.68	2.73
Malayalam	27	3.95	4.13	3.73	3.77	-	3.91	3.82
Tamil	22	3.13	-	-	3.54	3.2	2.81	3.22

Table 4: Mos scores for six Indian languages.

- Build a small footprint TTS system, so that it can be used in applications for mobile, PDA, ATM etc.
- Evaluate the TTS system by conducting objective tests for intelligibility and naturalness, using different measures including the Semantically Unpredictable Sentence (SUS) test.
- To extend this effort to other Indian languages.
- To develop full-fledged Bilingual voices. In the current system we use the Indian language corpus to synthesize English words. The complete bilingual voice would have an English corpus recorded in the same voice as the Indian language, so that the same speech quality can be provided to both English and Indian language input.

8 Conclusion

In this paper, we have briefly discussed the efforts taken towards integrating TTS systems in six Indian languages, with screen readers ORCA and NVDA. We have also described the issues that were faced while testing the system and the solutions to improve the system. Further, results of the subjective listening tests (MOS and DMOS evaluation) and System Usability tests conducted were discussed.

With the completion of this project, training programme in IIT Madras, can be conducted for visually challenged community, using screen readers NVDA and ORCA for Indian Languages, instead of JAWS. Figure 4 shows an active discussion among visually challenged candidates during the computer training using screen readers at IIT Madras.

9 Acknowledgement

The authors would like to acknowledge the contributions of the Consortium members, namely IIIT hyderabad, IIT Kharagpur, CDAC Thiruvananthapuram and CDAC Mumbai, towards the project.

This project has been supported by the Department of Information Technology, India. (Project number - CSE0809107DITXHEMA).

References

S.P. Kishore and A.W. Black 2003. *Unit size in unit selection speech synthesis, proceedings of EUROSPEECH, pp. 1317-1320, 2003*

A.W. Black and P. Taylor 1997 *Automatically clustering similar units for unit selection in speech synthesis Eurospeech97 (Rhodes, Greece, 1997), vol. 2, pp. 601-604*

M. Nageshwara Rao,S. Thomas, T. Nagarajan and Hema A. Murthy 2005 *Text-to-speech synthesis using syllable like units, proceedings of National Conference on Communication (NCC) 2005, pp. 227-280, IIT Kharagpur, India, Jan 2005.*

ITU-T Rec, P.85 1997 *Method for Subjective Performance Assessment of the Quality of Speech Voice Output Devices, ITU-T Rec, P.85, 1994, Int. Telecom. Union*

ITU-T Rec, P.800 1996 *Methods for subjective determination of transmission quality, ITU-T Rec, P.800, 1996, Int. Telecom. Union*

A. Black and K. Lenzo 2000 *Building voices in the Festival speech synthesis system* `http://festvox.org/bsv/`

A. Black, P. Taylor, and R. Caley 1998 *The Festival speech synthesis system* `http://festvox.org/festival`

Festival Speech Synthesis System
http://www.cstr.ed.ac.uk/projects/festival/

ORCA Screen reader.
http://live.gnome.org/Orca

NVDA Screen reader.
http://www.nvda-project.org/

Festival synthDriver for NVDA by Olga Yakovleva:
http://www.box.net/shared/jcnnzz7xu6

SCIM Input method.
http://apps.sourceforge.net/mediawiki/scim/index.php
https://help.Ubuntu.com/community/SCIM

Festival compilation in Windows.
http://www.eguidedog.net/doc_build_win_festival.php

Participatory Design Conference
http://www.publicsphereproject.org/drupal/node/235

J. Brooke 1996 *"SUS: a "quick and dirty" usability scale". In P. W. Jordan, B. Thomas, B. A. Weerdmeester, A. L. McClelland. Usability Evaluation in Industry.*
http://hell.meiert.org/core/pdf/sus.pdf

Nepali TTS User Manual. 2008.
http://www.bhashasanchar.org/textspeech_intro.php

JAWS Screen reader.
http://www.freedomscientific.com/jaws-hq.asp

espeak speech synthesis
http://espeak.sourceforge.net/

Training for Visually Challenged by IIT Madras
http://www.lantana.tenet.res.in/TTSconsortiumWiki/doku.php?id=start/

Acharya Multilingual Computing for literacy and education
http://acharya.iitm.ac.in/ Last updated on 2007-03-19

Chetna India
http://chetnaindia.org/our_values.htm

Per capita Income of India, 2011
http://www.financialexpress.com/news/Per-capita-income-in-India-is-Rs-46-492/744155/

Access India mailing list
http://accessindia.org.in/mailman/listinfo/accessindia_accessindia.org.in

Compilation of NVDA Synthdriver
http://www.lantana.tenet.res.in/TTSconsortiumWiki/doku.php?id=start

READ–IT: Assessing Readability of Italian Texts with a View to Text Simplification

Felice Dell'Orletta, Simonetta Montemagni and Giulia Venturi
Istituto di Linguistica Computazionale "Antonio Zampolli" (ILC–CNR)
via G. Moruzzi, 1 – Pisa (Italy)
{felice.dellorletta,simonetta.montemagni,giulia.venturi}@ilc.cnr.it

Abstract

In this paper, we propose a new approach to readability assessment with a specific view to the task of text simplification: the intended audience includes people with low literacy skills and/or with mild cognitive impairment. READ–IT represents the first advanced readability assessment tool for what concerns Italian, which combines traditional raw text features with lexical, morpho-syntactic and syntactic information. In READ–IT readability assessment is carried out with respect to both documents and sentences where the latter represents an important novelty of the proposed approach creating the prerequisites for aligning the readability assessment step with the text simplification process. READ–IT shows a high accuracy in the document classification task and promising results in the sentence classification scenario.

1 Introduction

Recently, there has been increasing interest in the exploitation of results from Natural Language Processing (NLP) for the development of assistive technologies. Here, we address this topic by reporting the first but promising results in the development of a software architecture for the Italian language aimed at assisting people with low literacy skills (both native and foreign speakers) or who have language disabilities in reading texts.

Within an information society, where everyone should be able to access all available information, improving access to written language is becoming more and more a central issue. This is the case, for instance, of administrative and governmental information which should be accessible to all members of the society, including people who have reading difficulties for different reasons: because of a low education level or because of the fact that the language in question is not their mother tongue, or because of language disabilities. Health related information represents another crucial domain which should be accessible to a large and heterogenous target group. Understandability in general and readability in particular is also an important issue for accessing information over the web as stated in the Web Content Accessibility Guidelines (WCAG) proposed by the Web Accessibility Initiative of the W3C.

In this paper, we describe the approach we developed for automatically assessing the readability of newspaper texts with a view to the specific task of text simplification. The paper is organized as follows: Section 2 describes the background literature on the topic; Section 3 introduces the main features of our approach to readability assessment, with Section 4 illustrating its implementation in the READ-IT prototype; Sections 5 and 6 describe the experimental setting and discuss achieved results.

2 Background

Readability assessment has been a central research topic for the past 80 years which is still attracting considerable interest nowadays. Over the last ten years, within the NLP community the automatic assessment of readability has received increasing attention: if on the one hand the availability of sophisticated NLP technologies makes it possible to monitor a wide variety of factors affecting the readability

Proceedings of the 2nd Workshop on Speech and Language Processing for Assistive Technologies, pages 73–83,
Edinburgh, Scotland, UK, July 30, 2011. ©2011 Association for Computational Linguistics

of a text, on the other hand there is a wide range of both human- and machine-oriented applications which can benefit from it.

Traditional readability formulas focus on a limited set of superficial text features which are taken as rough approximations of the linguistic factors at play in readability assessment. For example, the Flesch-Kincaid measure (the most common reading difficulty measure still in use, Kincaid (1975)) is a linear function of the average number of syllables per word and of the average number of words per sentence, where the former and latter are used as simple proxies for lexical and syntactic complexity respectively. For Italian, there are two readability formulas: an adaptation of the Flesh-Kincaid for English to Italian known as the Flesch-Vacca formula (Franchina and Vacca, 1986); the GulpEase index (Lucisano and Piemontese, 1988), assessing readability on the basis of the average number of characters per word and the average number of words per sentence.

A widely acknowledged fact is that all traditional readability metrics are quick and easy to calculate but have drawbacks. For example, the use of sentence length as a measure of syntactic complexity assumes that a longer sentence is more grammatically complex than a shorter one, which is often but not always the case. Word syllable count is used starting from the assumption that more frequent words are more likely to have fewer syllables than less frequent ones (an association that is related to Zipf's Law, Zipf (1935)); yet, similarly to the previous case, word length does not necessarily reflects its difficulty. The unreliability of these metrics has been experimentally demonstrated by several recent studies in the field: to mention only a few Si and Callan (2001), Petersen and Ostendorf (2006), Feng (2009).

On the front of the assessment of the lexical difficulty of a given text, a first step forward is represented by vocabulary-based formulas such as the Dale-Chall formula (Chall and Dale, 1995), using a combination of average sentence length and word frequency counts. In particular, for what concerns the latter it reconstructs the percentage of words not on a list of 3000 "easy" words by matching its own list to the words in the material being evaluated, to determine the appropriate reading level. If vocabulary-based measures represent an improvement in assessing the readability of texts which was possible due to the availability of frequency dictionaries and reference corpora, they are still unsatisfactory for what concerns sentence structure.

Over the last ten years, work on readability deployed sophisticated NLP techniques, such as syntactic parsing and statistical language modeling, to capture more complex linguistic features and used statistical machine learning to build readability assessment tools. A variety of different NLP-based approaches to the automatic readability assessment has been proposed so far, differing with respect to: a) the typology of features taken into account (e.g. lexical, syntactic, semantic, discourse), and, for each type, at the level of the inventory of used individual features; b) the intended audience of the texts under evaluation, which strongly influences the readability assessment, and last but not least c) the application within which readability assessment is carried out.

Interesting alternatives to static vocabulary-based measures have been put forward by Si and Callan (2001) who used unigram language models combined with sentence length to capture content information from scientific web pages, or by Collins-Thompson and Callan (2004) who adopted a similar language modeling approach (Smoothed Unigram model) to predict reading difficulty of short passages and web documents. These approaches can be seen as a generalization of the vocabulary-based approach, aimed at capturing finer-grained and more flexible information about vocabulary usage. If unigram language models help capturing important content information and variation of word usage, they do not cover other types of features which are reported to play a significant role in the assessment of readability. More recently, the role of syntactic features started being investigated (Schwarm and Ostendorf, 2005; Heilman et al., 2007; Petersen and Ostendorf, 2009): in these studies syntactic structure is tracked through a combination of features from n-gram (trigram, bigram and unigram) language models and parse trees (parse tree height, number of noun phrases, verb phrases and subordinated clauses or SBARs) with more traditional features.

Yet, besides lexical and syntactic complexity features there are other important factors, such as the structure of the text, the definition of discourse topic, discourse cohesion and coherence and so on, playing a central role in determining the reading difficulty of a text. More recent approaches esplored the role of these features in readability assessment: this is the case, for instance, of Barzilay and Lapata (2008) or Feng (2010). The last few years have been characterised by approaches based on the combination of features ranging over different linguistic levels, namely lexical, syntactic and discourse (see e.g. Pitler and Nenkova (2008), Kate (2010)).

Another important factor determining the typology of features to be considered for assessing readability has to do with the intended audience of readers: it is commonly agreed that reading ease does not follow from intrinsic text properties alone, but it is also affected by the expected audience. Among the studies addressing readability with respect to specific audiences, it is worth mentioning here: Schwarm and Ostendorf (2005) and Heilman et al. (2007) dealing with language learners, or Feng (2009) focussing on people with mild intellectual disabilities. Interestingly,Heilman et al. (2007) differentiate the typology of used features when addressing first (L1) or second (L2) language learners: they argue that grammatical features are more relevant for L2 than for L1 learners. Feng (2009) propose a set of cognitively motivated features operating at the discourse level specifically addressing the cognitive characteristics of the expected users. When readability is targeted towards adult competent language users a more prominent role is played by discourse features (Pitler and Nenkova, 2008).

Applications which can benefit from an automatic readability assessment range from the selection of reading material tailored to varying literacy levels (e.g. for L1/L2 students or low literacy people) and the ranking of documents by reading difficulty (e.g. in returning the results of web queries) to NLP tasks such as automatic document summarization, machine translation as well as text simplification. Again, also the application making use of the readability assessment, which is in turn strictly related to the intended audience of readers, strongly influences the typology of features to be taken into account.

Advanced NLP–based readability metrics developed so far typically deal with English, with a few attempts devoted to other languages, namely French (Collins-Thompson and Callan, 2004), Portuguese (Aluisio et al., 2010) and German (Brück, 2008).

3 Our Approach

Our approach to readability assessment was developed with a specific application in mind, i.e. text simplification, and addresses a specific target audience of readers, namely people characterised by low literacy skills and/or by mild cognitive impairment. Following the most recent approaches, we treat readability assessment as a classification task: in particular, given the available corpora for the Italian language as well as the type of target audience, we resorted to a binary classification aimed at discerning easy–to–read textual objects from difficult–to–read ones. The language dealt with is Italian: to our knowledge, this is the first attempt of an advanced methodology for readability assessment for this language. Our approach focuses on lexical and syntactic features, whose selection was influenced by the application, the intended audience and the language dealt with (both for its intrinsic linguistic features and for the fact of being a less resourced language). Following Roark (2007), in the features selection process we preferred easy-to-identify features which could be reliably identified within the output of NLP tools. Last but not least, as already done by Aluisio et al. (2010) the set of selected syntactic features also includes simplification oriented ones, with the final aim of aligning the readability assessment step with the text simplification process.

Another qualifying feature of our approach to readability assessment consists in the fact that we are dealing with two types of textual objects: documents and sentences. The latter represents an important novelty of our work since so far most research focused on readability classification at the document level (Skory and Eskenazi, 2010). When the target application is text simplification, we strongly believe that also assessing readability at the sentence level could be very useful. We know that methods developed so far perform well to characterize the level of an entire document, but they are unreliable for short texts and thus also for single sentences. Sentence-based readability assessment thus represents a further challenge we decided to tackle: in fact, if all sentences occurring in simplified texts can be assumed to be easy-to-read sentences, the reverse does not necessarily hold since not all sentences occurring in complex texts are difficult-to-read sentences. Since there are no training data at the sentence level, it becomes difficult – if not impossible – to evaluate the effectiveness of our approach, i.e. erroneous readability assessments within the class of difficult-to-read texts may either correspond to those easy–to–read sentences occurring within complex texts or represent real classification errors. In order to overcome this problem in the readability assessment of individual sentences, we introduced a notion of distance with respect to easy-to-read sentences. In this way, the prerequisites are created for the integration of the two processes of readability assessment and text simplification. Before, text readability was assessed with respect to the entire document and text simplification was carried out at the sentence level: due to the decoupling of the two processes, the impact of simplification operations on the overall readability level of the text was not always immediately clear. With sentence-based readability assessment, this should be no longer a problem.

4 READ–IT

Our approach to readability assessment has been implemented in a software prototype, henceforth referred to as READ–IT. READ–IT operates on syntactically (i.e. dependency) parsed texts and it assigns to each considered reading object - either a document or a sentence - a score quantifying its readability. READ–IT is a classifier based on Support Vector Machines using LIBSVM (Chang and Lin, 2001) that, given a set of features and a training corpus, creates a statistical model using the feature statistics extracted from the training corpus. Such a model is used in the assessment of readability of unseen documents and sentences.

The set of features used to build the statistical model can be parameterized through a configuration file: as we will see, the set of relevant features used for readability assessment at the document level differs from the those used at the sentence level. This also creates the prerequisites for specialising the readability assessment measure with respect to more specific target audiences: as pointed out in Heilman et al. (2007) different types of features come into play e.g. when addressing L1 or L2 language learners. Here follows the complete list of features used in the reported experiments.

4.1 Features

The features used for predicting readability are organised into four main categories: namely, raw text features, lexical features as well as morpho-syntactic and syntactic features. This proposed four–fold partition closely follows the different levels of linguistic analysis automatically carried out on the text being evaluated, i.e. tokenization, lemmatization, PoS tagging and dependency parsing. Such a partition was meant to identify those easy to extract features with high discriminative power in order to reduce the linguistic pre-processing of texts guaranteeing at the same time a reliable readability assessment.

Raw Text Features

They refer to those features typically used within traditional readability metrics. They include *Sentence Length*, calculated as the average number of words per sentence, and *Word Length*, calculated as the average number of characters per words.

Lexical Features

Basic Italian Vocabulary rate features: these features refer to the internal composition of the vocabulary of the text. To this end, we took as a reference resource the *Basic Italian Vocabulary* by De Mauro (2000), including a list of 7000 words highly familiar to native speakers of Italian. In particular, we calculated two different features corresponding to: *i)* the percentage of all unique words (types) on this reference list (calculated on a per–lemma basis); *ii)* the internal distribution of the occurring basic Italian vocabulary words into the usage classification classes of 'fundamental words' (very frequent words), 'high usage words' (frequent words) and 'high availability words' (relatively lower frequency words referring to everyday objects or actions and thus well known to speakers). Whereas the latter represents a novel feature in the readability assessment literature, the former originates from the Dale-Chall formula (Chall and Dale, 1995) and, as implemented here, it can be seen as the complement of the type out-of-vocabulary rate features used by Petersen and Ostendorf (2009).

Type/Token Ratio: this feature refers to the ratio between the number of lexical types and the number of tokens. This feature, which can be considered as an indicator of expressive language delay or disorder as shown in Wright (2003) for adults and in Retherford (2003) for children, has already been used for readability assessment purposes by Aluisio et al. (2010). Due to its sensitivity to sample size, this feature has been computed for text samples of equivalent length.

Morpho–syntactic Features

Language Model probability of Part-Of-Speech unigrams: this feature is based on a unigram language model assuming that the probability of a token is independent of its context. The model is simply defined by a list of types (POS) and their individual probabilities. This feature has already been shown to be a reliable indicator for automatic readability assessment (see, for example, Pitler and Nenkova (2008) and Aluisio et al. (2010)).

Lexical density: this feature refers to the ratio of content words (verbs, nouns, adjectives and adverbs) to the total number of lexical tokens in a text. Content words have already been used for readability assessment by Aluisio et al. (2010) and Feng (2010).

Verbal mood: this feature refers to the distribution of verbs according to their mood. It is a novel and language–specific feature exploiting the predictive power of the Italian rich verbal morphology.

Syntactic Features

Unconditional probability of dependency types: this feature refers to the unconditional probability of different types of syntactic dependencies (e.g. subject, direct object, modifier, etc.) and can be seen as the dependency-based counterpart of the 'phrase type rate' feature used by Nenkova (2010).

Parse tree depth features: parse tree depth can be indicative of increased sentence complexity as stated by, to mention only a few, Yngve (1960), Frazier (1985) and Gibson (1998). This set of features is meant to capture different aspects of the parse tree depth and includes the following measures: a) the *depth of the whole parse tree*, calculated in terms of the longest path from the root of the dependency tree to some leaf; b) the *average depth of embedded complement 'chains'* governed by a nominal head and including either prepositional complements or nominal and adjectival modifiers; c) the *probability distribution of embedded complement 'chains' by depth*. The first feature has already been used in syntax-based readability assessment studies (Schwarm and Ostendorf, 2005; Heilman et al., 2007; Nenkova, 2010); the latter two are reminiscent of the 'head noun modifiers' feature used by Nenkova (2010).

Verbal predicates features: this set of features captures different aspects of the behaviour of verbal predicates. They range from the *number of verbal roots* with respect to number of all sentence roots occurring in a text to their arity. The *arity of verbal predicates* is calculated as the number of instantiated dependency links sharing the same verbal head (covering both arguments and modifiers). Although there is no obvious relation between the number of verb dependents and sentence complexity, we believe that both a low and a high number of dependents can make sentence readability quite complex, although for different reasons (elliptical constructions in the former case, a high number of modifiers in the latter). Within this feature set we also considered the *distribution of verbal predicates by arity*. To our knowledge, this set of features has never been used so far for readability assessment purposes.

Subordination features: subordination is widely acknowledged to be an index of structural complexity in language. As in Aluisio et al. (2010), this set of features has been introduced here with a specific view to the text simplification task. A first feature was meant to measure the *distribution of subordinate vs main clauses*. For subordinates, we also considered their *relative ordering with respect to the main clause*: according to Miller and Weinert (1998), sentences containing subordinate clauses in post–verbal rather than in pre–verbal position are easier to read. Two further features were introduced to capture the depth of embedded subordinate clauses since it is a widely acknowledged fact that highly complex sentences contain deeply embedded subordinate clauses: in particular, a) the *average depth of 'chains' of embedded subordinate clauses* and b) the *probability distribution of embedded subordinate clauses 'chains' by depth*.

Length of dependency links feature: both Lin (1996) and Gibson (1998) showed that the syntactic complexity of sentences can be predicted with measures based on the length of dependency links. This is also demonstrated in McDonald and Nivre (2007) who claim that statistical parsers have a drop in accuracy when analysing long dependencies. Here, the dependency length is measured in terms of the words occurring between the syntactic head and the dependent. This feature is the dependency-based counterpart of the 'phrase length' feature used for readability assessment by Nenkova (2010) and Feng (2010).

5 The Corpora

One challenge in this work was finding an appropriate corpus. Although a possibly large collection of texts labelled with their target grade level (such as the Weekly Reader for English) would be ideal, we are not aware of any such collection that exists for Italian in electronic form. Instead, to test our approach to automatically identify the readability of a given text, we used two different corpora: a newspaper corpus, *La Repubblica* (henceforth, "Rep"), and an easy–to–read newspaper, *Due Parole* (henceforth, "2Par") which was specifically written for an audience of adults with a rudimentary literacy level or with mild intellectual disabilities. The articles in 2Par were written by Italian linguists expert in text simplification using a controlled language both at the lexicon and sentence structure levels (Piemontese, 1996) .

There are different motivations underlying the selection of these two corpora for our study. On the practical side, to our knowledge 2Par is the only available corpus of simplified texts addressing a wide audience characterised by a low literacy level. So, the use of 2Par represented the only possible option on the front of simplified texts. For the selection of the second corpus we opted for texts belonging to the same class, i.e. newspapers: this was aimed at avoiding interferences due to textual genre variation in the measure of text readability. This is confirmed by the fact that the two corpora show a similar behaviour with respect to a number of different parameters, which according to the literature on register variation (Biber, 2009) are indicative of textual genre differences: e.g. lexical density, the noun/verb ratio, the percentage of verbal roots, etc. On the other hand, the two corpora differ significantly with respect to the distribution of features typically correlated with text complexity, e.g. the composition of the used vocabulary (e.g. the percentage of words belonging to the *Basic Italian Vocabulary* in Rep is 4.14% and in 2Par is 48.04%) or, from the syntactic point of view, the average parse tree height (which in Rep is 5.71 and in 2Par 3.67), the average number of verb phrases per sentence (which in Rep is 2.40 and in 2Par 1.25), the depth of nested structures (e.g. the average depth of embedded complement 'chains' in Rep is 1.44 and in 2Par is 1.30), the proportion of main vs subordinate clauses (in Rep main and subordinate clauses represent respectively 65.11% and 34.88% of the cases; in 2Par there is 79.66% of main clauses and 20.33% of subordinate clauses).

The Rep/2Par pair of corpora is somehow reminiscent of corpora used in other readability studies, such as Encyclopedia Britannica and Britannica Elementary, but with a main difference: whereas the English corpora consist of paired original/simplified texts, which we might define as "parallel monolingual corpora", the selected Italian corpora rather present themselves as "comparable monolingual corpora", without any pairing of the full–simplified versions of the same article. Comparability is guaranteed here by the inclusion of texts belonging to the same textual genre: we expect such comparable corpora to be usefully exploited for readability assessment because of the emphasis on style over topic.

Although these corpora do not provide an explicit grade–level ranking for each article, broad categories are distinguished, namely easy–to–read vs difficult–to–read texts. The two paired complex/simplified corpora were used to train and test different language models described in Section 6. As already pointed out, such a distinction is reliable in a document classification scenario, while at the sentence classification level it poses the remarkable issue of discerning easy–to–read sentences within difficult–to–read documents (i.e. Rep).

6 Experiments and Results

READ–IT was tested on the 2Par and Rep corpora automatically POS tagged by the Part–Of–Speech tagger described in Dell'Orletta (2009) and dependency–parsed by the DeSR parser (Attardi, 2006) using Support Vector Machine as learning algorithm. Three different sets of experiments were devised to test the performance of READ-IT in the following subtasks: i) document readability classification, ii) sentence readability classification and iii) detection of easy–to–read sentences within difficult–

to–read texts.

For what concerns the document classification subtask, we used a corpus made up of 638 documents of which 319 were extracted from 2Par (taken as representative of the class easy–to–read texts) and 319 from Rep (representing the class of difficult–to–read texts). We have followed a 5–fold cross–validation process: the corpus was randomly split into 5 training and test sets. The test sets consisted of 20% of the individual documents belonging to the two considered readability levels, with each document being included in one test set only. With regard to the sentence classification subtask, we used a training set of about 3,000 sentences extracted from 2Par and of about 3,000 sentences from Rep and a test corpus of 1,000 sentences of which 500 were extracted from 2Par (hereafter, *2Par test set*) and 500 from Rep (hereafter, *Rep test set*). In the third experiment, readability assessment was carried out by READ–IT with respect to a much bigger corpus of 2,5 milion of words extracted from the newspaper *La Repubblica* (hereafter, *Rep 2.5*), for a total of 123,171 sentences, with the final aim of detecting easy–to–read sentences.

All the experiments were carried out using four different readability models, described as follows:

1. **Base Model**, using *raw text* features only;
2. **Lexical Model**, using a combination of *raw text* and *lexical* features;
3. **MorphoS Model**: using *raw text*, *lexical* and *morpho–syntactic* features;
4. **Syntax Model**: combining all feature types, namely *raw text*, *lexical*, *morpho–syntactic* and *syntactic* features.

Note that in the Lexical and Syntax Models, different sets of features were selected for the subtasks of document and sentence classification. In particular, for sentence–based readability assesment we did not take into account the Type/Token Ratio feature, all features concerning the distribution of 'chains' of embedded complements and subordinate clauses and the distribution of verbal predicates by arity.

Since, to our knowledge, a machine learning readability classifier does not exist for the Italian language we consider the *Base Model* as our baseline: this can be seen as an approximation of the GulpEase index, which is based on the same raw text features (i.e. sentence and word length).

6.1 Evaluation Methodology

Different evaluation methods have been defined in order to assess achieved results in the three aforementioned experiment sets. The performance of both document and sentence classification experiments have been evaluated in terms of i) overall Accuracy of the system and ii) Precision and Recall.

In particular, Accuracy is a global score referring to the percentage of documents or sentences correctly classified, either as easy–to–read or difficult–to–read objects. Precision and Recall have been computed with respect to two the target reading levels: in particular, Precision is the ratio of the number of correctly classified documents or sentences over the total number of documents and sentences classified by READ–IT as belonging to the easy–to–read (i.e. 2Par) or difficult–to–read (i.e. Rep) classes; Recall has been computed as the ratio of the number of correctly classified documents or sentences over the total number of documents or sentences belonging to each reading level in the test sets. For each set of experiments, evaluation was carried out with respect to the four models of the classifier.

Following from the assumption that 2Par contains only easy–to–read sentences while Rep does not necessarily contain only difficult–to–read ones, we consider READ–IT errors in the classification of 2Par sentences as erroneously classified sentences. On the other hand, classification errors within the set of Rep sentences deserve an in–depth error analysis, since we need to discern real errors from misclassifications due to the fact that we are in front of easy–to–read sentences occurring in a difficult–to–read context. In order discern errors from 'correct' misclassifications, we introduced a new evaluation methodology, based on the notion of *Euclidean distance* between feature vectors. Each feature vector is a n–dimensional vector of linguistic features (see Section 4.1) that represents a set of sentences. Two vectors with 0 distance represent the same set of sentences, i.e. those sentences sharing the same values for the monitored linguistic features. Conversely, the bigger the distance between two vectors is, the more distant are the two represented sets of sentences with respect to the monitored features.

The same notion of distance has also been used to test which model was more effective in predicting the readability of n–word long sentences.

6.2 Results

In Table 1, the Accuracy, Precision and Recall scores achieved with the different READ–IT models in the document classification subtask are reported. It can be noticed that the *Base Model* shows the lowest performance, while the *MorphoS Model* outperforms all other models. Interestingly, the *Lexical Model* shows a high accuracy for what concerns the document classification subtask (95.45%), by significantly improving the accuracy score of the *Base Model* (about +19%). This result demonstrates that for assessing the readability of documents a combination of raw and lexical features provides reliable results which can be further improved (about +3%) by also taking into account morpho-syntax.

		2Par		*Rep*	
Model	Accuracy	Prec	Rec	Prec	Rec
Base	76.65	74.71	80.56	78.91	72.73
Lexical	95.45	95.60	95.30	95.31	95.61
MorphoS	**98.12**	**98.12**	**98.12**	**98.12**	**98.12**
Syntax	97.02	97.17	96.87	96.88	97.18

Table 1: Document classification results

Consider now the sentence classification subtask. Table 2 shows that in this case the most reliable results are achieved with the *Syntax Model*. It is interesting to note that the morpho–syntactic and syntactic features allow a much higher increment in terms of Accuracy, Precision and Recall scores than in the document classification scenario: i.e. the difference between the performance of the *Lexical Model* and the best one in the document classification experiment (i.e. the *MorphoS Model*) is equal to 2.6%, while in the sentence classification case (i.e. *Syntax Model*) is much higher, namely 17% .

In Table 3, we detail the performance of the best READ–IT model (i.e. the *Syntax Model*) on the *Rep test set*. In order to evaluate those sentences which were erroneously classified as belonging to 2Par, we calculated the distance between 2Par and i) these sentences (140 sentences referred to as *wrong* in the Table), ii) the correctly classified sentences

		2Par		*Rep*	
Model	Accuracy	Prec	Rec	Prec	Rec
Base	59.6	55.6	95.0	82.9	24.2
Lexical	61.6	57.3	91.0	78.1	32.2
MorphoS	76.1	72.8	83.4	80.6	68.8
Syntax	**78.2**	**75.1**	**84.4**	**82.2**	**72.0**

Table 2: Sentence classification results

(360 sentences, referred to as *correct* in the Table), iii) the whole *Rep test set*. As we can see, the distance between the *wrong* sentences and 2Par is much lower than the distance holding between 2Par and the correcly classified sentences (*correct*). This entails that the sentences which were erroneously classified as easy–to–read sentences (i.e. belonging to 2Par) are in fact more readable than the correctly classified ones (as belonging to Rep).It is obvious that the *Rep test set*, which contains both *correct* and *wrong* sentences, has an intermediate distance value with respect to 2Par.

	Distance
Correct	52.072
Rep test set	45.361
Wrong	37.843

Table 3: Distances between 2Par and Rep on the basis of the *Syntax Model*

In Table 4, the percentage of *Rep 2.5* sentences classified as difficult–to–read is reported. The results show that the *Syntax Model* classifies the higher number of sentences as difficult–to–read, but from these results we cannot say whether this model is the best one or not since *Rep 2.5* sentences are not annotated with readability information. Therefore, in order to compare the performance of the four READ–IT models and to identify which is the best one, we computed the distance between the sentences classified as easy–to–read and 2Par, which is reported, for each model, in Table 5. It can be noticed that the *Syntax Model* appears to be the best one since it shows the lowest distance with respect to 2Par; on the other hand, the whole *Rep 2.5* corpus shows a higher distance since it contains both difficult– and easy–to–read sentences. Obviously, the sentences classified as difficult–to–read by the *Syntax Model* (*Diff Syntax* in the Table) show the broader distance.

	Accuracy
Base	0.234
Lexical	0.387
MorphoS	0.705
Syntax	**0.755**

Table 4: Accuracy in sentence classification of *Rep 2.5*.

	Distance
Diff Syntax	66.526
Rep 2.5	64.040
Base	61.135
Lexical	60.529
MorphoS	55.535
Syntax	**51.408**

Table 5: Distance between 2Par and i) difficult–to–read sentences according to the *Syntax Model*, ii) *Rep 2.5*, iii) easy–to–read sentences by the four models.

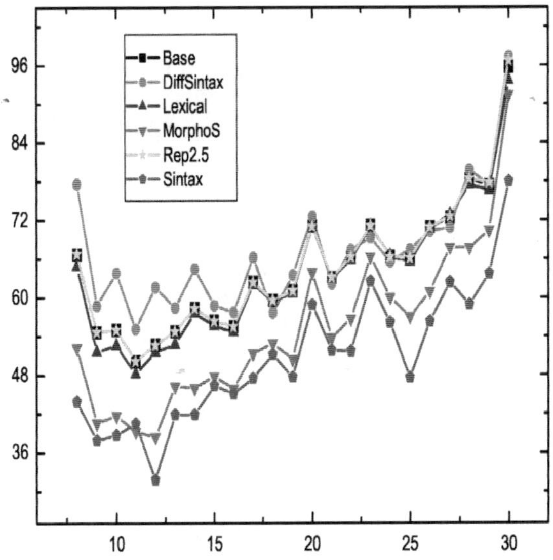

Figure 1: Distance between 2Par and i) difficult–to–read sentences according to the *Syntax Model*, ii) *Rep 2.5*, iii) easy–to–read sentences by the four models for sets of sentences of fixed length

In order to gain an in–depth insight into the different behaviour of the four READ–IT models, we evaluated their performances for sentences of a fixed length. We considered sentences whose length ranges between 8 and 30. For every set of sentences of the same legth, we compared the easy–to-read sentences of *Rep 2.5* classified by the four models with respect to 2Par. In Figure 1, each point represents the distance between a set of sentences of the same length and the same n–word long set of sentences in the 2Par corpus. As it can be seen, the bottom line which represents the sentences classified as easy–to–read by the *Syntax Model* is the closest to the 2Par sentences of the same length. On the contrary, the line representing the sentences classified by the *Base Model* is the most distant amongst the four READ–IT models. Interestingly, it overlaps with the line representing the *Rep 2.5* sentences: this suggests that a classification model based only on raw text features (i.e. sentence and word length) is not able to identify easy–to-read sentences if we consider sets of sentences of a fixed length. Obviously, the line representing the sentences classified as difficult–to–read by the *Syntax Model* shows the broadest distance. This experiment has shown that linguistically motivated features (and in particular syntactic ones) have a fundamental role in the sentence readability assessment subtask.

7 Conclusion

In this paper, we proposed a new approach to readability assessment with a specific view to the task of text simplification: the intended audience includes people with low literacy skills and/or with mild cognitive impairment. The main contributions of this work can be summarised as follows: i) READ–IT represents the first advanced readability assessment tool for what concerns Italian; ii) it combines traditional raw text features with lexical, morpho-syntactic and syntactic information; iii) readability assessment is carried out with respect to both documents and sentences. Sentence–based readability assessment is an important novelty of our approach which creates the prerequisites for aligning readability assessment with text simplification. READ–IT shows a high accuracy in the document classification task and promising results in the sentence classification scenario. The two different tasks appear to enforce different requirements at the level of the underlying linguistic features. To overcome the lack of an Italian reference resource annotated with readability information at the sentence level we introduced the notion of distance to assess READ–IT performance.

Acknowledgements

The research reported in the paper has been partly supported by the national project "Migrations" of the National Council of Research (CNR) in the framework of the line of research *Advanced technologies and linguistic and cultural integration in the school*. In particular the authors would like to thank Eva Maria Vecchi who contributed to the prerequisites of the proposed readability assessment methodology reported in the paper.

References

Sandra Aluisio, Lucia Specia, Caroline Gasperin and Carolina Scarton. 2010. *Readability assessment for text simplification*. In Proceedings of the NAACL HLT 2010 Fifth Workshop on Innovative Use of NLP for Building Educational Applications, pp. 1–9.

Giuseppe Attardi. 2006. *Experiments with a multilanguage non-projective dependency parser*. In Proceedings of the Tenth Conference on Computational Natural Language Learning (CoNLL-X '06), New York City, New York, pp. 166–170.

Regina Barzilay and Mirella Lapata. 2008. *Modeling local coherence: An entity-based approach*. In Computational Linguistics, 34(1), pp. 1–34.

Douglas Biber and Susan Conrad. 2009. *Register, genre, and style*. Cambridge, Cambridge University Press.

Tim vor der Brück, Sven Hartrumpf, Hermann Helbig. 2008. *A Readability Checker with Supervised Learning using Deep Syntactic and Semantic Indicators*. In Proceedings of the 11th International Multiconference: Information Society - IS 2008 - Language Technologies, Ljubljana, Slovenia, pp. 92–97.

Jeanne S. Chall and Edgar Dale. 1995. *Readability Revisited: The New Dale–Chall Readability Formula*. Brookline Books, Cambridge, MA.

Chih-Chung Chang and Chih-Jen Lin. 2001. *LIBSVM: a library for support vector machines*. Software available at `http://www.csie.ntu.edu.tw/~cjlin/libsvm`

Kevyn Collins-Thompson and Jamie Callan. 2004. *A language modeling approach to predicting reading difficulty*. In Proceedings of the HLT / NAACL, pp. 193–200.

Felice Dell'Orletta. 2009. *Ensemble system for Part-of-Speech tagging*. In Proceedings of Evalita'09, Evaluation of NLP and Speech Tools for Italian, Reggio Emilia, December.

Tullio De Mauro. 2000. *Il dizionario della lingua italiana*. Torino, Paravia.

Lijun Feng, Martin Jansche, Matt Huenerfauth and Noémie Elhadad. 2010. *A comparison of features for automatic readability assessment*. In Proceedings of the 23rd International Conference on Computational Linguistics (COLING 2010), pp. 276–284.

Lijun Feng, Noémie Elhadad and Matt Huenerfauth. 2009. *Cognitively motivated features for readability assessment*. In Proceedings of the 12th Conference of the European Chapter of the Association for Computational Linguistics (EACL '09), pp. 229–237.

V. Franchina and Roberto Vacca. 1986. *Adaptation of Flesh readability index on a bilingual text written by the same author both in Italian and English languages*. In Linguaggi (3), pp. 47–49.

Lyn Frazier. 1985. *Syntactic complexity*. In D.R. Dowty, L. Karttunen and A.M. Zwicky (eds.), *Natural Language Parsing*, Cambridge University Press, Cambridge, UK.

Edward Gibson. 1998. *Linguistic complexity: Locality of syntactic dependencies*. In *Cognition*, 68(1), pp. 1-76.

Michael J. Heilman, Kevyn Collins and Jamie Callan. 2007. *Combining Lexical and Grammatical Features to Improve Readability Measures for First and Second Language Texts*. In Proceedings of the Human Language Technology Conference, pp. 460–467.

Michael J. Heilman, Kevyn Collins and Maxine Eskenazi. 2008. *An analysis of statistical models and features for reading difficulty prediction*. In Proceedings of the Third Workshop on Innovative Use of NLP for Building Educational Applications (EANL '08), pp. 71–79.

Rohit J. Kate, Xiaoqiang Luo, Siddharth Patwardhan, Martin Franz, Radu Florian, Raymond J. Mooney, Salim Roukos, Chris Welty. 2010. *Learning to Predict Readability using Diverse Linguistic Features*. In Proceedings of the 23rd International Conference on Computational Linguistics (COLING 2010), pp. 546–554.

J. Peter Kincaid, Lieutenant Robert P. Fishburne, Richard L. Rogers and Brad S. Chissom. 1975. *Derivation of new readability formulas for Navy enlisted personnel*. Research Branch Report, Millington, TN: Chief of Naval Training, pp. 8–75.

George Kingsley Zipf. 1988. *The Psychobiology of Language*. Houghton–Miflin, Boston.

Dekan Lin. 1996. *On the structural complexity of natural language sentences*. In Proceedings of COLING 1996, pp. 729–733.

Pietro Lucisano and Maria Emanuela Piemontese. 1988. *Gulpease. Una formula per la predizione della difficoltà dei testi in lingua italiana*. In Scuola e Città (3), pp. 57–68.

Ryan McDonald and Joakim Nivre. 2007. *Characterizing the Errors of Data-Driven Dependency Parsing Models*. In Proceedings of EMNLP-CoNLL, 2007, pp. 122-131.

Jim Miller and Regina Weinert. 1998. *Spontaneous spoken language. Syntax and discourse*. Oxford, Clarendon Press.

Ani Nenkova, Jieun Chae, Annie Louis, and Emily Pitler. 2010. *Structural Features for Predicting the Linguistic Quality of Text Applications to Machine Translation, Automatic Summarization and Human–Authored Text*. In E. Krahmer, M. Theune (eds.), *Empirical Methods in NLG*, LNAI 5790, Springer-Verlag Berlin Heidelberg, pp. 222–241.

Sarah E. Petersen and Mari Ostendorf. 2006. *A machine learning approach to reading level assessment*. University of Washington CSE Technical Report.

Sarah E. Petersen and Mari Ostendorf. 2009. *A machine learning approach to reading level assessment*. In Computer Speech and Language (23), pp. 89–106.

Maria Emanuela Piemontese. 1996. *Capire e farsi capire. Teorie e tecniche della scrittura controllata* Napoli, Tecnodid.

Emily Pitler and Ani Nenkova. 2008. *Revisiting readability: A unified framework for predicting text quality*. In Proceedings of the 2008 Conference on Empirical Methods in Natural Language Processing, pp. 186–195.

Kristine Retherford. 2003. *Normal development: a database of communication and related behaviors*. Eau Claire, WI: Thinking Publications.

Brian Roark, Margaret Mitchell and Kristy Hollingshead. 2007. *Syntactic complexity measures for detecting mild cognitive impairment*. In Proceedings of the Workshop on BioNLP 2007: Biological, Translational, and Clinical Language Processing, pp. 1–8.

Sarah E. Schwarm and Mari Ostendorf. 2005. *Reading level assessment using support vector machines and statistical language models*. In Proceedings of the 43rd Annual Meeting on Association for Computational Linguistics (ACL 05), pp. 523–530.

Luo Si and Jamie Callan. 2001. *A statistical model for scientific readability*. In Proceedings of the tenth international conference on Information and knowledge management, pp. 574–576.

Adam Skory and Maxine Eskenazi. 2010. *Predicting cloze task quality for vocabulary training*. In Proceedings of the NAACL HLT 2010 Fifth Workshop on Innovative Use of NLP for Building Educational Applications, pp. 49–56.

Victor H.A. Yngve. 1960. *A model and an hypothesis for language structure*. In Proceedings of the American Philosophical Society, pp. 444-466.

Heather Harris Wright, Stacy W. Silverman and Marilyn Newhoff. 2003. *Measures of lexical diversity in aphasia*. In Aphasiology, 17(5), pp. 443-452.

Source Language Categorization for improving a Speech into Sign Language Translation System

V. López-Ludeña, R. San-Segundo, S. Lutfi, J.M. Lucas-Cuesta, J.D. Echevarry, B. Martínez-González
Grupo de Tecnología del Habla
Universidad Politécnica de Madrid
{veronicalopez|lapiz|syaheerah|juanmak|jdec|beatrizmartinez}@die.upm.es

Abstract

This paper describes a categorization module for improving the performance of a Spanish into Spanish Sign Language (LSE) translation system. This categorization module replaces Spanish words with associated tags. When implementing this module, several alternatives for dealing with non-relevant words have been studied. Non-relevant words are Spanish words not relevant in the translation process. The categorization module has been incorporated into a phrase-based system and a Statistical Finite State Transducer (SFST). The evaluation results reveal that the BLEU has increased from 69.11% to 78.79% for the phrase-based system and from 69.84% to 75.59% for the SFST.

Keywords: Source language categorization, Speech into Sign Language translation. Lengua de Signos Española (LSE).

1 Introduction

In the world, there are around 70 million people with hearing deficiencies (information from World Federation of the Deaf http://www.wfdeaf.org/). Deafness brings about significant communication problems: most deaf people are unable to use written languages, having serious problems when expressing themselves in these languages or understanding written texts. They have problems with verb tenses, concordances of gender and number, etc., and they have difficulties when creating a mental image of abstract concepts. This fact can cause deaf people to have problems when accessing information, education, job, social relationship, culture, etc. According to information from INE (Statistic Spanish Institute), in Spain, there are 1,064,000 deaf people. 47% of deaf population do not have basic studies or are illiterate, and only between 1% and 3% have finished their studies (as opposed to 21% of Spanish hearing people). Another example are the figures from the National Deaf Children's Society (NDCS), Cymru, revealing for the first time a shocking attainment gap between deaf and hearing pupils in Wales. In 2008, deaf pupils were 30% less likely than hearing pupils to gain five A*-C grades at General Certificate of Secondary Education (GCSE) level, while at key stage 3 only 42% of deaf pupils achieved the core subject indicators, compared to 71% of their hearing counterparts. Another example is a study carried out in Ireland in 2006; of 330 respondents "38% said they did not feel confident to read a newspaper and more than half were not fully confident in writing a letter or filling out a form" (Conroy, 2006).

Deaf people use a sign language (their mother tongue) for communicating and there are not enough sign-language interpreters and communication systems. In Spain, there is the Spanish Sign Language (Lengua de Signos Española LSE) that is the official sign language. In the USA, there are 650,000 Deaf people (who use a sign language). Although there are more people with hearing deficiencies, there are only 7,000 sign-language interpreters, i.e. a ratio of 93 deaf people to 1 interpreter. In Finland we find the best ratio, 6 to 1, and in Slovakia the worst with 3,000 users to 1 interpreter (Wheatley and Pabsch, 2010). In Spain this ratio is 221 to 1. This information shows the need to develop automatic translation systems with new technologies for helping hearing and Deaf people to communicate between themselves.

Proceedings of the 2nd Workshop on Speech and Language Processing for Assistive Technologies, pages 84–93,
Edinburgh, Scotland, UK, July 30, 2011. ©2011 Association for Computational Linguistics

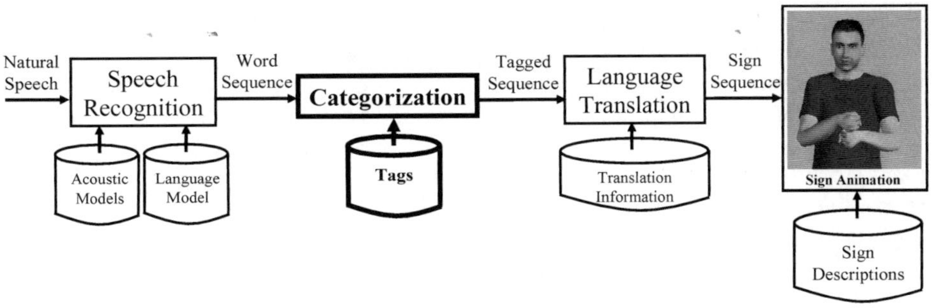

Figure 1. Spanish into LSE translation system.

It is necessary to make a difference between "deaf" and "Deaf": the first one refers to non-hearing people, and the second one refers to hearing and non-hearing people who use a sign language to communicate between them, being part of the "Deaf community". Each country has a different sign language, but there may even be different sign languages in different regions.

This paper describes a categorization module for improving the performance of a Speech into Sign Language Translation System. This system helps Deaf people to communicate with government employees in a restricted domain: the renewal of Identity Documents and Driver's License (San-Segundo et al., 2008). This system has been designed to translate the government employee's explanations into LSE when government employees provide these face-to-face services. The system is made up of a speech recognizer (for decoding the spoken utterance into a word sequence), a natural language translator (a phrase-based system for converting a word sequence into a sequence of signs belonging to the sign language), and a 3D avatar animation module (for playing back the signs) (Figure 1). This paper proposes to include a fourth module named "categorization" between the speech recognition and language translation modules (Figure 1). This categorization module replaces Spanish words with associated tags as will be shown further.

For the natural language translation module, two different statistical strategies have been analyzed: a phrase-based system (Moses) and a Statistical Finite State Transducer (SFST). The proposed categorization module has been incorporated into and evaluated with both translation strategies.

This paper is organized as follows: section 2 describes the state of the art. Section 3 describes the parallel corpus used in these experiments. The main characteristics of the LSE are presented in section 4. Section 5 details the two main translation strategies considered. The categorization module is described in section 6. Section 7 includes the main experiments and the obtained results, and finally, sections 8 and 9 include the main conclusions and the future work.

2 State of the art

In recent years, several groups have developed prototypes for translating Spoken language into Sign Language: example-based (Morrissey, 2008), rule-based (Marshall and Sáfár, 2005; San-Segundo et al. 2008), full sentence (Cox et al., 2002) or statistical approaches (Stein et al., 2006; Morrissey et al., 2007; Vendrame et al., 2010) approaches.

Given the sparseness of data for researching in Sign Languages, in the last five years, several projects have started to generate more resources: in American Sign Language (Dreuw et al.., 2008), British Sign Language (Schembri, 2008), Greek Sign Language (Efthimiou and Fotinea, 2008), in Irish Sign Language (Morrissey et al., 2010), NGS (German Sign Language) (Hanke et al., 2010), and Italian Sign Language (Geraci et al., 2010). For LSE, the biggest database was generated two years ago in a Plan Avanza project (www.traduccionvozlse.es) (San-Segundo et al., 2010) and it is has been used in this work. Not only the data but also new practice (Forster et al., 2010) and new uses of traditional annotation tools (Crasborn et al., 2010) have been developed.

The work presented in this paper describes experiments with a relevant database Despite the small amount of data available for research into sign languages, the system presented in this paper demonstrates a very good performance compared to similar systems previously developed. The presented results are also the best results for translating Spanish into LSE using the biggest database that includes these languages.

In Europe, the two main research projects involving sign languages are DICTA-SIGN (Hanke et al., 2010; Efthimiou et al., 2010) and SIGN-SPEAK (Dreuw et al., 2010a and 2010b), both financed by The European Commission within the Seventh Frame Program. DICTA-SIGN (http://www.dictasign.eu/) aims to develop the technologies necessary to make Web 2.0 interactions in sign language possible: users sign to a webcam using a dictation style. The computer recognizes the signed phrases, converts them into an internal representation of sign language, and then it has an animated avatar that signs them back to the users. In SIGN-SPEAK (http://www.signspeak.eu/), the overall goal is to develop a new vision-based technology for recognizing and translating continuous sign language into text.

3 Parallel corpus

This section describes the first Spanish-LSE parallel corpus developed for language processing in two specific domains: the renewal of the Identity Document (ID) and Driver's License (DL). This corpus has been obtained with the collaboration of Local Government Offices where these services are provided. Over several weeks, the most frequent explanations (from the government employees) and the most frequent questions (from the user) were taken down. In this period, more than 5,000 sentences were noted and analyzed.

Not all the sentences refer to ID or DL renewal (Government Offices provide more services), so sentences had to be selected manually. This was possible because every sentence was tagged with the information about the service being provided when it was collected. Finally, 1360 sentences were collected: 1,023 pronounced by government employees and 337 by users. These sentences have been translated into LSE, both in text (sequence of glosses) and in video (containing replayed sentences by native LSE signers), and compiled in an excel file. Videos are not used in this study but they were collected for generating a complete parallel corpus.

This corpus was increased to 4,080 by incorporating different variants for Spanish sentences (maintaining the LSE translation) (San-Segundo et al. 2010). Table 1 summarizes the main features of this database.

	Spanish	LSE
Sentence pairs	4,080	
Different sentences	3,342	1,289
Words/signs per sentence	7.7	5.7
Running words	31,501	23,256
Vocabulary	1,232	636

Table 1. Main statistics of the corpus

For the experiments presented in this paper, this database has been divided randomly into three sets: training (75%), development (12.5%) and test (12.5%). The training set was used for tuning the speech recognizer (vocabulary and language model) and training the translation models. The development set was used for tuning the translation systems and finally, the test set was used for evaluating the categorization module.

4 Spanish Sign Language (LSE)

Spanish Sign Language (LSE), just like other sign languages, has a visual-gestural channel, but it also has grammatical characteristics similar to spoken languages. Sign languages have complex grammars and professional linguists have found all of the necessarily linguistic characteristics for classifying sign languages as "true languages". In linguistic terms, sign languages are as complex as spoken languages, despite the common misconception that they are a "simplification" of spoken languages. For example, The United Kingdom and USA share the same language. However, British Sign Language is completely different from American Sign Language. W. Stokoe (Stokoe, 1960) supports the idea that sign languages have four dimensions (three space dimensions plus time), and spoken languages have only one dimension, time, so it cannot say that sign languages are a simplification of any other language.

One important difference between spoken languages and sign languages is sequentially. Phonemes in spoken languages are produced in a sequence. On the other hand, sign languages have a large non-sequential component, because fingers, hands and face movements can be involved in a sign simultaneously, even two hands moving in different directions. These features give a complexity to sign languages that traditional spoken languages do not have. This fact makes it very difficult to write sign languages. Traditionally, signs have been written using words (in capital letters) in Spanish (or English in the case of BSL, British Sign Language) with a similar meaning to the sign meaning. They are called glosses (i.e. 'CAR' for the sign 'car').

In the last 20 years, several alternatives, based on specific characteristics of the signs, have appeared in the international community: HamNoSys (Prillwitz et al, 1989), SEA (Sistema de Escritura Alfabética) (Herrero, A., 2004) and SignWriting (http://www.signwriting.org/). HamNoSys and SignWriting require defining a specific picture font to be used by computers. SignWriting includes face features in the notation system but HamNoSys and SEA do not include them. All of these alternatives are flexible enough for dealing with different sign languages including LSE. However, in this work, glosses have been considered for writing signs because it is the most familiar and extended alternative according to the Spanish Deaf Association. These glosses include non-speech indicators (i.e. PAY or PAY? if the sign is localized at the end of an interrogative sentence) and finger spelling indicators (i.e. DL-PETER that must be represented letter by letter P-E-T-E-R).

LSE has some characteristics that differ from Spanish. One important difference is the order of arguments in sentences: LSE has a **SOV** (subject-object-verb) order in contrast to **SVO** (subject-verb-object) Spanish order. An example that illustrates this behaviour is shown below:

Spanish: Juan ha comprado las entradas (Juan has bought the tickets) **LSE**: JUAN ENTRADAS COMPRAR (JUAN TICKETS TO-BUY)

There are other typological differences that are not related to predication order:

- Gender is not usually specified in LSE, in contrast to Spanish.
- In LSE, there can be concordances between verbs and subject, receiver or object and even subject and receiver, but in Spanish there can be only concordance between verb and subject:
  - Spanish: Te explica (*he explains to you*)
  - LSE: EXPLICAR-él-a-ti (*EXPLAIN-HIM-TO-YOU*)
- The use of classifiers is common in LSE, but they are not in Spanish.
  - Spanish: debe acercarse a la cámara (*you must approach the camera*)
  - LSE: FOTO CLD_GRANDE_NO CLL_ACERCARSE DEBER (*PHOTO CLD_BIG_NO CLL_APPROACH MUST*)
- Articles are used in Spanish, but not in LSE.
- Plural can be descriptive in LSE, but not in Spanish.
- In Spanish, there is a copula in non-verbal predications (the verb 'to be', *ser* and *estar* in Spanish), but there is not in LSE.
- There are Spanish impersonal sentences, but not in LSE.
- LSE is more lexically flexible than Spanish, and it is perfect for generating periphrasis through its descriptive nature and because of this, LSE has fewer nouns than Spanish. (i.e. mud is translated into SAND+WATER)
- To finish, LSE has less glosses per sentence (5.7 in our database) than Spanish (7.7 in our database).
- LSE has smaller vocabulary variability. LSE has a vocabulary of around 10,000 signs while Spanish has several millions of different words. Good examples are the different verb conjugations.

5 Statistical translation strategies

In this paper, two different statistical strategies have been considered: a phrase-based system and a Statistical Finite State Transducer. The proposed automatic categorization has been evaluated with both translation strategies. This section describes the architectures used for the experiments.

5.1 Phrase-based translation system

The Phrase-based translation system is based on the software released at the 2009 NAACL Workshop on Statistical Machine Translation (http://www.statmt.org/wmt09/) (Figure 2).

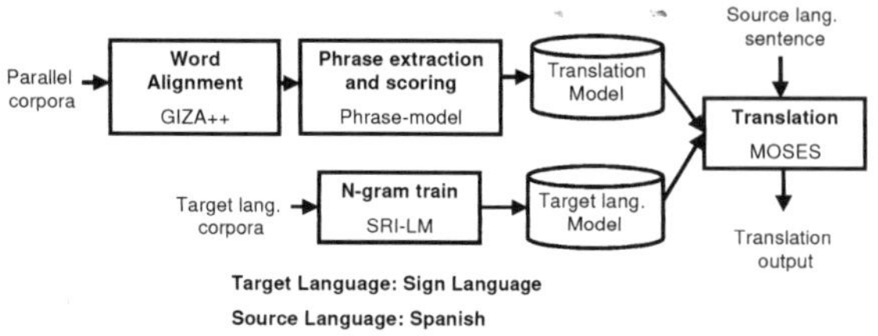

Figure 2. Phrase-based translation architecture.

In this study, a phrase consists of a subsequence of words (in a sentence) that intends to have a meaning. Every sentence is split in several phrases automatically so this segmentation can have errors. But, the main target, when training a phrase-based model, is to split the sentence in several phrases and to find their corresponding translations in the target language.

The phrase model has been trained starting from a word alignment computed using GIZA++ (Och and Ney, 2003). GIZA++ is a statistical machine translation toolkit that is used to train IBM Models 1-5 and an HMM word alignment model. In this step, the alignments between words and signs in both directions (Spanish-LSE and LSE-Spanish) are calculated. The "alignment" parameter has been fixed to "target-source" as the best option (based on experiments over the development set): only this target-source alignment was considered (LSE-Spanish). In this configuration, alignment is guided by signs: this means that in every sentence pair alignment, each word can be aligned to one or several signs (but not the opposite), and also, it is possible that some words were not aligned to any sign. When combining the alignment points from all sentences pairs in the training set, it is possible to have all possible alignments: several words aligned to several signs.

After the word alignment, the system performs a phrase extraction process (Koehn et al. 2003) where all phrase pairs that are consistent with the word alignment (target-source alignment in our case) are collected. In the phrase extraction, the maximum phrase length has been fixed at 7 consecutive words, based on development experiments over the development set (see previous section).

Finally, the last step is phrase scoring. In this step, the translation probabilities are computed for all phrase pairs. Both translation probabilities are calculated: forward and backward.

For the translation process, the Moses decoder has been used (Koehn, 2010). This program is a beam search decoder for phrase-based statistical machine translation models. In order to obtain a 3-gram language model, the SRI language modeling toolkit has been used (Stolcke, 2002).

5.2 Phrase-based translation system

The translation based on SFST is carried out as set out in Figure 3.

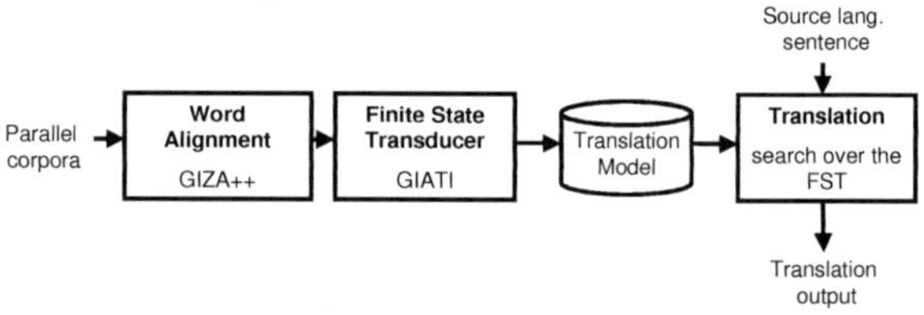

Figure 3. Diagram of the FST-based translation module.

The translation model consists of an SFST made up of aggregations: subsequences of aligned source and target words. The SFST is inferred from the word alignment (obtained with GIZA++) using the GIATI (Grammatical Inference and Alignments for Transducer Inference) algorithm (Casacuberta and Vidal, 2004). The SFST probabilities are also trained from aligned corpora. The software used in this paper has been downloaded from http://prhlt.iti.es/content.php?page=software.php.

6 Categorization module

As it was presented in Figure 1, the categorization module proposed in this paper analyzes the source language sentence (sentence in Spanish) and replaces Spanish words with their associated tags. This module uses a list of 1014 Spanish words (the vocabulary in this restricted domain) and the corresponding tags. For every word, only one syntactic-semantic tag is associated. In the case of homonyms, the most frequent meaning has been considered for defining the syntactic-semantic tag. Figure 4 shows an extract of the word-tag list. This list is composed of Spanish words and their corresponding tags, including the English translation in parenthesis.

word TAG (word and tag in English)
...
cerrado CERRAR-YA (*closed CLOSE-ALREADY*)
cerramos CERRAR (*we close CLOSE*)
cerrar CERRAR (*to close CLOSE*)
cobradas COBRAR-YA (*charged CHARGE-ALREADY*)
cobro COBRAR (*I charge CHARGE*)
coge COGER (*you get GET*)
cogido COGER-YA (*gotten GET-ALREADY*)
coja COGER (*you get GET*)
...

Figure 4. Extract of the word-tag list.

The categorization module executes a simple procedure: for all words in a Spanish sentence, the categorization module looks for this word in the list and replaces it with the associated tag. It is important to comment two main aspects. The first one is that there is a tag named "non-relevant" associated to those words that are not useful for translating the sentence. The second one is that if the Spanish word is not in the list (it is an Out Of Vocabulary word: OOV), this word is not replaced with any tag: this word is kept as it is.

In order to train the statistical translation modules when using the categorization module, it is necessary to retrain the translation models considering the tagged source language, not the original word sentences, and using the training set. This way, the translation models learn the relationships between tags and signs.

The main issue for implementing the categorization module is to generate the list of the Spanish words with the associated tags. In this work, the categorization module considers the categories used in the rule-based translation system previously developed for this application domain (San-Segundo et al., 2008). These categories were generated manually during one week, approximately. In this case, the natural language translation module was implemented using a rule-based technique considering a bottom-up strategy. The translation process is carried out in two steps. In the first one, every word is mapped into one syntactic-pragmatic tag. After that, the translation module applies different rules that convert the tagged words into signs by means of grouping concepts or signs and defining new signs. These rules can define short and large scope relationships between the concepts or signs.

When implementing the categorization module, several strategies for dealing with the "non-relevant" words have been proposed:

- In the first alternative, all the words are replaced by their tags with the exception of those words that they do not appear in the list (OOV words). As, it was commented before, they are kept as they are. In the word-tag list, there is a "non-relevant" tag mapped to words that are not relevant for the translation process (named "basura" (non-relevant)). This alternative will be referred in the experiments like "**Base categorization**". For example:
  - Source sentence: debes pagar las tasas en la caja (*you must pay the taxes in the cash desk*)
  - Categorizated source sentence: DEBER PAGAR basura DINERO basura basura DINERO-CAJA (*MUST PAY non-relevant MONEY non-relevant non-relevant CASH-DESK*)
  - Target sentence: VENTANILLA ESPECÍFICO CAJA TU PAGAR (*WINDOW SPECIFIC CASH-DESK YOU PAY*)
- The second proposed alternative was not to tag any word in the source language but removing non-relevant words from the source lexicon (associated to the "non-relevant" tag). This alternative will be referred in the experiments like "**Non-relevant word deletion**". For example:
  - Source sentence: debes pagar las tasas en la caja (*you must pay the taxes in the cash desk*)
  - Categorizated source sentence: debes pagar tasas caja
  - Target sentence: VENTANILLA ESPECÍFICO CAJA TU PAGAR (*WINDOW SPECIFIC CASH-DESK YOU PAY*)
- Finally, the third alternative proposes to replace words with tags (with the exception of OOVs) and to remove "non-relevant" tags. This alternative will be referred in the experiments like "**Categorization and non-relevant word deletion**". For example:
  - Source sentence: debes pagar las tasas en la caja (*you must pay the taxes in the cash desk*)
  - Categorizated source sentence: debes|DEBER pagar|PAGAR tasas|DINERO caja|DINERO-CAJA
  - Target sentence: VENTANILLA ESPECÍFICO CAJA TU PAGAR (WINDOW SPECIFIC CASH-DESK YOU PAY)

In the next section, all the alternatives will be evaluated and discussed.

7 Experiments and discussion

For the experiments, the corpus (described in section 3) was divided randomly into three sets: training (75%), development (12.5%) and test (12.5%). Results are compared with a baseline. This baseline consists of training models with original source and target corpus without any type of factorization, i.e, sentences contain words and signs from the original database. For example: this sentence "debes pagar las tasas en la caja" (*you must pay the taxes in the cash desk*) is translated into "VENTANILLA ESPECÍFICO CAJA TU PAGAR" (*WINDOW SPECIFIC CASH-DESK YOU PAY*).

For evaluating the performance of the translation systems, the BLEU (BiLingual Evaluation Understudy) metric (Papineni et al., 2002) has been used. BLEU is one of the most well-known metric for evaluating automatic translation systems because this metric presents a good correlation with human evaluations. This metric has been also adopted to evaluate speech into sign language translation systems (Stein et al., 2006; Morrissey et al., 2007; Vendrame et al., 2010, San-Segundo et al. 2008). In order to analyze the significance of the differences between several systems, for every BLEU result, the confidence interval (at 95%) is also presented. This interval is calculated using the following formula:

$$\pm\Delta = 1{,}96\sqrt{\frac{BLEU(100-BLEU)}{n}} \qquad (1)$$

n is the number of signs used in evaluation, in this case n=2,906. An improvement between two systems is statistically significant when there is no overlap between the confidence intervals of both systems.

Related to the speech recognizer, it is important to comment that the Word Error Rate (WER) obtained in these experiments has been 4.7%.

Table 2 compares the baseline system and the system with the categorization module for translating the references (Reference) and the speech recognizer outputs (ASR output) using the phrase-based translation system.

Phrase-based translation System		**BLEU**	**±Δ**
Baseline	Reference	73.66	1.60
	ASR output	**69.11**	**1.68**
Base categorization	Reference	81.91	1.40
	ASR output	**74.55**	**1.58**
Non-relevant words deletion	Reference	80.02	1.45
	ASR output	**73.89**	**1.60**
Categorization and non-relevant word deletion	Reference	84.37	1.32
	ASR output	**78.79**	**1.49**

Table 2. Evaluation results for the phrase-based translation system.

Table 3 compares the baseline system and the system with the categorization module for translating the references (Reference) and the speech recognizer outputs (ASR output) using the SFST-based translation system.

SFST		**BLEU**	**±Δ**
Baseline	Reference	71.17	1.65
	ASR output	**69.84**	**1.67**
Base categorization	Reference	71.86	1.63
	ASR output	**68.73**	**1.69**
Non-relevant words deletion	Reference	76.71	1.54
	ASR output	**72.77**	**1.62**
Categorization and non-relevant word deletion	Reference	81.48	1.41
	ASR output	**75.59**	**1.56**

Table 3. Evaluation results for the SFST-based translation system.

Comparing the three alternatives for dealing with the non-relevant words, it is shown that adding tags to the words and removing "non-relevant" words are complementary actions that allow reaching the best results.

In order to better understand the main causes of this improvement, an error analysis has been carried out, establishing a relationship between these errors and the main differences between Spanish and LSE.

The most important type of error (35% of the cases) is related to the fact that in Spanish there are more words than signs in LSE (7.7 for Spanish and 5.7 for LSE in this corpus). This circumstance provokes different types of errors: generation of many phrases in the same output, producing a high number of insertions. When dealing with long sentences there is the risk that the translation model cannot deal properly with the big distortion. This produces important changes in order and sometimes the sentence is truncated producing several deletions.

The second most important source of errors (25% of the cases) is related to the fact that when translating Spanish into LSE, there is a relevant number of words in the testing set that they do not appear in the training set due to the higher variability presented in Spanish. These words are named Out Of Vocabulary words. For example, in Spanish there are many verb conjugations that are translated into the same sign sequence. So, when a new conjugation appears in the evaluation set, it is an OOV that provokes a translation error.

Other important source of errors corresponds to ordering errors provoked by the different order in predication: LSE has a SOV (Subject-Object-Verb) while Spanish SVO (Subject-Verb-Object). In this case, the frequency is close to 20%

Finally, there are others causes of errors like the wrong generation of the different classifiers needed in LSE and not presented in Spanish (11%) and the existence of some deletions when translating very specific names, even when they are in the training set. Some of these names (i.e. 'mud' is translated into SAND + WATER) need some periphrasis in LSE that not always are properly generated.

Based on this error analysis, the main causes of the translation errors are related to the different variability in the vocabulary for Spanish and LSE (much higher in Spanish), the different number for words or signs in the sentences (higher in Spanish) and the different predication order.

The categorization module allows reducing the variability in the source language (for example, several verb conjugations are tagged with the same tag) and also the number of tokens composing the input sentence (when removing non-relevant words). Also, reducing the source language variability and the number of tokens provoke an important reduction on the number of source-target alignments the system has to train. When having a small corpus, as it is the case of many sign languages, this reduction of alignment points permits to obtain better training models with less data, improving the results. These aspects allow increasing the system performance. Presumably, if there were a very large corpus of Spanish-to-Spanish-Sign-Language available, the system could learn better translation models and the improvement reached with this categorization module would be lower.

The evaluation results reveal that the BLEU has increased from 69.11% to 78.79% for the phrase-based system and from 69.84% to 75.59% for the SFST.

8 Conclusions

This paper describes a categorization module for improving a Spanish into Spanish Sign Language Translation System. This module allows incorporating syntactic-semantic information during the translation process reducing the source language variability and the number of words composing the input sentence. These two aspects reduce the translation error rate considering two statistical translation systems: phrase-based and SFST-based translation systems. This system is used to translate government employee's explanations into LSE when providing a personal service for renewing the Identity Document and Driver's License.

9 Future work

The main issue for implementing the categorization module is to generate the list of the Spanish words with the associated tags. Generating this list manually is a subjective, slow and difficult task. Because of this, in the near future, authors will work on the possibility to define a procedure for calculating this list automatically.

Acknowledgments

The authors would like to thank the eSIGN consortium for permitting the use of the eSIGN Editor and the 3D avatar. The authors would also like to thank discussions and suggestions from the colleagues at GTH-UPM. This work has been supported by Plan Avanza Exp Nº: TSI-020100-2010-489), INAPRA (MEC ref: DPI2010-21247-C02-

02), and SD-TEAM (MEC ref: TIN2008-06856-C05-03) projects and FEDER program.

References

Casacuberta F., E. Vidal. 2004. "Machine Translation with Inferred Stochastic Finite-State Transducers". Computational Linguistics, Vol. 30, No. 2, pp. 205-225, 2004.

Conroy, P. 2006. Signing in and Signing Out: The Education and Employment Experiences of Deaf Adults in Ireland. Research Report, Irish Deaf Society, Dublin. 2006.

Cox, S.J., Lincoln M., Tryggvason J., Nakisa M., Wells M., Mand Tutt, and Abbott, S., 2002 "TESSA, a system to aid communication with deaf people". In ASSETS 2002, Edinburgh, Scotland, pp 205-212, 2002.

Crasborn O., Sloetjes H. 2010. "Using ELAN for annotating sign language corpora in a team setting". In 4th Workshop on the Representation and Processing of Sign Languages: Corpora and Sign Language Technologies (CSLT 2010), Valletta, Malta, 2010. pp 61-65

Dreuw P., Neidle C., Athitsos V., Sclaroff S., and Ney H. 2008. "Benchmark Databases for Video-Based Automatic Sign Language Recognition". In International Conference on Language Resources and Evaluation (LREC), Marrakech, Morocco, May 2008. pp 1115-1121.

Dreuw P., Ney H., Martinez G., Crasborn O., Piater J., Miguel Moya J., and Wheatley M., 2010 "The SignSpeak Project - Bridging the Gap Between Signers and Speakers". In 4th Workshop on the Representation and Processing of Sign Languages: Corpora and Sign Language Technologies (CSLT 2010), Valletta, Malta, 2010a. pp 73-80.

Dreuw P., Forster J., Gweth Y., Stein D., Ney H., Martinez G., Verges Llahi J., Crasborn O., Ormel E., Du W., Hoyoux T., Piater J., Moya Lazaro JM, and Wheatley M. 2010 "SignSpeak - Understanding, Recognition, and Translation of Sign Languages". In 4th Workshop on the Representation and Processing of Sign Languages: Corpora and Sign Language Technologies (CSLT 2010), Valletta, Malta, May 2010b. pp 65-73

Efthimiou E., and Fotinea, E., 2008 "GSLC: Creation and Annotation of a Greek Sign Language Corpus for HCI" LREC 2008. pp 1-10.

Efthimiou E., Fotinea S., Hanke T., Glauert J., Bowden R., Braffort A., Collet C., Maragos P., Goudenove F. 2010. "DICTA-SIGN: Sign Language Recognition, Generation and Modelling with application in Deaf Communication". In 4th Workshop on the Representation and Processing of Sign Languages: Corpora and Sign Language Technologies (CSLT 2010), Valletta, Malta, May 2010. pp 80-84.

Forster J., Stein D., Ormel E., Crasborn O., Ney H. 2010. "Best Practice for Sign Language Data Collections Regarding the Needs of Data-Driven Recognition and Translation". In 4th Workshop on the Representation and Processing of Sign Languages: Corpora and Sign Language Technologies (CSLT 2010), Valletta, Malta, May 2010. pp 92-98.

Geraci C., Bayley R., Branchini C., Cardinaletti A., Cecchetto C., Donati C., Giudice S., Mereghetti E., Poletti F., Santoro M., Zucchi S. 2010. "Building a corpus for Italian Sign Language. Methodological issues and some preliminary results". In 4th Workshop on the Representation and Processing of Sign Languages: Corpora and Sign Language Technologies (CSLT 2010), Valletta, Malta, May 2010. pp 98-102.

Hanke T., König L., Wagner S., Matthes S. 2010. "DGS Corpus & Dicta-Sign: The Hamburg Studio Setup". In 4th Workshop on the Representation and Processing of Sign Languages: Corpora and Sign Language Technologies (CSLT 2010), Valletta, Malta, May 2010. pp 106-110.

Herrero, A., 2004 "Escritura alfabética de la Lengua de Signos Española" Universidad de Alicante. Servicio de Publicaciones.

Koehn P., F.J. Och D. Marcu. 2003. "Statistical Phrase-based translation". Human Language Technology Conference 2003 (HLT-NAACL 2003), Edmonton, Canada, 2003. pp. 127-133.

Koehn, Philipp. 2010. "Statistical Machine Translation". phD. Cambridge University Press.

Marshall, I., Sáfár, E. (2005) "Grammar Development for Sign Language Avatar-Based Synthesis", In Proceedings HCII 2005, 11th International Conference on Human Computer Interaction (CD-ROM), Las Vegas, USA, July 2005. pp 1-10.

Morrissey S., Way A., Stein D., Bungeroth J., and Ney H., 2007 "Towards a Hybrid Data-Driven MT System for Sign Languages. Machine Translation Summit (MT Summit)", Copenhagen, Denmark, 2007. pp 329-335.

Morrissey, S. 2008. "Data-Driven Machine Translation for Sign Languages". Thesis. Dublin City University, Dublin, Ireland.

Morrissey S., Somers H., Smith R., Gilchrist S., Dandapat S., 2010 "Building Sign Language Corpora for Use in Machine Translation". In 4th Workshop on the Representation and Processing of Sign Languages: Corpora and Sign Language Technologies (CSLT 2010), Valletta, Malta, May 2010. pp 172-178.

Och J., Ney. H., 2003. "A systematic comparison of various alignment models". Computational Linguistics, Vol. 29, No. 1, 2003. pp. 19-51.

Papineni K., S. Roukos, T. Ward, W.J. Zhu. 2002 "BLEU: a method for automatic evaluation of machine translation". 40th Annual Meeting of the Association for Computational Linguistics (ACL), Philadelphia, PA. 2002. pp. 311-318.

Prillwitz, S., R. Leven, H. Zienert, T. Hanke, J. Henning, et-al. 1989. "Hamburg Notation System for Sign Languages – An introductory Guide". International Studies on Sign Language and the Communication of the Deaf, Volume 5. Institute of German Sign Language and Communication of the Deaf, University of Hamburg, 1989.

San-Segundo R., Barra R., Córdoba R., D'Haro L.F., Fernández F., Ferreiros J., Lucas J.M., Macías-Guarasa J., Montero J.M., Pardo J.M, 2008. "Speech to Sign Language translation system for Spanish". Speech Communication, Vol 50. 2008. pp. 1009-1020.

San-Segundo, R., Pardo, J.M., Ferreiros, F., Sama, V., Barra-Chicote, R., Lucas, JM., Sánchez, D., García. A., "Spoken Spanish Generation from Sign Language" Interacting with Computers, Vol. 22, No 2, 2010. pp. 123-139.

Schembri. A., 2008 "British Sign Language Corpus Project: Open Access Archives and the Observer's Paradox". Deafness Cognition and Language Research Centre, University College London. LREC 2008. pp 1-5.

Stein, D., Bungeroth, J. and Ney, H.: 2006 "Morpho-Syntax Based Statistical Methods for Sign Language Translation". 11th Annual conference of the European Association for Machine Translation, Oslo, Norway, June 2006. pp 223-231.

Stolcke A., 2002. "SRILM – An Extensible Language Modelling Toolkit". Proc. Intl. Conf. on Spoken Language Processing, vol. 2, Denver USA, 2002. pp. 901-904,

Stokoe W., Sign Language structure: an outline of the visual communication systems of the American deaf, Studies in Linguistics, Buffalo University Paper 8, 1960.

Vendrame M., Tiotto G., 2010. ATLAS Project: Forecast in Italian Sign Language and Annotation of Corpora. In 4th Workshop on the Representation and Processing of Sign Languages: Corpora and Sign Language Technologies (CSLT 2010), Valletta, Malta, May 2010. pp 239-243.

Wheatley, M., Annika Pabsch, 2010. "Sign Language in Europe". In 4th Workshop on the Representation and Processing of Sign Languages: Corpora and Sign Language Technologies. LREC. Malta 2010. pp 251-255.

What does it mean to communicate (not) emotionally?

Jan-Oliver Wülfing
Fraunhofer Centre Birlinghoven IZB
Schloß Birlinghoven
D-53754 Sankt Augustin
jan-oliver.wuelfing
@izb.fraunhofer.de

Lisa Hoffmann
Fraunhofer Institute for
Applied Information Technology FIT
Schloß Birlinghoven
D-53754 Sankt Augustin
lisa.hoffmann@fit.fraunhofer.de

Abstract

Communication is an essential part of our life. Though, not only communication is the key – it is all about emotional (prosodic) communication. Due to empirical research, people, who are augmentative communicators and speak with a voice output communication aid, want to express their emotions in the same way as everybody else – it is one of their deepest interests (Portnuff, 2006; Hoffmann and Wülfing, 2010). So far, current devices lack the opportunity of emotional utterances. This circumstance leads not only to a huge usability deficit, but furthermore, it is an obstacle to develop emotional competence and to behave as well as regulate one´s emotion adequately (Blackstone and Wilkins, 2009). This article aims to increase the sensitivity for the importance of emotional communication. Furthermore, it tries to give first suggestions for implementing an usable device that supports users with a voice output communication aid to express emotional utterances. This could be done by using phrase-generation, as mentiond by Vanderheyden and Pennigton (1998).

1 Introduction

One can hardly imagine how it would be to communicate without an emotional output. If we talk to each other, every conversation is influenced by our emotions. Sometimes we want to hide our feelings; however, more often we want to send an underlying message with our prosodic utterance. For example, imagine someone goes for a walk with their best friend, the sun is shining and the birds are chirping – this kind of situation and the feeling it evokes will probably be reflected by their prosodic utterance: "Dude, it`s awesome weather today!" Or imagine furthermore, the same person gets into a fight with this friend while walking in the sun; it certainly must not be pointed out that the emotion and therefore the reaction would differ. Though, communication and emotion seem inevitably associated, it is still not possible for people with complex communication needs to talk emotionally, since current voice output communication aids (VOCA) do not offer prosodic speech output. A circumstance that leads to several drawbacks; starting with disadvantages in social and academic arrangements.

1.1 What is a prosodic utterance?

Prosodic utterances are the key for daily communication processes. They depend on the emotion, i.e. it is reflected by an utterance through the pitch, the rhythm, and the volume of the voice. These differences are called prosody and, hence, it is possible to express very different types of emotions. Prosodic utterances influence the behaviour of the listener (Strom, 1998). The one and the same utterance can differ in their meaning. A good example of this is irony or subtle utterances. They may or may not be serious depending also on their prosodic features. Either way, the listener is going to react and this reaction relies not only on the accurate comprehension but also on the prosody of the speaker´s intended utterance (Battachi et al., 1997). In the case of augmentative communicators and their use of a

Proceedings of the 2nd Workshop on Speech and Language Processing for Assistive Technologies, pages 94–100,
Edinburgh, Scotland, UK, July 30, 2011. ©2011 Association for Computational Linguistics

VOCA, these aspects are not fully fulfilled. Instead of underlining their utterances with one or more prosodic features in order to convey their emotions to the listener, they must transcribe their current emotion in text input of the VOCA. In turn, the VOCA renders this in a monotonic, mostly synthetic voice output, which leads to two objections:

Firstly, the listener misinterprets the augmented communicator´s utterance, which may have dramatically effects for a follow-up conversation. Secondly, the listener becomes just bored and the conversation does not last long. In both ways, the augmented communicator´s situation becomes worse, since it influences their social environments and, thus, themselves (Balandin, 2005).

2 Emotional competence as a pre-condition for social participation

Emotions are seen to be an essential factor of social communication. To be a part of social relationships, it is necessary to develop emotional competence in some kind. Janke (2008) postulates emotional competence as the ability to express and regulate the own emotions and, furthermore, it describes the ability to understand emotions – the own one´s and other one´s. However, without the possibility to talk emotionally, it is hard to develop emotional competence. Research, in fact, has shown that users of a VOCA often have deficits in this area which leads to difficulties in forming relationships and the adequate emotion regulation is influenced as well (Brinton and Fujiki, 2009; Blackstone and Wilkins, 2009). Furthermore, there is a significant correlation between children´s emotional knowledge and the degree of peer popularity (Janke, 2008). Brinton and Fujiki (2009) even suggest that emotional competence has impact on academic learning. Due to the fact that the development of emotional competence is learned in day-to-day interactions with other people and that emotional utterances are a necessary pre-condition for exactly these interactions, it becomes clear that the development of a VOCA which does support prosodic communication would be an important factor for increasing the user´s Quality of Life. Among other things, it includes warm interpersonal relationships and academic achievements.

2.1 Development of social behaviour

Recent psychological theories focus on mutual-information processing systems for explaining social behaviour. Strack and Deutsch (2004) postulate two determinants to guide one´s decision-making: the reflective and the impulsive system. Though, both systems are interacting, they are different in their characteristics and functioning. The reflecting system is rather rational; it includes knowledge about facts and (social) values on which it bases its decision. The impulsive system, on the other hand, is lacking rational reasoning. It is rather impulsive, quick, and affected by motivational factors. Whereas the impulsive system is part of every decision making process, the reflective system is not. As, for instance, it needs more cognitive resources while operating and is easily disturbed.

When transferring the model onto emotional processing and electronic communication aids, it appears that alternative communicators are challenged in both, the impulsive and the reflective system. By definition, emotions are impulsive, quick, and the decisions based on them are often lacking rational reason. Thus, most of the time, emotional behaviour is driven by the impulsive system. Due to slow input-rates, users of a VOCA, indeed, are not able to communicate their emotions quickly and impulsively. They have to rely on the reflecting system. In some cases one might argue that this is the better opportunity as impulsive emotional utterances are regretted at times. On that account children learn that in some situations it is important to not follow their (inappropriate) impulsive behaviour while growing up (Blackstone and Wilkins, 2009). But due to the fact that alternative communicators are often disadvantaged in developing appropriate emotional behaviour (Brinton and Fujiki, 2009; Blackstone and Wilkins, 2009), it is also difficult to provide an adequate basis of knowledge for the reflective system. Thus, in particular for children, is important to communicate impulsively as it also strengthens the ability to make rational choices. Taking Strack´ and Deutsch´s theory (2004) into account it becomes clear that for the purpose of impulsive reactions an intended prosodic VOCA requires a possibility for a fast input-rate.

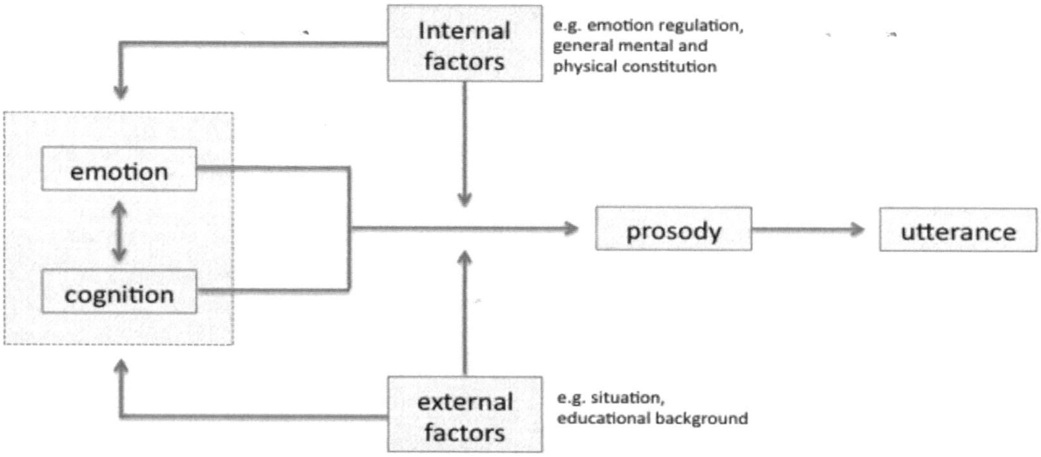

Fig. 1: The origin of prosodic utterances which reflects the emotional state. Internal and external factors have both influence on the emotion and cognition development as well as on the utterance itself.

3 Usability deficits

Empirical research in Usability Engineering shows that users of a VOCA claim for emotional communication (Hoffmann and Wülfing, 2010). Though, they typically honour the prospects given by the devices, they still describe the missing opportunity to talk emotionally (Portnuff, 2006; Hoffmann and Wülfing, 2010). If we take Maslow´s (1970) 'Hierarchy of Needs' into account, it is indeed not surprising that people, who have complex communication needs, want to talk in a very normal way. Maslow´s purpose is to show that every human being has specific needs. These needs are ordered hierarchically. The lowest frame depicts physiological needs like nutrition, sex, and the activity of the autonomous nervous system which are mostly involuntary (e.g. breathing). Then, the next layer symbolises all the aspects of safety. If these needs are fulfilled, it comes to friendship and love needs, those include emotional talk, social relationships, and emotional competence. His hierarchy underlines the assumption that a communication without prosody is acceptable but not satisfying, since emotional talk is an essential factor for being part of social relationships. Here, we go one step forward, because if we say that a product must be usable as described in ISO 9241-11 (1998), it must also be satisfying. The ISO standard defines Usability as: "The extent to which a product can be used by specified users to achieve specified goals with effectiveness, efficiency, and satisfaction in a specified context of use." The effectiveness means the accuracy in achieving the specific goal. Efficiency is time and effort the user needs for the achievement. And, satisfaction is the positive attitude towards the system. The three aspects are arranged hierarchically as shown in figure 2. Taking this definition into account and extending it on electronic communication aids, it becomes clear that the missing possibility for emotional communication can not only be seen as a satisfactory-failure but also as an effective-failure: the user is not able to achieve their goal accurately. Imagine, for instance, a human being cannot move because they have a significant impairment. The person is sitting in a wheelchair in one corner of a room and has a VOCA mounted on the wheelchair. Via the device the user asks the people in the room to move their chair, however, no one listens and helps due to the monotonous voice. In this scenario the VOCA fails and the user is not able to achieve their goal. The device, therefore, is not effective. But would this happen if the VOCA would have a prosodic voice output? We believe that this would not happen. With a prosodic voice it is possible to get attention more easily. In a normal situation, if we could use our voice, we would rather become angry more and more if no one listens to us. Our cadence would unveil our emotion (Scherer and Banse, 1991) and, hence, would underline our intention. For augmented communicators, this would be an important step forward to not only communicate the semantic content of their utterances, but also the emotion underlying those. The actual relevance of the made-up scenario above is also supported by VOCA user Collin Portnuff. He claimed in a speech, given in 2006, a device capable of shouting to gain attention in certain situations (Portnuff, 2006).

Fig. 2: Hierarchical steps of Usability based on ISO 9241-11 (1998)

The elimination of the uability deficit described above would also strengthen the user´s position in a communication and most likely the duration of a communication. We all love more to talk to people whose voice contains prosodic features than to face anyone whose voice is rather monotonous. Due to the fact that human beings are empathic, we like to have an impression of the opposite´s emotion. And how do we get such an impression? Through the mimic, gesture, and the tone of voice. So, an emotional device is a Win-Win situation: The listener can respond adequately and the speaker can express his intention through a verbal prosodic utterance. It becomes clear that even from the listener´s point of view it is easier and more comfortable to have a conversation with an augmented communicator who has a prosodic VOCA, since it would fulfil at least some constraints of a fluent conversation (Todman and Alm, 2003). Or as Collin Portnuff (2006) puts it: "And when you help someone communicate, you are not just helping that person, but all the people with whom he or she interacts."

4 Often heard criticism

Often heard criticism about a prosodic speech output of a VOCA typically embraces the following three aspects:

a. Emotional conversation would increase the input rate,

b. emotional utterances are not possible without a synthetic voice that supports emotional output and

c. emotions and emotional conversations are too complex to work on a VOCA.

Even though these aspects are not to be dismissed, we assume that it is possible to find proper solutions for each of them.

a. Increasing input rate: The speech generic device of a VOCA with a specific prosodic tool should enable the possibility of an emotional conversation without increasing the input time. Instead, emotional utterances will extend the duration of a conversation. So far augmentative communicators use their VOCA often to communicate common needs as "I´m hungry" or to answer simple yes-/no-questions (Blackstone and Wilkins, 2009). Lasting conversations as for example talking about a film watched just before at a cinema and the experienced emotions while doing so are rather rare. In the latter kind of conversations emotional utterances are very important, since a lack of them would shorten a conversation dramatically. Also one can guess that the user´s need to have an emotional equipped VOCA is higher than the expense of one more additional keystroke. Nevertheless it is important to keep any additional effort to the lowest to truly fulfil the user´s requirements. However, the missing lasting conversations are to be seen as a gap in the Quality of Life. In order to bridge this gap along with the gaps mentioned above (e.g. the missing emotional competence and Usability deficits) the development of a VOCA, that does support prosodic communication, seems inevitable.

b. Synthetic voice: Starting with a prototype of VOCA, the emotional utterances can easily be pronounced naturally instead of using synthesized speech, since emotional speech is rather limited in current VOCAs (Higginbotham; 2010). Nonetheless, there has been some notable efforts in recent years (e.g. CereProc Ltd.[1]). They make use of what they call 'Emotional Continum'. It is possible to simulate a wide range of underlying emotions of the voice. Or, if we look at the work of the World Wide Web Consortium, they currently work on the EmotionML (2011) which should facilitate synthetic voices to become annotated with emotional tags. So, it is to assume that in the near future emotional synthetic utterances will be possible. In the meantime, however, a natural recorded voice of an actor is an acceptable solution as current existing synthetic voices are often experienced as alien (Hoffmann and Wülfing, 2010). Furthermore, user experience shows some people find it difficult to listen to the same intonations given by the devices while the meaning of the words change (Portnuff, 2006), a problem that can be solved by using natural voice output.

c. Complexity: In order to limit the complexity of such a formation, it is necessary to start with isolating a reasonable amount of emotions. It is also important to not use indifferent emotions, as for example cold anger and panic fear, as people seem to have problems distinguishing them (Banse and Scherer, 1996) which may lead to frustration in conversations later on. The three emotions happiness, anger, and sadness are quite different in their prosody. Thus, a listener can recognise them very well, as Burkhardt (2001) mentioned. They belong to the so-called basic emotions as well (Ekman, 1999). Therefore, it seems to be a reasonable choice to choose them for a start-up project. Another possibility to lower the complexity is to attach the emotions to certain situations; this restricts the context of utterances.

5 Initial approaches

The proposed project aims at a spontaneous emotional communication in context-specific situations for VOCA users. This includes the idea of identifying a user-specific and context-specific vocabulary based on phrase-generation. As shown above there are certain requirements for an authentic emotional communication: Any emotional utterance consists of its semantic content, its prosodic characteristic, and a certain degree of impulsiveness. The presented initial approaches keep these requirements in mind as well as the beforehand mentioned criticism. It is important to note that these initial approaches are first propositions which are based on current knowledge. Possibly some adjustments need to be made in the development of the prosodic VOCA in order to keep the device truly usable.

Yet, based on current experiences we propose a system where users firstly select their emotion and secondly compose the prosodic utterance, since the emotion does typically not change after each utterance. Thus, the user does not need to change the prosodic filter option every time. In this way, the input-rate will not enhance unnecessarily as often criticised. To render the possibility of impulsive, spontaneous, and agile communication, the prosodic VOCA needs to support the user with a sample of potential utterances fitting the user´s emotion in the specific situation. Therefore, the development of a phrased-based vocabulary is necessary. It is important to guarantee the validity of the possible utterances given by the device as otherwise they will not be perceived authentic. That is why the potential samples of utterances must not be chosen at random. Instead they should be based on empirical settings. This will be done by investigating specific contexts and identifying emotional phrases given by a specific subpopulation. The probability enhances that the device offers the user an utterance which he or she actually needs in the specific situation by using empirical based methods. The established vocabulary should be user-specific by all means. There are age-based differences in the way people speak and express their emotions. A user-specific vocabulary needs to keep these age-differences in mind for identifying phrases that fit the phraseology of specific users. Therefore, the sample of potential utterances should also be based on colloquial speech. This is a good example in order to enrich a conversation more lively and ongoing. In particular, colloquial speech enables the augmentative communicators to be perceived more authentic by their social environment. It also supports the user in developing emotional competence using impulsive speech. In turn the environment´s feedback increases the adequate

[1] www.cereproc.com (accessed 06/24/2011)

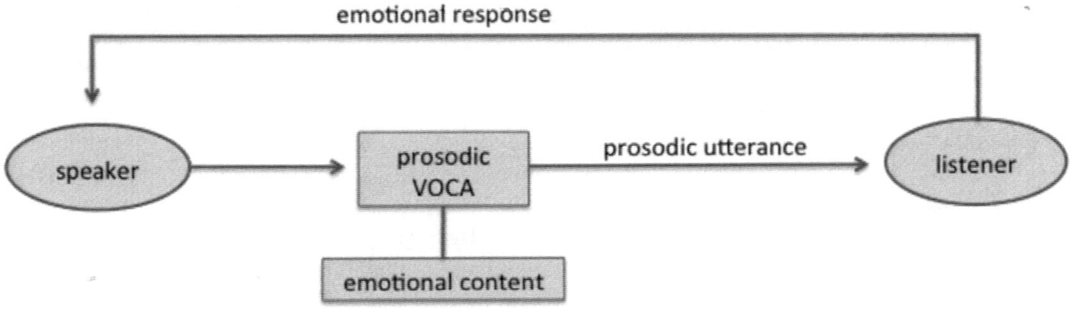

Fig. 3: Model of emotional communication using a prosodic Voice Output Communication Aid which allows the listener an appropriate emotional response to the speaker`s (augmented communicator) intented message.

handling of emotions in specific situations (s. Fig. 3). In addition to the possibility of using the utterances given by the device the user still needs the alternative to form contents individually. A prosodic VOCA does not aim at depriving the users of the power to speak independently. It rather serves as an adequate support in order to enhance the promptness of a statement which is an important requirement for an authentic conversation. As already mentioned, natural recorded voices could be used for the potential utterances as an alternative to synthetic speech output. However, it is important to note that the utterances must resemble the appropriate prosody. Hence, the pitch, the rhythm, and the volume of the voice need to fit the content of the utterance. Sorrow e.g. should be presented rather quiet while enragement requires a higher sound level.

All things considered, it becomes clear that the development of a prosodic VOCA goes along with some important requirements that reflect the user´s needs. In order to develop a device, which supports these needs, the Usability has to be seen as an essential factor. Thus, it is important to include the user throughout the whole process of developing. A constraint for designing usable devices that fit the Usability definition is the ISO standard 9241-11 (1998). This kind of Usability-Setting include interviews with users and when indicated a monitoring with a 'Thinking aloud-'method, which helps to formalise specific usability problems with the specific system in that specific context.

Summarised, the requirements for a prosodic VOCA should be based on:

- phrase-generation
- specific contexts
- appropriate emotions
- user-specific phraseology
- adequate prosody
- usability standards

To validate these and additional assumptions for a specific sample of users, they must be confirmed in an emprical setting. A frist step was done by showing the importance of emotional utterances for augmented communicators (Hoffmann and Wülfing, 2010).

6 Conclusion

Emotional communication is an essential part of everyday life - this is true for people with and without disabilities. Lacking the opportunity of talking emotional means to miss out many aspects of a fulfilling life, since emotional output has an enormous impact on social relationships, the developing of emotional competence, and even on academic achievements. Furthermore, this circumstance leads to a huge usability deficit. Augmented communicators´ own expressiveness of emotions by gesture and mimic means is limited and prosodic communication is not possible, yet. Precisely because, prosodic VOCA is a real innovation. It gives people with complex communications needs the opportunity to express themselves emotionally. It would encourage their participation in social life and, thus, also their Quality of Life. Still, there is a lot of criticism involving this topic, however, with adequate methods and ideas it does seem possible that some day in the future users of a VOCA will be able to communicate emotionally.

References

Susan Balandin (2005). Ageing and AAC: Start early, age well! In Jens Boenisch and Karin Otto (eds.), Leben im Dialog – Unterstützte Kommunikation über die gesamte Lebensspanne (466-478). Von Loeper, Karlsruhe.

Marco W. Battachi, Thomas Suslow, and Margherita Renna (1997). Emotion & Sprache – Zur Definition der Emotion und ihren Beziehungen zu kognitiven Prozessen, dem Gedächtnis und der Sprache. Peter Lang, Frankfurt a.M.

Rainer Banse and Klaus R. Scherer (1996). Acoustic profiles in vocal emotion expression. In: Journal of Personality and Social Psychology, 70(3), 614-636.

Sarah W. Blackstone and David P. Wilkins (2009). Exploring the Importance of Emotional Competence in Children With Complex Communication Needs. In: Perspectives on Augmentative and Alternative Communication, 18, 78-87.

Felix Burkhardt (2001). Simulation emotionaler Sprechweise mit Sprachsyntheseverfahren. In: Reihe Berichte aus der Kommunikationstechnik. Shaker, Aachen.

Bonnie Brinton and Martin Fujiki (2009). Meet me more than half way: Emotional competence in conversation using AAC. In: Perspectives on Augmentative and Alternative Communication, 18, 73-77.

Paul Ekman (1999). Basic Emotions. In: Tim Dalgleish and Mick Power (Eds.), Handbook of Cognition and Emotion. John Wiley & Sons, Sussex, U.K.

Emotion Markup Language 1.0 (2011) W3C working draft. http://www.w3.org/TR/2011/WD-emotionml-20110407/ (accessed 06/24/2011).

Jeffrey Higginbotham (2010). Humanizing Vox Artificialis: The Role of Speech Synthesis in Augmentative and Alternative Communication. In: John Mullennix and Steven Stern (Eds.), Computer Synthesized Speech Technologies – Tools for Aiding Impairment (50-70). IGI Global, Hershey, PA.

Lisa Hoffmann and Jan-O. Wülfing (2010). Usability of Electronic Communication Aids in the Light of Daily Use. In: Proceedings of the 14th Biennial Conference of the International Society for Augmentative and Alternative Communication (259). Barcelona, Spain

ISO 9241-11 (1998). Ergonomic requirements for office work with visual display terminals (VDTs) – Part 11: Guidance on usability.

Bettina Janke (2008). Emotionswissen und Sozialkompetenz von Kindern im Alter von drei bis zehn Jahren. In: Empirische Pädagogik, 22(2), 127-144.

Abraham H. Maslow (1970). Motivation and Personality. Harper & Row, New York, NY.

Colin Portnuff (2006). AAC: A user´s perspective. Webcast available as part of the AAC-RERC Webcast Series. http://aac-rerc.psu.edu/index-8121.php.html (accessed 03/30/2011).

Klaus R. Scherer, Rainer Banse, Harald G. Wallbott, and Thomas Goldbeck (1991). Vocal Cues in Emotion Encoding and Decoding. In: Motivation and Emotion, 15(2), 123-148.

Fritz Strack and Roland Deutsch (2004). Reflective and Impulsive Determinants of Social Behavior. In: Personality and Social Psychology Review, 8(3), 220-247.

Volker F. Strom (1998). Automatische Erkennung von Satzmodus, Akzentuierung und Phrasengrenzen. PhD thesis, University of Bonn.

John Todman and Norman Alm (2003). Modelling conversational pragmatics in communications aids. In: Journal of Pragmatics, 35, 523-538.

Peter B. Vanderheyden and Christopher A. Pennigton (1998). An Augmentative Communication Interface Based on Conversational Schemata. In: Vibhu O. Mittal, Holly A. Yanco, John Aronis, Richard C. Simpson and Richard Simpson (Eds.): Assistive Technology and AI, LNAI 1458, 109-125.

Arabic Text to Arabic Sign Language Translation System for the Deaf and Hearing-Impaired Community

Abdulaziz Almohimeed
University of Southampton
United Kingdom
aia07r@ecs.soton.ac.uk

Mike Wald
University of Southampton
United Kingdom
mw@ecs.soton.ac.uk

R. I. Damper
University of Southampton
United Kingdom
rid@ecs.soton.ac.uk

Abstract

This paper describes a machine translation system that offers many deaf and hearing-impaired people the chance to access published information in Arabic by translating text into their first language, Arabic Sign Language (ArSL). The system was created under the close guidance of a team that included three deaf native signers and one ArSL interpreter. We discuss problems inherent in the design and development of such translation systems and review previous ArSL machine translation systems, which all too often demonstrate a lack of collaboration between engineers and the deaf community. We describe and explain in detail both the adapted translation approach chosen for the proposed system and the ArSL corpus that we collected for this purpose. The corpus has 203 signed sentences (with 710 distinct signs) with content restricted to the domain of instructional language as typically used in deaf education. Evaluation shows that the system produces translated sign sentences outputs with an average word error rate of 46.7% and an average position error rate of 29.4% using leave-one-out cross validation. The most frequent source of errors is missing signs in the corpus; this could be addressed in future by collecting more corpus material.

1 Introduction

Machine translation (MT) has developed rapidly since 1947, when Warren Weaver first suggested the use of computers to translate natural languages (Augarten, 1984). Presently, this technology offers a potential chance for ArSL signers to benefit by, for instance, giving them access to texts published in Arabic. ArSL and general sign language (SL) have inherent ambiguity problems that should be taken into account while designing any ArSL translation system. Therefore, ArSL translation must be done through close collaboration with the deaf community and signing experts. This paper describes a full prototype MT system that translates Arabic texts into deaf and hearing-impaired peoples' first language, Arabic Sign Language (ArSL). It is the result of extended collaboration between engineers and a team consisting of three deaf native signers and one ArSL interpreter.

Most existing systems have wrongly assumed that ArSL is dependent on the Arabic language (Mohandes, 2006; Alnafjan, 2008; Halawani, 2008; Al-Khalifa, 2010). These systems make word-to-sign translations without regard to ArSL's unique linguistic characteristics, such as its own grammar, structure, and idioms, as well as regional variations (Abdel-Fateh, 2004) or translate into finger-spelling signs that only exist in Arabic, not in ArSL.

This paper begins by providing a brief background of ArSL. It then addresses the problems and misconceptions plaguing previous ArSL systems. Thereafter, it describes related works built on the assumption of one of the two misconceptions mentioned above. The rest of the paper will present an example-based machine translation (EBMT) system that translates published Arabic texts to make them accessible to deaf and hearing-impaired people who use ArSL.

Proceedings of the 2nd Workshop on Speech and Language Processing for Assistive Technologies, pages 101–109,
Edinburgh, Scotland, UK, July 30, 2011. ©2011 Association for Computational Linguistics

2 Background

SL is composed of basic elements of gesture and location previously called 'cheremes' but modern usage has changed to the even more problematic 'optical phoneme' (Ojala, 2011). These involve three components: hand shape (also called hand configuration), position of the hand in relation to the signer's body, and the movement of direction of the hand. These three components are called manual features (MFs). In addition, SL may involve non-manual features (NMFs) that involve other parts of the body, including facial expression, shoulder movements, and head tilts in concurrence with MFs. Unlike written language, where a text expresses ideas in a linear sequence, SL employs the space around the signer for communication, and the signer may use a combination of MFs and NMFs. These are called multi-channel signs. The relationship between multi-channel signs may be parallel, or they may overlap during SL performance. MFs are basic components of any sign, whereas NMFs play an important role in composing signs in conjunction with MFs. NMFs can be classified into three types in terms of their roles. The first is essential: If an NMF is absent, the sign will have a completely different meaning.

An example of an essential NMF in ArSL is the sign sentence: "Theft is forbidden", where as shown in Figure 1(a), closed eyes in the sign for "theft" are essential. If the signer does not close his or her eyes, the "theft" sign will mean "lemon". The second type of NMF is a qualifier or emotion. In spoken language, inflections, or changes in pitch, can express emotions, such as happiness and sadness; likewise, in SL, NMFs are used to express emotion as in Figure 1(b). The third type of NMF actually plays no role in the sign. In some cases, NMFs remain from a previous sign and are meaningless. Native signers naturally discard any meaningless NMFs based on their knowledge of SL.

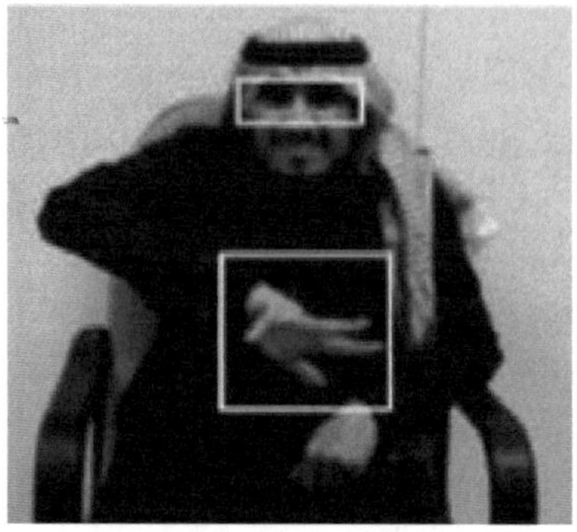

(a) Essential NMF

(b) Emotion NMF

Figure 1: (a) The sign for "theft", in which the signer uses the right hand while closing his eyes. (b) His facial expressions show the emotion of the sign.

3 Problem Definition

ArSL translation is a particularly difficult MT problem for four main reasons, which we now describe.

The first of the four reasons is the lack of linguistic studies on ArSL, especially in regard to grammar and structure, which leads to a major misunderstanding of natural language and misleads researchers into failing to build usable ArSL translation systems. These misunderstandings about ArSL can be summed up by the following:

- SL is assumed to be a universal language that allows the deaf anywhere in the world to communicate, but in reality, many different SLs exist (e.g., British SL, Irish SL, and ArSL).
- ArSL is assumed to be dependent on the Arabic language but it is an independent language that has its own grammar, structure, and idioms, just like any other natural language.
- ArSL is not finger spelling of the Arabic alphabet, although finger spelling is used for names and places that do not exist in ArSL or for other entities for which no sign exists (e.g., neologisms).

The related work section will describe an ArSL translation system that was built based on one of these misunderstandings.

The second factor that should be taken into account while building an ArSL translation system is the size of the translation corpus, since few linguistic studies of ArSL's grammar and structure have been conducted. The data-driven approach adopted here relies on the corpus, and the translation accuracy is correlated with its size. Also, ArSL does not have a written system, so there are no existing ArSL documents that could be used to build a translation corpus, which must be essentially visual (albeit with annotation). Hence, the ArSL corpus must be built from scratch, limiting its size and ability to deliver an accurate translation of signed sentences.

The third problem is representing output sign sentences. Unlike spoken languages, which use sounds to produce utterances, SL employs 3D space to present signs. The signs are continuous, so some means are required to produce novel but fluent signs. One can either use an avatar or, as here, concatenate video clips at the expense of fluency.

The last problem is finding a way to evaluate SL output. Although this can be a problem for an MT system, it is a particular challenge here as SL uses multi-channel representations (Almohimeed et al., 2009).

4 Related Works

As mentioned above, we deem it necessary for engineers to collaborate with the deaf community and/or expert signers to understand some fundamental issues in SL translation. The English to Irish Sign Language (ISL) translation system developed by Morrissey (2008) is an example of an EBMT system created through strong collaboration between the local deaf community and engineers. Her system is based on previous work by Veale and Way (1997), and Way and Gough (2003; 2005) in which they use tags for sub-sentence segmentation. These tags represent the syntactic structure. Their work was designed for large tagged corpora.

However, as previously stated, existing research in the field of ArSL translation shows a poor or weak relationship between the Arab deaf community and engineers. For example, the system built by Mohandes (2006) wrongly assumes that ArSL depends on the Arabic language and shares the same structure and grammar. Rather than using a data-driven or rule-based approach, it uses so-called "direct translation" in which words are transliterated into ArSL on a one-to-one basis.

5 Translation System

The lack of linguistic studies on ArSL, especially on its grammar and structure, is an additional reason to favour the example-based (EMBT) approach over a rule-based methodology. Further, the statistical approach is unlikely to work well given the inevitable size limitation of the ArSL corpus, imposed by difficulties of collecting large volumes of video signing data from scratch. On the other hand, EBMT relies only on example-guided suggestions and can still produce reasonable translation output even with existing small-size corpora. We have adopted a chunk-based EBMT system, which produces output sign sentences by comparing the Arabic text input to matching text fragments, or 'chunks'. As Figure 2 shows, the system has two phases. Phase 1 is run only once; it pre-compiles the chunks and their associated signs. Phase 2 is the actual translation system that converts Arabic input into ArSL output. The following sections will describe each component in Figure 2.

5.1 Google Tashkeel Component

In Arabic, short vowels usually have diacritical marks added to distinguish between similar words in terms of meaning and pronunciation. For example, the word كُتُب means *books*, whereas كَتَبَ means *write*. Most Arabic documents are written without the use of diacritics. The reason for this is that Arabic speakers can naturally infer these diacritics from context. The morphological analyser used in this system can accept Arabic input without diacritics, but it might produce many different analysed outputs by making different assumptions about the missing diacritics. In the end, the system needs to select one of these analysed outputs, but it might not be equivalent to the input meaning. To solve this problem, we use Google Tashkeel (`http://tashkeel.googlelabs.com/`) as a component in the translation system; this software tool adds missing diacritics to Arabic text, as shown in Figure 3. (In Arabic, *tashkeel* means "to add shape".) Using this component, we can guarantee

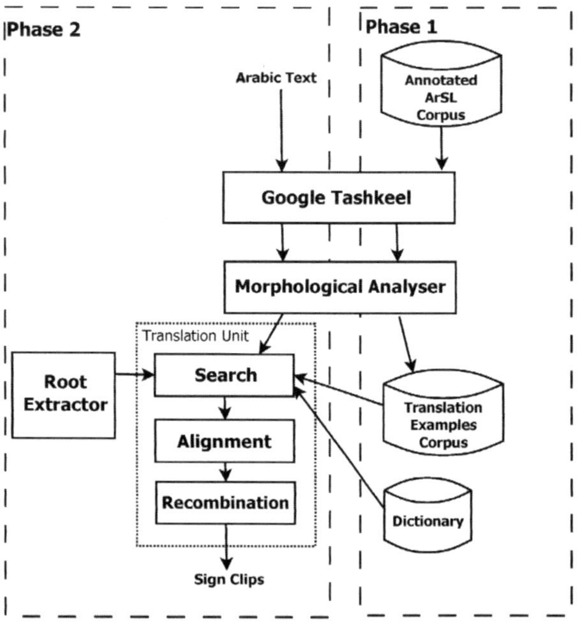

Figure 2: Main components of the ArSL chunks-based EBMT system. Phase 1 is the pre-compilation phase, and Phase 2 is the translation phase.

that the morphological analyser described immediately below will produce only one analysed output.

5.2 Morphological Analyser

The Arabic language is based on root-pattern schemes. Using one root, several patterns, and numerous affixes, the language can generate tens or hundreds of words (Al Sughaiyer and Al Kharashi, 2004). A *root* is defined as a single morpheme

Figure 3: An example of an input and output text using Google Tashkeel. The input is a sentence without diacritics; the output shows the same sentence after adding diacritics. English translation: *You should read the explanation.*

that provides the basic meaning of a word. In Arabic, the root is also the original form of the word, prior to any transformation process (George, 1990). In English, the root is the part of the word that remains after the removal of affixes. The root is also sometimes called the stem (Al Khuli, 1982). A *morpheme* is defined as the smallest meaningful unit of a language. A *stem* is a single morpheme or set of concatenated morphemes that is ready to accept affixes (Al Khuli, 1982). An *affix* is a morpheme that can be added before (a prefix) or after (a suffix) a root or stem. In English, removing a prefix is usually harmful because it can reverse a word's meaning (e.g., the word *disadvantage*). However, in Arabic, this action does not reverse the meaning of the word (Al Sughaiyer and Al Kharashi, 2004). One of the major differences between Arabic (and the Semitic language family in general) and English (and similar languages) is that Arabic is 'derivational' (Al Sughaiyer and Al Kharashi, 2004), or non-catenative, whereas English is concatenative.

Figure 4 illustrates the Arabic derivational system. The three words in the top layer (كتب, خبر, ذهب) are roots that provide the basic meaning of a word. Roman letters such as *ktb* are used to demonstrate the pronunciation of Arabic words. After that, in the second layer, "xAxx" (where the small letter x is a variable and the capital letter A is a constant) is added to the roots, generating new words (كاتب, خابر, ذاهب) called stems. Then, the affix "ALxxxx" is added to stems to generate words (الكاتب, الخابر, الذاهب).

Morphology is defined as the grammatical study of the internal structure of a language, which includes the roots, stems, affixes, and patterns. A morphological analyser is an important tool for predicting the syntactic and semantic categories of unknown words that are not in the dictionary. The primary functions of the morphological analyser are the segmentation of a word into a sequence of morphemes and the identification of the morpho-syntactic relations between the morphemes (Semmar et al., 2005).

Due to the limitation of the ArSL corpus size, the syntactic and semantic information of unmatched chunks needs to be used to improve the translation system selection, thereby increasing the system's

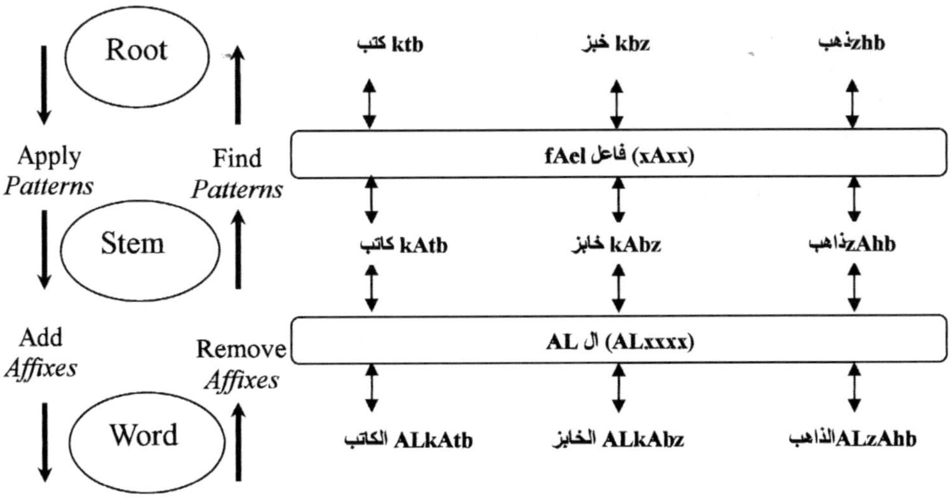

Figure 4: An example of the Arabic derivational system. The first stage shows some examples of roots. An Arabic root generally contains between 2 and 4 letters. The second stage shows the generated stems from roots after adding the pattern to the roots. The last stage shows the generated words after the prefixes are added to the stems.

accuracy. To analyse this information, Buckwalter's morphological analyser was used (Buckwalter, 2004). In addition, we implemented a root extractor based on a tri-literal root extraction algorithm (Momani and Faraj, 2007). In this work, sentences without diacritics are passed to the morphological analyser, which therefore produces multiple analyses (distinguished by different assumptions about the missing diacritics) from which the 'best' one must be chosen. This is not an easy decision for a computer system to make. The approach we have implemented uses the Google Tashkeel output in conjunction with the Levenshtein distance (Levenshtein, 1966) to select among the multiple analyses delivered by Buckwalter's morphological analyser. Figure 5 gives an example showing how the morphological and root extractor analyses the syntactic, semantic and root information.

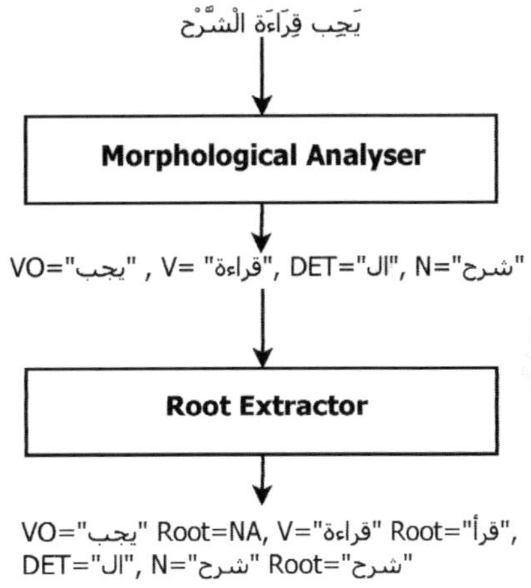

Figure 5: An example showing how the morphological analyser and root extractor are utilised for the same sentence as in Fig. 3.

5.3 Corpus

An annotated ArSL corpus is essential for this system, as for all data-driven systems. Therefore, we collected and annotated a new ArSL corpus with the help of three native ArSL signers and one expert interpreter. Full details are given in Almohimeed et al. (2010). This corpus's domain is restricted to the kind of instructional language used in schools for deaf students. It contains 203 sentences with 710 distinct signs. The recorded signed sentences were annotated using the ELAN annotation tool (Brugman and Russel, 2004), as shown in Figure 6. Signed sentences were then saved in EUDICO Annotation Format (EAF).

The chunks database and sign dictionary are de-

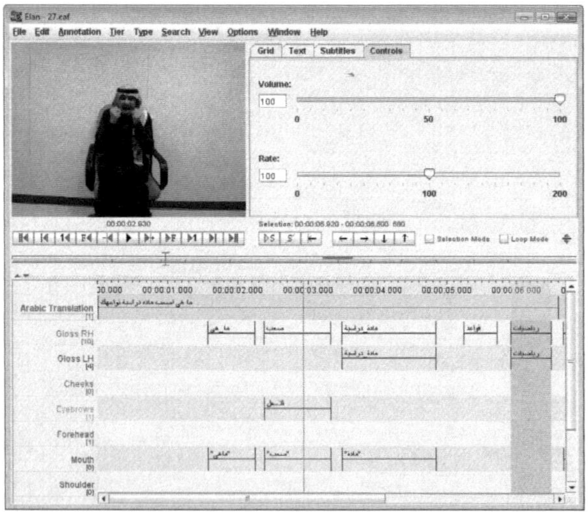

Figure 6: An example of a sign sentence annotated by the ELAN tool.

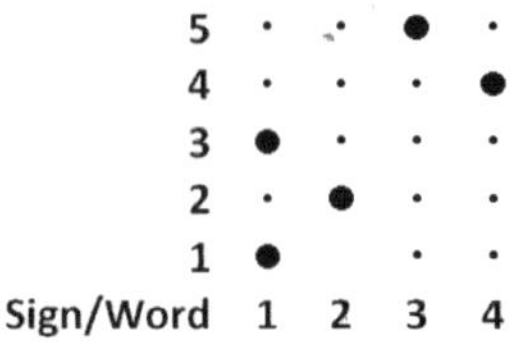

Starting from Word #	T1	T2	T3	T4
1	[1-1,3]	[1,2-1,2,3]	[1,2,3-1,2,3,5]	[1,2,3,4-1,2,3,4,5]
2	[2-2]	[2,3-2,5]	[2,3,4-2,4,5]	
3	[3-5]	[2,3-4,5]		
4	[4,4]			

Figure 7: An example of how the system finds chunks by finding continuous words and signs.

rived from this corpus by parsing the EAF file to extract the MFs and NMFs to build a parallel corpus of ArSL and associated Arabic chunks. Before detecting and extracting chunks, words are linked with their equivalent signs in each sentence. After a manual words-to-signs alignment, chunk extraction begins. This is done automatically by finding consistent word/sign sequence pairs. The refined technique proposed by Och and Ney (2003) is employed in this system to extract chunks. Figure 7 illustrates how the system does so.

The chunks table has four fields. The first contains all the Arabic words in the chunk, and the second contains an identifier for the video clips of the signs. The third field contains syntactic and semantic information about the Arabic words. The last field indicates the relative position of the parallel ArSL and text chunks. After extraction of the chunks, the database is sorted from largest chunks (in terms of words) to smallest. Details of the tool that carries out these steps will be published in a future paper.

5.4 Translation Unit

As depicted earlier in Figure 2, the translation unit contains three components. The first is the search component, which is responsible for finding chunks that match the input. It starts matching words from the beginning of the chunks table and scans the table until the end. Overlapping chunks have higher priority for selection than separate chunks. Then, for any remaining unmatched input words, it starts matching stems from the beginning through to the end of the chunks table. The second is the alignment component, which replaces chunks with their equivalent signs. For the remaining input words that do not have a chunk match, a sign dictionary is used to translate them. If the word does not appear in the dictionary (which is possible due to the size of the corpus), the system starts searching for the stem of the word and compares it with the stems in the dictionary. If the stem also does not appear in the database or dictionary, the system searches for a matching root. This process will increase the chance of translating the whole input sentence. The last component is recombination, which is responsible for delivering sign output using the sign location on both the chunks table and dictionary. The component will produce a series of sign clips, and between two clips, it will insert a transition clip, as shown in Figure 8.

The output representation has been tested by the team of three native signers on several hundred

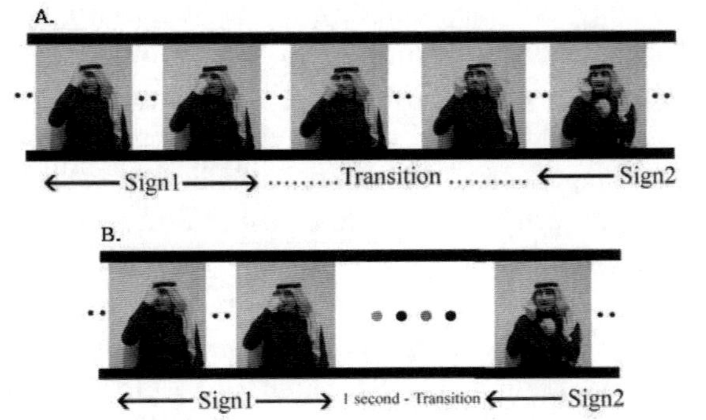

Figure 8: Image A shows an example of the original representation, while B shows the output representation.

selected sign sentences in which natural transitions were replaced by a one-second pause. Moreover, the sign in actual sentences has been replaced by the equivalent sign in the sign dictionary. This test showed that the meaning of the sentences was clearly expressed to the signers; all three evaluated the test sentences by giving them 5 points out of 5, which means the sentence clearly expresses its meaning. In addition, the fluency of sentences was deemed acceptable since the evaluators choose 4 points out of 5. In view of this positive result, we did not feel it worthwhile to evaluate the effect of variation in (one-second) pause duration, although this will be adjustable by the user in the final implementation.

6 Illustration

In this section, we illustrate the workings of the prototype system on three example sentences.

Figures 9, 10, and 11 shows the main stages of the translation of Arabic sentence to ArSL for some selected inputs. The input sentence in Figure 9 is 2 words, 5 in Figure 10, and 7 in Figure 11. As shown in the figures, the system starts collecting the morphological details of the Arabic input. Then, it passes it to the translation unit where it first searches for a matching chunk in the chunks table. When many matches are received, the system takes the largest chunk (recall that the system gives overlapping chunks higher priority than isolated chunks and that when no chunks are found in the table, the system uses the stem rather than the word to find a match). When a match is not found, the system uses the dictionary to translate the sign by looking for the word. In the next stage, alignment, the system identifies the corresponding translation chunk from both the chunks table and dictionary. The system uses the location field in the chunks table and dictionary to determine the location of the translated chunk. The last stage is recombination, during which the system delivers a sign sentence in a Windows Media Video (WMV) format, as shown in Figure 8.

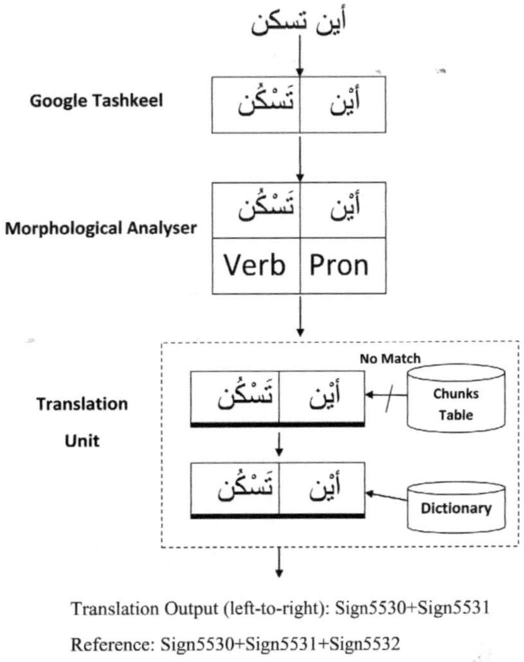

Figure 9: Example translation from the first Arabic sentence to ArSL. The square selection represents a chunk match. The crossed arrow means that there was no chunk match and that it has been translated using the dictionary. In this case, the output is incorrect (Sign5532 is missing). English translation: *Where do you live?*

7 Leave-One-Out Cross Validation

The full evaluation results (203 sentences) were acquired using leave-one-out cross validation. This technique removes a test sentence from the dataset and then uses the remaining dataset as the translation corpus. The word error rate (WER) was, on average, 46.7%, whereas the position-independent word error rate (PER) averaged 29.4%. The major source of

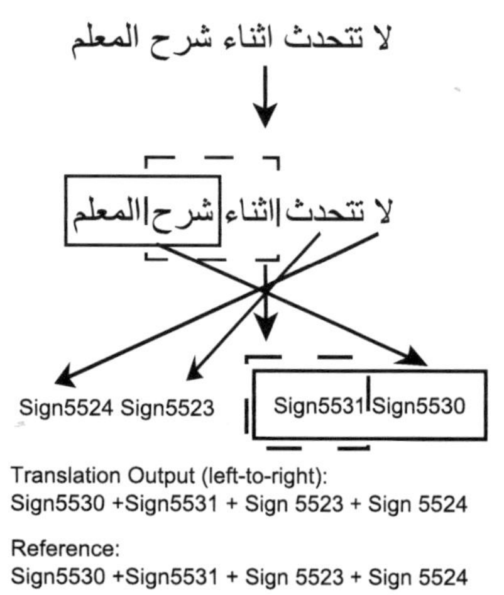

Figure 10: Example translation from the second Arabic sentence to ArSL. In this case, the output is correct. English translation: *Don't talk when the teacher is teaching.*

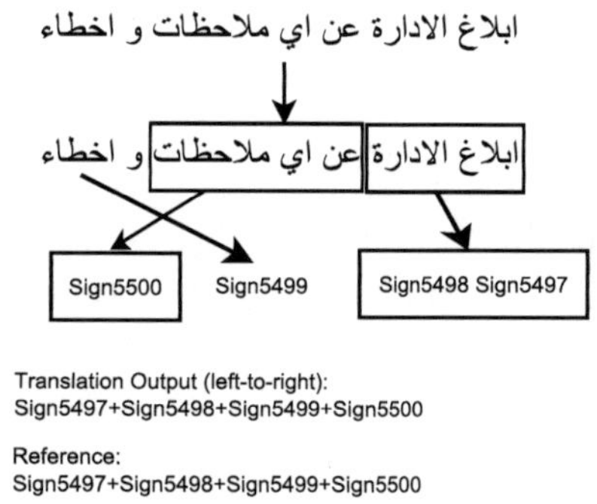

Figure 11: Example translation from the third Arabic sentence to ArSL. Again, the output is correct. English translation: *Let the Principal know about any suggestions or comments that you have.*

error is that signs in some translated sentences do not have equivalent signs in the dictionary. In principle, this source of error could be reduced by collection of a larger corpus with better coverage of the domain, although this is an expensive process.

8 Conclusion

This paper has described a full working prototype ArSL translation system, designed to give the Arabic deaf community the potential to access published Arabic texts by translating them into their first language, ArSL. The chunk-based EBMT approach was chosen for this system for numerous reasons. First, the accuracy of this approach is easily extended by adding extra sign examples to the corpus. In addition, there is no requirement for linguistic rules; it purely relies on example-guided suggestions. Moreover, unlike other data-driven approaches, EBMT can translate using even a limited corpus, although performance is expected to improve with a larger corpus. Its accuracy depends primarily on the quality of the examples and their degree of similarity to the input text. To overcome the limitations of the relatively small corpus, a morphological analyser and root extractor were added to the system to deliver syntactic and semantic information that will increase the accuracy of the system. The chunks are extracted from a corpus that contains samples of the daily instructional language currently used in Arabic deaf schools. Finally, the system has been tested using leave-one-out cross validation together with WER and PER metrics. It is not possible to compare the performance of our system with any other competing Arabic text to ArSL machine translation system, since no other such systems exist at present.

Acknowledgments

This work would not have been done without the hard work of the signers' team: Mr. Ahmed Alzaharani, Mr. Kalwfah Alshehri, Mr. Abdulhadi Alharbi and Mr. Ali Alholafi.

References

Mahmoud Abdel-Fateh. 2004. Arabic Sign Language: A perspective. *Journal of Deaf Studeis and Deaf Education*, 10(2):212–221.

Hend S. Al-Khalifa. 2010. Introducing Arabic sign language for mobile phones. In *ICCHP'10 Proceedings of the 12th International Conference on Computers Helping People with Special Needs*, pages 213–220 in Springer Lecture Notes in Computer Science, Part II, vol. 6180, Linz, Austria.

Muhammad Al Khuli. 1982. *A Dictionary of Theoretical Linguistics: English-Arabic with an Arabic-English Glossary*. Library of Lebanon, Beirut, Lebanon.

Imad Al Sughaiyer and Ibrahim Al Kharashi. 2004. Arabic morphological analysis techniques: A comprehensive survey. *Journal of the American Society for Information Science and Technology*, 55(3):189–213.

Abdulaziz Almohimeed, Mike Wald, and R. I. Damper. 2009. A new evaluation approach for sign language machine translation. In *Assistive Technology from Adapted Equipment to Inclusive Environments, AAATE 2009, Volume 25*, pages 498–502, Florence, Italy.

Abdulaziz Almohimeed, Mike Wald, and Robert Damper. 2010. An Arabic Sign Language corpus for instructional language in school. In *Proceedings of the Seventh International Conference on Language Resources and Evaluation, LREC*, pages 81–91, Valetta, Malta.

Abeer Alnafjan. 2008. Tawasoul. Master's thesis, Department of Computer Science, King Saud University, Riyadh, Saudi Arabia.

Stan Augarten. 1984. *Bit by Bit: An Illustrated History of Computers*. Tickner and Fields, New York, NY.

Hennie Brugman and Albert Russel. 2004. Annotating multimedia/multi-modal resources with ELAN. In *Proceedings of the Fourth International Conference on Language Resources and Evaluation, LREC*, pages 2065–2068, Lisbon, Portugal.

Tim Buckwalter. 2004. Issues in arabic orthography and morphology analysis. In *Proceedings of the Workshop on Computational Approaches to Arabic Script-based Languages, CAASL*, pages 31–34, Geneva, Switzerland.

Metri George. 1990. *Al Khaleel: A Dictionary of Arabic Syntax Terms*. Library of Lebanon, Beirut, Lebanon.

Sami M. Halawani. 2008. Arabic Sign Language translation system on mobile devices. *IJCSNS International Journal of Computer Science and Network Security*, 8(1):251–256.

Vladimir I. Levenshtein. 1966. Binary codes capable of correcting deletions, insertions, and reversals. *Soviet Physics Doklady*, 10(8):707–710.

Mohamed Mohandes. 2006. Automatic translation of Arabic text to Arabic Sign Language. *ICGST International Journal on Artificial Intelligence and Machine Learning*, 6(4):15–19.

Mohanned Momani and Jamil Faraj. 2007. A novel algorithm to extract tri-literal arabic roots. In *Proceedings ACS/IEEE International Conference on Computer Systems and Applications*, pages 309–315, Amman, Jordan.

Sara Morrissey. 2008. *Data-Driven Machine Translation for Sign Languages*. Ph.D. thesis, Dublin City University, Dublin, Ireland.

Franz Josef Och and Hermann Ney. 2003. A systematic comparison of various statistical alignment models. *Computational Linguistics*, 29(1):19–51.

Sinja Ojala. 2011. Studies on individuality in speech and sign. Technical Report No. 135, TUCS Dissertations, Turku Centre for Computer Science, University of Turku, Finland.

Nasredine Semmar, Faïza Elkateb-Gara, and Christian Fluhr. 2005. Using a stemmer in a natural language processing system to treat Arabic for cross-language information retrieval. In *Proceedings of the Fifth Conference on Language Engineering*, pages 1–10, Cairo, Egypt.

Tony Veale and Andy Way. 1997. Gaijin: A bootstrapping approach to example-based machine translation. In *Proceedings of the Second Conference on Recent Advances in Natural Language Processing, RANLP*, pages 27–34, Tzigov Chark, Bulgaria.

Andy Way and Nano Gough. 2003. wEBMT: developing and validating an example-based machine translation system using the world wide web. *Computational Linguistics*, 29(3):421–457.

Andy Way and Nano Gough. 2005. Comparing example-based and statistical machine translation. *Natural Language Engineering*, 11(3):295–309.

Lekbot: A talking and playing robot for children with disabilities

Peter Ljunglöf
Computer Science and Engineering
University of Gothenburg, Sweden
peter.ljunglof@gu.se

Britt Claesson
Ingrid Mattsson Müller
DART: Centre for AAC and AT
Queen Silvia Children's Hospital
Gothenburg, Sweden
{britt.claesson,ingrid.mattsson-muller}@vgregion.se

Stina Ericsson
Cajsa Ottesjö
Philosophy, Linguistics and
Theory of Science
University of Gothenburg, Sweden
{stina.ericsson,cajsa.ottesjo}@gu.se

Alexander Berman
Fredrik Kronlid
Talkamatic AB
Gothenburg, Sweden
{alex,fredrik}@talkamatic.se

Abstract

This paper describes an ongoing project where we develop and evaluate a setup involving a communication board and a toy robot, which can communicate with each other via synthesised speech. The purpose is to provide children with communicative disabilities with a toy that is fun and easy to use together with peers, with and without disabilities. When the child selects a symbol on the communication board, the board speaks and the robot responds. This encourages the child to use language and learn to cooperate to reach a common goal. Throughout the project, three children with cerebral palsy and their peers use the robot and provide feedback for further development. The multimodal interaction with the robot is video recorded and analysed together with observational data in activity diaries.

1 Background

The vision of our project is to utilise current technology in human computer interaction and dialogue systems to provide young people with communication disabilities with a fun and exciting toy. Currently there are not many opportunities for children with severe disabilities to play independently and to interact on equal terms with typically developing children. Our hope is that the toy will give children, with and without disabilities, the opportunity to interact and play with each other. As a side effect this can also help them develop their communicative skills.

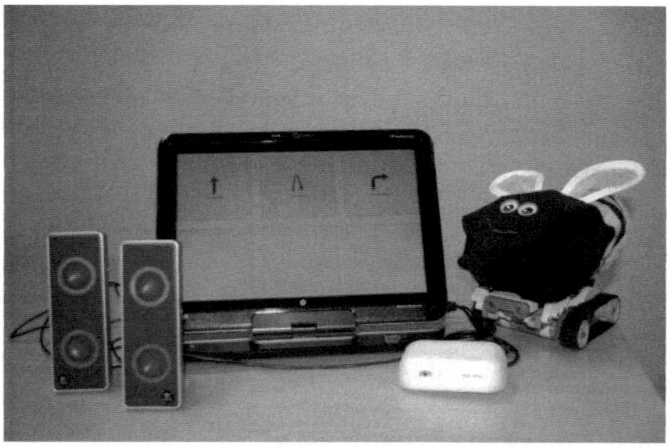

Figure 1: The robot and the communication board

We are developing a remote-controlled robot that can be used by children with severe physical and/or communicative disabilities, such as cerebral palsy or autism. The child communicates by selecting a symbol on a communication board, which is translated into an utterance using a speech synthesiser. The robot responds using synthesised utterances and physical actions, that the child in turn can respond to. The communication board acts as an extension of the child, by giving the child speech as a means of communication. The robot and its communication board is shown in Figure 1.

Technically the robot is controlled wirelessly,

Proceedings of the 2nd Workshop on Speech and Language Processing for Assistive Technologies, pages 110–119,
Edinburgh, Scotland, UK, July 30, 2011. ©2011 Association for Computational Linguistics

with no speech recognition. The spoken dialogue is there for the benefit of the child, and enables the child to engage in a spoken dialogue, without having the physical and/or cognitive ability to do so. Our hope is that this will facilitate the child's own language development while having fun with the radio-controlled robot.

1.1 The Lekbot project

The Lekbot project is a collaboration between DART,[1] Talkamatic AB and the University of Gothenburg. It is funded by VINNOVA[2] and runs from March 2010 to August 2011.

The project is similar to the TRIK project (Ljunglöf et al., 2009), which developed a drawing robot that was controlled in the same manner as above. The very limited user study that was conducted suggested that the product had great potential. The current project can be seen as a continuation of TRIK, where we perform a more full-scale user study, with video recording, transcription, interaction analyses, etc.

1.2 Dialogue systems and robots

Most existing dialogue systems are meant to be used by competent language users without physical, cognitive or communicative disabilities; either they are supposed to be spoken to (e.g., phone based systems), or one has to be able to type the utterances (e.g., the interactive agents that can be found on the web). Dialogue systems for users with disabilities have so far been targeted at people with physical disabilities, who need help in performing daily activities.

Dialogue systems have also been used for second language learning; i.e., learning a new language for already language competent people. Two examples are the artificial agent "Ville: The Virtual Language Tutor" (Beskow et al., 2004), and "SCILL: Spoken Conversational Interface for Language Learning", a system for practicing Mandarin Chinese (Seneff et al., 2004).

However, we are not aware of any examples where a dialogue system is used for communicating with people with communication disorders.

With the advent of tablet computers, there now exist several spoken-language and touch-screen apps for children's games and interactive and linguistic training. In these apps, the interaction is between the child and the tablet, whereas in Lekbot the child and the tablet act together as one dialogue participant, interacting with the robot. The Lekbot robot is also a physical agent, acting in the world, thus adding another dimension to the interaction.

When it comes to robots, there are a number of past and present research projects on robots and children. An early inspiration is the LOGO robot developed at Massachusetts Institute of Technology for teaching children to use computers and program simple applications (Papert, 1993). There are several robots focusing on children with disabilities (Robins et al., 2008; Saldien et al., 2006; Kozima et al., 2007; Lee et al., 2008; Arent and Wnuk, 2007), and most commonly autism. Some of these communicate with children in different ways. For instance, KASPAR is a child-sized humanoid robot for children with autism, and it trains interactional capabilities through gesture imitation.[3] Probo, developed for hospitalised children, produces nonsense speech intended to convey different feelings.[4] KOALA is a small round ball that interacts with children with autism using lights and sounds (Arent and Wnuk, 2007). However, none of these robots and research projects involves natural language communication in any form between the child and the robot.

2 Project description

Our basic idea is to use a dialogue system to stimulate play and interaction for children with severe communicative disabilities. There are already communication boards connected to speech synthesis in the form of communication software on computers. The main values that this project adds to existing systems are that:

- the child is offered an exciting, creative and fun activity

[1] Centre for AAC and AT at the Queen Silvia Children's Hospital

[2] The Swedish Governmental Agency for Innovation Systems

[3] `http://kaspar.feis.herts.ac.uk/`

[4] `http://probo.vub.ac.be/`

- the child can play and interact with other peers on equal terms
- the child can explore language in stimulating cooperation with the robot and with other children

By being able to use a symbol-based communication board the children are given an opportunity to play, interact, explore language, and at the same time learn to use tools for alternative and augmentative communication.

2.1 Description of the system

The child has a communication board that can talk; when the child points at one of the symbols it is translated to an utterance which the board expresses via speech synthesis in Swedish. This is recognised by a robot that moves around in the room, and performs the commands that the child expresses through the board. The robot has an incarnation as a toy animal, currently a bumblebee. It has a very basic personality which means that it can take the initiative, without the child telling it, refuse actions, or even negotiate with the child.

The inspiration for the robot comes from robot toys such as babies, dogs and dinosaurs, but also from electronic pets such as Tamagotchi and Talking Tom. The main difference is that our robot is able to have a dialogue with the child, to find out what to do, or just to be teasingly playful.

The Lekbot robot can move forward and backward, and turn right and left. Furthermore it can perform actions such as laughing, dancing, yawning, farting and eating. The functionality is constantly improving during the evaluation, to keep the children interested in playing with the robot.

2.2 Needs and potential

The target audience is children with severe physical, cognitive or communicative disabilities. These children depend on assistive devices and persons to be able to interact with other people and artifacts. The idea is that the robot will be a fun toy that gives the child an opportunity to control the artifacts itself, without the help of other people. Hopefully this will increase the child's confidence, and also promote language development.

2.2.1 The importance of play

Play may be defined by the following terms (Knutsdotter Olofsson, 1992):

- spontaneous; the child takes the initiative, not the adults
- not goal-oriented; the game does not have an explicit purpose
- fun and pleasurable
- repeating; that it can be played many times as one wants
- voluntary

For children with severe disabilities, playing requires adult help, and it is difficult for the adult not to control the game, especially if the child has problems communicating what it wants. Often play is used as a tool for development training, and many times play is so scheduled that it is no longer spontaneous (Brodin and Lindstrand, 2007). A toy that is always available for the child to play with whenever it wants, and on its own terms can help the child to play "for real".

Children learn from each other, and a toy that is used on equal terms by children, with and without disabilities, encourages interaction that otherwise would not have been possible between children with such diverse backgrounds.

2.2.2 Educational advantages

As discussed in section 3.3 later, the setup works without the robot and the communication board actually listening to each others' speech – instead, they communicate wirelessly. However, there is an important educational point in having them (apparently) communicate using spoken language. It provides the child with an experience of participating in a spoken dialogue, even though the child is not physically able to speak. For children who are more advanced in their language development, the robot can offer the opportunity to understand the basic properties of the dialogue, such as taking turns, asking and answering questions, the importance of providing sufficient information, and cooperating to achieve a shared goal. Another educational advantage is that the child learns to use tools for alternative and augmentative communication.

3 Implementation

This section describes some technical aspects of the implementation of the Lekbot system.

3.1 Components

The final Lekbot setup consists of the following components:

- a simple LEGO Mindstorms robot which can turn and move in all directions, can perform different specialised actions, and has a "costume" which makes it look like a bumble-bee
- a touch-screen computer which functions as a communication board, and a custom support frame for the computer
- the dialogue system GoDiS (Larsson, 2002), using Acapela Multimedia text-to-speech with Swedish voices
- Bluetooth communication and wireless audio transmission, from the touch-screen computer to the robot, and two sets of loudspeakers, for the computer and the robot

If the target user already has his or her own Windows based communication device, with adapted accessibility for him or her, this special software for the robot play can be installed on this device.

Note that it is the communication board computer that controls the robot via the dialogue system, but the intention is that it should seem like the robot is autonomous. Every utterance by the robot is executed by the speech synthesiser, and then sent to the robot via radio.

3.2 LEGO Mindstorms

The robot is built using LEGO Mindstorms NXT,[5] a kind of technical lego which can be controlled and programmed via a computer. Apart from being cheap, this technology makes it easy to build a prototype and to modify it during the course of the project.

[5]http://mindstorms.lego.com/

3.3 Perfect speech recognition

Typically, the most error-prone component of a spoken dialogue system is speech recognition; the component responsible for correctly interpreting speech. This of course becomes even more problematic when working with language learning or communication disorders, since in these situations it is both more difficult and more important that the computer correctly hears and understands the user's utterances. An advantage of the Lekbot setup is that we will, in a sense, have "perfect speech recognition", since we are cheating a bit. The robot does not actually have to listen for the speech generated by the communication board; since the information is already electronically encoded, it can instead be transferred wirelessly. This means that the robot will never hear "go forward and then stop" when the communication board actually says "go forward seven steps".

3.4 The GoDiS dialogue manager

A dialogue system typically consists of several components: speech recogniser, natural language interpreter, dialogue manager, language generator, speech synthesiser and a short-term memory for keeping track of the dialogue state. One can make a distinction between dialogue systems, which (ideally) are general and reusable over several domains, and dialogue system applications, which are specific to a certain domain. The dialogue manager is the "intelligence" of the system, keeping track of what has been said so far and deciding what should be said next.

The GoDiS dialogue manager (Larsson, 2002) has been developed at the Department of Philosophy, Linguistics and Theory of Science at the University of Gothenburg over several years. It is designed to be easily adaptable to new domains, but nevertheless be able to handle a variety of simpler or more complex dialogues. For example, GoDiS can either take initiative and prompt a user for information, or take a back seat and let the experienced user provide information in any desired order, without having to wait for the right question from the system.

From the viewpoint of dialogue systems research, there are some interesting aspects in the Lekbot setting:

- *Constantly changing environment*: the surroundings of the robot can change all the time, and the dialogue system needs to adapt
- *Alternative input modalities*: instead of speech input, we are using a touch screen interface, on which the symbols on the screen also changes depending on the current dialogue state
- *Utterance generation*: it is important for everyone, but in particular children with communicative disabilities, that information is presented in a correct way – with correct and consequent grammar, lexicon and pronunciation

3.5 Utterance generation

Clear pronunciation is important, and perhaps even more important when we are dealing with communicative disabilities. We are experimenting with using different utterance generation strategies and stressing important words to make the children understand the robot better. Interestingly, user feedback from children and preschools during the project has also indicated when default intonation does not work and needs to be modified.

The Lekbot system uses two different voices, one for the touch screen, acting as the child's voice, and one for the robot. Whereas the touch-screen voice is a vocalisation of something the child has already seen on the screen, the utterances of the robot have no visualisations. Hence, it is particularly important that the robot's utterances are as clear as possible, and the TTS voice chosen for the robot is therefore the voice that was determined to have the best and most flexible intonation in informal perception tests at the start of the project.

3.5.1 Contextual intonation

We have incorporated models of information structure in GoDiS to enable the appropriate assignment of phonological emphasis (Ericsson, 2005).

Lekbot uses a fairly basic dialogue-move-to-string mapping for the creation of output utterances, which are then fed to the speech synthesiser. Determining the information structure of an utterance to be generated, involves the determination of what is informative in the utterance – the focus – and what is a reflection of something already in the context – the ground (Vallduví, 1992). The system assigns emphasis to all alternatives, that is, all contrasting elements, in alternative questions, that are produced by the robot. Consider the following example:

> *User*: Go forward.
>
> *Robot*: Do you want me to go forward a lot or go forward a little?

For the generation of the robot utterance, the system determines "go forward a lot" and "go forward a little" as alternatives, and assigns emphasis to these. Future development of the system may involve the inclusion of information structure also for utterances other than non-alternative questions, to determine appropriate intonation assignment more generally.

Unfortunately, we have not yet been able to use this feature in the actual demonstration system, since the Swedish TTS voices do not emphasise properly with regard to the markup. Instead we have tuned the utterances lexically and syntactically to make the best possible use of the default TTS intonation.

4 Evaluation

We are evaluating the Lekbot system during spring and summer 2011, in parallel with continued development, in the spirit of eXtreme Programming (XP). Some major themes in XP that were deemed particularly interesting in this project are i) the need to involve the users in the development process, ii) to work in short iterations with frequent releases to get a nearly constant feedback from users, and iii) to always prioritise the tasks that provide the greatest benefit to users.

4.1 Users

A test group was recruited consisting of three target children with peers and staff, at three different pre-schools, was recruited. The target children, two boys and one girl are in the ages 4–6 years, two boys and one girl. They have cerebral palsy with complex communication needs. They also have a poor gross motor control, but are able to use their hands for activating a touch screen on a computer. They serve as the test group and as a basis for the specifications of the further development of the system. During the course of development the children in the test group use the system to verify that it works as intended and help to identify the most important qualities to develop. The project group works with one month iterations with a new public release every second month. Therefore, the users have in the end used about six releases of the robot.

Along with the target children, three typically developed peers, of the same age, or slightly younger, were recruited at each pre-school. The three peers were all girls. Hence, there are three groups of children playing with the robot. At various occasions other children in the pre-school group are involved in the robot play.

The children were assessed regarding their receptive language levels by using Test for Reception of Grammar (TROG) (Bishop et al., 1998). Their communication levels were estimated by the project group in cooperation with the pre-school staff using Communication Function Classification System (CFCS) for Individuals with Cerebral Palsy (Hidecker et al., 2009). The pre-school staff also completed Swedish Early Communicative Development Inventories (SECDI) forms for each child (Eriksson and Berglund, 1999; Berglund and Eriksson, 2000). A pre-school form (Förskoleformulär) was also completed (Granlund and Olsson, 1998). It consists of questions concerning the child's engagement in various situations, the pre-school teacher's perception of the interaction between her and the child as well as the interaction between the child and other children.

With the two youngest target children TROG testing was not feasible, while the oldest one appeared to have some difficulties in understanding verbs, prepositions and sentences containing these components, thus a bit lower than his age. The three peers showed results matching their age. From here on the target children will be named Per, Hans and Greta.

The purpose of CFCS is to classify the every day communication performance of an individual with cerebral palsy. The levels are ranged between 1 and 5, where 1 is the highest and 5 the lowest.

- The 6 year old Per shows a level of 3: Effective sender *and* effective receiver with familiar partners.
- The 5 year old Hans is estimated to level 5: Seldom effective sender and effective receiver with familiar partners, and
- The 4 year old Greta is at level 4: Inconsistent sender and/or receiver with familiar partners.
- All the peers, of course, reach the level of 1.

The CFCS levels will be estimated over again when the Lekbot testing is finished.

The results of SECDI and the pre-school form will be presented at a later stage of the Lekbot project, as they will be redistributed.

4.2 Evaluation tools and methods

The tools used to evaluate the robot play are three:

- Talking Mats,[6] which is an established communication tool that uses a mat with attached symbols as the basis for communication. It is designed to help people with communicative and cognitive difficulties to think about issues discussed with them, and provide them with a way to effectively express their opinions. Both the target children and their peers were interviewed about the robot and the interaction, in order to get

[6] `http://www.talkingmats.com`

feedback for evaluation and for developing the system.

They were asked questions about the behaviour of the robot and answered by putting symbol cards either at the "fun" side of the mat or at the "boring/not nice" side. It is also possible to put symbols between "fun" and "boring/not nice". The answers were then checked and evaluated together with the children. An example is shown in Figure 2.

- Video recordings during the robot play were made by the project group from January to May 2011, six recordings from each peer group, in all 18 recordings. The duration is between 20 and 30 minutes each and shot with one camera by one of the project members. Short sequences from the videos have been transcribed and analysed with focus on cooperation between the children and joyfulness. Transcriptions were made in CLAN[7] with detailed descriptions of the non-verbal actions, signs and gaze. We got permissions to do the recordings from the parents of the children.

- Weekly Activity diaries were kept by the pre-school staff, where they could provide their reflections about the play sessions. The diaries included headings regarding numbers of play occasions, duration of the play, persons participating, what happened in the play, functionality of the robot, suggestions for improvement and the children's satisfaction with the play perceived by the staff.

Furthermore, the interaction between the communication board and the robot is logged by the system, providing valuable information.

Beside these evaluation tools there have also been discussions with the designated staff at the current pre-schools.

[7] http://childes.psy.cmu.edu/clan/

Figure 2: Talking Mats

4.3 Preliminary evaluation results from the activity diaries

According to the activity diaries, Lekbot was used 56 times during releases 2–5; just below 10 times each for the early releases, and 20 times each for releases 4 and 5. There is a great variation in numbers of performed play sessions and in completed activity diaries, mainly due to illness in children or staff, orthopedic surgery in one child and holidays. In the beginning there was always the same peer, and only that one, attending the play sessions. Further on in the project the staff chose to engage more peers from the pre-school. That means that sometimes there was a different peer than originally and sometimes there was a group of peers interacting in the play. The support person attending the play sessions was always the same. She also was the one completing the activity diaries.

4.3.1 Functionality

15 comments were given about the system working well, where release 5 got the best scores. Problems with the system were reported 16 times. Comments were given about rebooting the system, loosing the commands, or problems with activating them. Dissatisfaction with the actions of the Lekbot was reported 5 times, mainly about the delay between activating a command and the activation of the robot. There were also reports of improved accessibility of the system, by finding a mobile piece of furniture

for the stand and by changing the angle of the display.

4.3.2 Interaction

The project group chose not to give strict instructions on what to do in the play, just to let everyone use the Lekbot at suitable level. Thus, there was a variation in complexity of the comments, as the headings in the activity diaries gave a structure of open questions. The collected, written comments were categorised in five groups; Preparations for the Lekbot play, Explicit support from adult, Target child's activity and perception of the play, Peer's activity and perception of the play and Shared activity and perception of the play between target child and peer(s). The three latter are reported together release by release.

Preparation for the Lekbot play occurred mainly for Per's group, where he and his peers built different tracks for the robot to follow. Explicit support by adult is mentioned only for Per's group, where the adult chose target point for the robot and she used the play for educational matters regarding letter teaching. She also mediated between the children which improved their cooperation. In the final sessions Per initiated turn taking after being urged by the adult.

4.3.3 Activity and perception

Target child's activity and perception of the play is mentioned a lot, especially for Per and Greta. Most frequent among the comments are those concerning Shared activity and perception of the play between target child and peer(s).

Release 2: Per initiates turn taking, reacts to the event followed by the activation of the command on the display, protests when his peer choses "the wrong command". Together they repeatedly perform turn taking and use Per's digital communication device in the Lekbot activity. Hans and his peers make a tunnel and the children give commands that make the robot go through it. Greta has high expectations on the play before the session. Repeatedly she is unwilling to stop the play and she gives oral comments to the activities of the robot.

Release 3: Per explores the commands and what happens when using them to answer the newly implemented supplementary questions. Around Hans there is turn taking. Several children are playing together and the children most frequently choose the dance command. Greta is excited and unwilling to stop the play. She protests when the adult makes the choice for the robot.

Release 4: Per shows the new commands for his peer, and the children imitate the robot. Per and his original peer chose one new peer each. Interaction between the children takes place through dancing and hand clapping. Hans plays with the robot together with adults from outside the preschool. Greta likes going backwards, turning and hitting things with the robot. She starts telling her peer how to act by using the commands on the display and her paper communication chart. Her peer enjoys following Greta's "instructions" and she likes dancing. There are repeated turn taking between them and they enjoy to cooperate getting the robot to move from one spot to another.

Release 5: Per plays with the new commands, by himself. He finds strategies for the robot in finding food. When there are more than two children in the play, Per chooses to be the one controlling the display. He cooperates more – waits for his turn and shows better understanding for the other's turn. All children repeatedly use communication charts and Blissymbolics to express themselves. They imitate the robot and they act instead of it when it is out of order. In Hans's group there is dancing and looking for food play. Turn taking takes place and all children want to participate in the Lekbot play. Greta decides whose turn it is to control the robot. Her peer likes the play of finding food.

4.3.4 Satisfaction

Starting in release 3, the level of satisfaction with the play session was noted in the activity diary. The staff was asked to estimate how satisfied the target child and the peer were on a scale from 1 to 5, where 1 is the lowest and 5 the highest. This was done every time at some pre-schools and some times at others. The tendency is that the target children seem to be more satisfied with the play than their peers from the start of the play session. This is most protruding regarding the oldest pair. At release 4 where Per and his peer interact as a group for the first time, the scores suddenly are reversed so the Per is perceived to 3 on the satisfactory scale and the peer(s) at 5. In release 5 the scores get a more even variation.

4.4 Video recordings

Most of the interviews with Talking Mats were video recorded. The full analysis will be done later in the project. The analysis of the video recordings of the robot interaction is an ongoing work were three of the project members participate. This part of the work is time consuming and only minor sequences are transcribed and analysed so far. Through micro analysis the fine grained interactional movements and the cooperation between the children and the teacher appears, as well as the joy of playing.

Figure 3 contains a segment from the transcription. The participants are Per, his peer Selma and his teacher Isa; and the Computer and the Robot. In the excerpt we can see how Per asks for Selma's attention and with the help of Isa and the communication map tells Selma to take her turn, which is to make a new command for the robot to perform. Finally they both dance to the music.

126 %gaze: Per looks at Selma

127 %move: Selma is standing on her knees, sits down on her heels, keeps booths hands on her skirt

128 %gaze: Selma looks toward the mirror on the wall

129 %move: Per touches the left hand of Selma, keeps his arm stretched when Selma moves a bit

131 %gaze: Isa looks at Per's hand

132 *Selma: ——————

133 %comment: Selma is singing while Per stretches toward her left hand

134 %gesture: Isa draws the pointing map closer

135 %gaze: Per looks down at the map

136 %gaze: Selma looks down at the map

137 *Per: ——————

138 %move: Selma stands up on her knee, departs on a movement forward

139 *Isa: eh::: (0.3) your turn (0.3) Selma's turn

140 %gesture: Isa moves her finger back and forth over the 6th picture on the map

141 %gesture: Isa rests her finger at the picture, then withdraws it

142 %gesture: Per points at the map

143 %move: Selma moves toward the screen

144 (2.1)

145 %action: Selma makes a fast press at the screen

146 %gaze: Per looks at the screen

147 *Selma: dance: my king ——————

148 %move: Selma moves left with arms swinging, bends forward, landing on hands and knees

149 %action: Per looks at Selma, smiles

150 *Computer: dance

151 *Selma: mi:ine ñ: ñ: —(1.8)—

152 *Robot: okay I gladly dance

153 (1.0)

154 *Robot: plays music 11 sec

155 %comment: both children are dancing, Selma on her knees and Per sitting down

Figure 3: An example transcription segment, translated to English

4.5 Conclusion

All target children have enjoyed the Lekbot play from the beginning. The more commands and abilities the robot has received the more appreciated has the play become also by the peers. Improved play and interaction skills can be observed in varying degrees depending on the level of each child. The Lekbot has been a nice and fun artefact for the children to gather round and it has given both the target children and their peers experiences of playing with each other. From Talking Mats interviews performed with Per and Greta it was revealed that they had no problems handling the computer display or seeing and hearing the display and the robot. Making the same interview with Hans was not feasible, though the project group experienced that he seemed to deal pretty well with the system, although he needed a little more support than the two other children, who were able to control the toy autonomously. More results will be presented when the video sequences are analysed, later on in the project.

5 Acknowledgements

We are grateful to 5 anonymous referees for their valuable comments. The Lekbot project is financed by Vinnova, and Acapela has kindly provided us with speech synthesis.

References

K. Arent and M. Wnuk. 2007. Remarks on behaviours programming of the interactive therapeutic robot Koala based on fuzzy logic techniques. In *First KES International Symposium on Agent and Multi-Agent Systems: Technologies and Applications*, Wroclaw, Poland.

E. Berglund and M. Eriksson. 2000. Communicative development in Swedish children 16–28 months old: The Swedish early communicative development inventory – words and sentences. *Scandinavian Journal of Psychology*, 41(2):133–144.

Jonas Beskow, Olov Engwall, Björn Granström, and Preben Wik. 2004. Design strategies for a virtual language tutor. In *INTERSPEECH 2004*.

Dorothy Bishop, Eva Holmberg, and Eva Lundälv. 1998. *TROG: Test for Reception of Grammar (Swedish version)*. SIH Läromedel.

J. Brodin and P. Lindstrand. 2007. *Perspektiv på IKT och lärande för barn, ungdomar och vuxna med funktionshinder*. Studentlitteratur.

Stina Ericsson. 2005. *Information Enriched Constituents in Dialogue*. Ph.D. thesis, University of Gothenburg, Gothenburg, Sweden.

M. Eriksson and E. Berglund. 1999. Swedish early communicative development inventory – words and gestures. *First Language*, 19(55):55–90.

M. Granlund and C. Olsson. 1998. *Familjen och habiliteringen*. Stiftelsen ALA.

M. J. C. Hidecker, N. Paneth, P. Rosenbaum, R. D. Kent, J. Lillie, and B. Johnson. 2009. Development of the Communication Function Classification System (CFCS) for individuals with cerebral palsy. *Developmental Medicine and Child Neurology*, 51(Supplement s2):48.

B. Knutsdotter Olofsson. 1992. *I lekens värld*. Almqvist och Wiksell.

H. Kozima, C. Nakagawa, and Y. Yasuda. 2007. Children-robot interaction: a pilot study in autism therapy. *Progress in Brain Research*, 164:385–400.

Staffan Larsson. 2002. *Issue-based Dialogue Management*. Ph.D. thesis, Department of Linguistics, University of Gothenburg, Sweden.

C.H. Lee, K. Kim, C. Breazeal, and R.W. Picard. 2008. Shybot: Friend-stranger interaction for children living with autism. In *CHI2008*, Florence, Italy.

Peter Ljunglöf, Staffan Larsson, Katarina Mühlenbock, and Gunilla Thunberg. 2009. TRIK: A talking and drawing robot for children with communication disabilities. In *Nodalida'09: 17th Nordic Conference of Computational Linguistics*. Short paper and demonstration.

Seymour Papert. 1993. *Mindstorms: Children, Computers, and Powerful Ideas*. Basic Books.

B. Robins, K. Dautenhahn, R. te Boekhorst, and C.L. Nehaniv. 2008. Behaviour delay and expressiveness in child-robot interactions: a user study on interaction kinesics. In *HRI'08, 3rd ACM/IEEE International Conference on Human Robot Interaction*, Amsterdam, Netherlands.

J. Saldien, K. Goris, B. Verrelst, R. Van Ham, and D. Lefeber. 2006. ANTY: The development of an intelligent huggable robot for hospitalized children. In *CLAWAR, 9th International Conference on Climbing and Walking Robots*, Brussels, Belgium.

Stephanie Seneff, Chao Wang, and Julia Zhang. 2004. Spoken conversational interaction for language learning. In *InSTIL/ICALL 2004 Symposium on Computer Assisted Learning: NLP and Speech Technologies in Advanced Language Learning Systems*.

E. Vallduví. 1992. *The Informational Component*. Garland.

Using lexical and corpus resources for augmenting the AAC lexicon

Katarina Heimann Mühlenbock
Dept of Swedish Language
University of Gothenburg
Gothenburg
katarina.heimann.muhlenbock@gu.se

Mats Lundälv
Dart
Queen Silvia Children's Hospital
Gothenburg
mats.lundalv@vgregion.se

Abstract

A corpus of easy-to-read texts in combination with a base vocabulary pool for Swedish was used in order to build a basic vocabulary. The coverage of these entries by symbols in an existing AAC database was then assessed. We finally suggest a method for enriching the expressive power of the AAC language by combining existing symbols and in this way illustrate additional concepts.

1 Introduction

A considerable proportion of the population, among 1.3 % of all individuals (Beukelman and Mirenda, 2005) are affected by severe communication disorders, making them more or less unable to use written and/or spoken language. Different language supportive aids for these persons have evolved over the years, mainly as graphical systems containing symbols and pictures, simplified supportive signing (derived from sign language vocabulary), or a combination of these, possibly comprising speech synthesis and speech recognition. All these supportive measures and methods are referred to as Augmentative and Alternative Communication (AAC).

A vocabulary comprising 20,878 lemma or base forms from different sources was analysed in terms of frequency and dispersion. The primary issue in this study was to analyse to what extent the concepts in the main AAC symbol databases mirror the vocabulary needed to produce and understand everyday Swedish language. Another goal was to investigate the possibility of extending the AAC symbol databases by combining separate basic words from the vocabulary into compounds.

2 Background

A fundamental aspect for participation in the society is the possibility to acquire information and to communicate. For the majority of citizens, getting information on every-day issues is hardly a task entailing any specific problems. There is, however, a substantial number of persons who have substantial difficulties to benefit from ordinary written and spoken sources, being dependent upon other modalities, either to express themselves, or as a support for interpretation, or both. For this purpose, AAC resources in the shape of pictures and symbols have been designed for use in low-tech solutions such as communication books and boards, and high-level technologies such as computer programs and eye-tracking devices. AAC resources at hand are, however, burdened by two major problems. First, manual production requires much effort and time. New concepts have to be identified and a uniform agreement has to be reached among different parties on how to visually present the concept. Second, accessibility in the sense of a consumer's or developer's possibility and freedom to use available resources, is strongly restricted by distribution, copyright and licensing issues. Different projects have been carried out with the goal to develop and implement some suggested open standards for syntactic and semantic encoding of AAC material. The European IST project WWAAC (World Wide Augmentative & Alternative Communication, 2004) was

Proceedings of the 2nd Workshop on Speech and Language Processing for Assistive Technologies, pages 120–127,
Edinburgh, Scotland, UK, July 30, 2011. ©2011 Association for Computational Linguistics

a pan-european initiative to make the web more accessible for a wide range of persons with language and/or cognitive impairments.

An essential part of language lies within its ambiguity on the lexical as well as structural level. When it comes to computerized processing, semantic variation between word forms, morphological relationships within different word forms, and multiword items claim specific handling, especially when enriching an existing vocabulary with new entries. In fact, comparing wordlists and frequencies from different sources is a task affected by a couple of complications. One problem encountered in a comparative study of word frequencies is how a *word* is defined, which in fact has been put under debate by for instance Gardner (2007). In the present study, we consider the *lemma*, i.e. the look up form of a word, to be the key unit. The idea behind the use of lemma frequencies as units of study is that the human mental or computational processing of lemmas and inflected forms profit from each other, which is in favour of a theory implying that a morphological decomposition takes place for the recognition of inflected forms.

Knowledge of the vocabulary is an essential part of both conveying and understanding messages, verbally as well as non-verbally. Together with the system of rules generating grammatical combinations, the words in the vocabulary contribute to the infinite expressive power of language. With a narrow vocabulary, the possible means to produce and achieve adequate information decreases. Researchers have attempted to identify lists of words that could be included in a core vocabulary (Thorndike and Lorge, 1944), (Spache, March 1953) and more specifically for people who use AAC (Balandin and Iacono, 1998), (Banajee et al., 2003). There have also been efforts to investigate how much of the vocabulary a person needs to know in order to grasp the content of written texts without having to struggle with isolated, unknown words (Hirsch and Nation, 1992). In the latter study, a list of around 2,000 high frequency words of English, compiled by West (1953), was used in order to investigate if knowledge of these words was actually sufficient for reading unsimplified short novels. It was found that a person with this restricted vocabulary was familiar with about 90-92% of the total words. It is worth noting that the word frequency counts here reflect the number of times a word pertaining to a certain *word family* occurs in a text. The idea behind a word family is that inflected and regulary derived forms of a known base word can also be considered as known words if the affixes are known. This implies that nouns, adverbs, verbs and adjectives sharing a common base will be treated as one word, contrary to the lexicographical traditions (for Swedish), where the lemma or base form is the conventional unit of study.

With this in mind, it follows that a database containing a core vocabulary of a language has to contain enough information for identification of different lexemes. For our purposes in this study, it was also necessary to add another source of information in order to retrieve the semantic identifiers for subsequent illustration of different concepts into AAC symbols.

3 Experimental design

A corpus of easy-to-read texts and children's fiction was used in order to retrieve candidates for inclusion into a database of basic Swedish. The hypothesis is that by using a corpus of plain texts produced with the aim of being easy to understand, we can derive appropriate data for further statistical analysis of which words or word forms are to be considered as pertaining to a basic vocabulary. The candidates retrieved by excerption of high-frequency lemmas from the corpus were subsequently compared to the base-form words in a Swedish base vocabulary, where the lemmas obtaining the highest rank in both sets were integrated into a database of core vocabulary. The AAC symbol coverage of these database entries was then assessed by addressing an existing AAC symbol database. Finally, attempts were made to expand the existing AAC vocabulary through a semantic analysis of new words, simple as well as compounds, and in that way make it possible to illustrate new concepts.

4 Material

The material used comprise corpora as well as lexica. Some of the resources are freely available from the public domain, while other are used under specific permissions.

4.1 AAC material

Pictures and symbols aiding language and communication have been developed over decades. Some of the symbol systems have a visual structure that supports different parts of speech. For this study, the Widgit symbols library (Widgit Software, 2011) and vocabulary in Swedish (preliminary version 11) was used, covering around 11,000 symbols and 64,000 words (including synonyms and inflected forms). Some of the symbols are produced in order to illustrate different concepts rather than isolated words, which to some extent had a negative impact on the comparison of different wordlists. The focus of interest has been on content words, i.e. nouns, verbs, adjectives and adverbs, since the functional words normally don't appear as independent items. In total, a wordlist of 20,907 entries was extracted, normally the lemma form. Proper nouns and numbers were excluded in the study.

4.2 Corpora

4.2.1 LäSBarT

The primary corpus material for this study is LäSBarT, an acronym for *Lättläst Svenska och Barnbokstext* 'Easy-to-read Swedish and Children's fiction Texts' (Mühlenbock, 2008). It is a specialized corpus of 1.3 million tokens, compiled with the objective to mirror simple vocabulary and syntax. The main text types include works from different domains and genres, such as fiction, official documents from the government, parliament, county council, municipality and daily news. The common denominator for all the texts is that they are all intended to be read by persons that do not fully master everyday Swedish language.

The size of the corpus, 1.3 million tokens, was compensated for by making text representativeness be decisive during compilation. The supply of easy-to-read material is limited and subsequently, the variation range is quite narrow. Contrary to many other writing tasks, the production of easy-to-read text is elicited by a specific need from the society and we cannot expect a large variety of genres. Three genres of easy-to-read texts were identified for obtaining a representative sample, namely fiction, news and community information, which for the target group of readers can be regarded as being a balanced corpus.

4.2.2 SUC 2.0

SUC 2.0 is a balanced corpus of 1 million words in written Swedish, originating from the 1990's. It is designed according to the Brown corpus (Francis and Kucera, 1979) and LOB corpus (Johansson et al., 1978) principles, which means that it consists of 500 samples of text with a length of about 2,000 words each. The state-of-the-art markup language at the time of compilation was SGML, and this annotation schema is kept also in the acctual, revised version. All entries are annotated with parts-of-speech, morphological analysis and lemma, or rather base form. The corpus is also provided with a wide range of structural tags and functionally interpreted tags, according to the TEI standards Sperberg, (Consortium, TEI, 2007).

At the lexeme level, about 23% of the SUC corpus is covered by nouns, while verbs amounts to 17%, adjectives to 9%, proper nouns to 4%, adverbs to 9%, prepositions 12%, conjunctions 8%, numbers 2%, pronouns 10% and determiners to 6% of the total words. The total vocabulary has 69,371 base forms.

4.3 Lexica

4.3.1 LäSBarT wordlist

The wordlist obtained from the LäSBarT corpus, *LäSBarT-listan* (henceforward referred to as LBL) contains 22,041 lemmas in total, covering 43,364 lexemes, proper nouns excluded. It contains information about lexical frequency, baseform, part-of-speech tag, and lemma/lexeme form. The lemma/lexeme information tells us that a word like *sticka* has three different lemma/lexeme forms, namely **sticka.1** for the noun *sticka* 'splinter; knitting needle', and **sticka.2** or **sticka.3** for the two different verb lexemes with the meanings 'prick, sting; put' and 'knit', respectively. This information is necessary for further semantic disambiguation of polysemous words.

The overall part-of-speech distribution is listed in Table 1. In this study, 2,277 verbs, 14,856 nouns, 2,715 adjectives and 1,030 adverbs were extracted for further analysis.

Part-of-speech	% lemmas	% lexemes
Nouns	67.4	20.1
Verbs	10.1	25.3
Adjectives	12.3	6.2
Adverbs	4.7	10.0
Prepositions	0.4	17.4
Conjunctions	0.1	7.1
Pronouns	1.2	12.6
Determiners	0.1	4.0

Table 1: POS-distribution in LBL

It is interesting to note a large discrepancy in verbal representation between SUC (17 %) and LäSBarT (25 %). The most probable explanation to this is the tendency among authors of easy-to-read texts to paraphrase a complicated sentence by two or more simpler ones, each necessitating a new head verb.

4.3.2 The Swedish Base Vocabulary Pool

The Swedish base lemma vocabulary pool (henceforward referred to as SBV) (Forsbom, 2006) is derived from the SUC corpus. The units of the SBV are the base forms from SUC annotation disambiguated for part-of-speech. This means for example that a polysemous and homonymous word pertaining to different parts-of-speech such as a noun and a verb is represented both as its nominal and its verbal form. No information is, however, given at the lexeme or semantic level. The version presently used contains 8,215 entries, where the lemmas are ranked according to relative frequency weighted with dispersion, i.e. how evenly spread-out they are across the subcorpora. Instead of using frequency alone, the formula for adjusted frequency calculation was used (Rosengren, 1972):

$$AF = (\sum_{i=1}^{n} \sqrt{d_i x_i})^2$$

where
AF = adjusted frequency
d_i = relative size of category i
x_i = frequency in category i
n = number of categories

The SBV was used as reference material for the comparison of dispersion of word base forms to LäSBarT.

4.3.3 SALDO

SALDO (Borin and Forsberg, 2009) is a modern Swedish semantic and morphological lexicon. The organization differs in a fundamental way from the widely used lexical-semantic database Princeton WordNet (Fellbaum, 1998), even though both are based on psycholinguistic principles. While Princeton WordNet and its descendant Swedish WordNet (Viberg et al., 2002), are organized in encoded concepts in terms of sets of synonyms, called synsets, the associative relations between the entries in SALDO are based on metaphorical kinships that are specified as strictly hierarchical structures. Every entry in SALDO must have a mother, which in practice often is either a hyperonym or a synonym. At the top of the hierarchy is an artificial most central entry, the PRIM, which is used as the mother of 50 semantically unrelated entries. In this way, all entries become totally integrated into a single rooted tree without cycles.

5 Comparative results

The lemma forms of 2,277 verbs (Fig. 1), 14,856 nouns (Fig. 2), 2,715 adjectives (Fig. 3) and 1,030 adverbs (Fig. 4) in LBL were compared against the SBV in order to obtain lemmas occurring in both lists, i.e. the intersection of two high-frequency and evenly distributed sets of words in the two corpora *LäSBarT* and *SUC*. This yielded a remaining set of 961 verbs, 2,390 nouns, 692 adjectives and 425 adverbs, illustrated as the top two rectangles of each figure. In order to analyse to what extent the AAC symbols really supported this basic vocabulary, an additional comparison was made, focusing on the intersection of words with and without symbol coverage in the two sets. It turned out that as much as 95 % (916 out of 961) of the verbs present in both LBL and SBV also were represented by symbols. For nouns, the corresponding ratio was 76 %, and for adjectives and adverbs 71 % and 60 %, respectively. Figures 1-4 illustrate the overall ratios.

5.1 Verbs

Adjusted frequency of the 44 verbs not represented in the symbol database ranged between 14.97 and 1.38, implying a moderate dispersion and frequency. In addition, the majority were compounds with an adverb or preposition as prefix, predominantly composite particle verbs. Authors of easy-to-read texts normally avoid composite particle verbs and prefer to use a paraphrase or synonym, since the former lexical structure can be perceived as old-fashioned and therefore difficult to understand. Furthermore, as many as 29 of the verbs lemmas were hapax words.

Some interesting features must also be mentioned regarding the verbal semantic fields of the words not supported by symbols. Many of the verbs seem to fall into a group of socially motivated actions, such as *bestraffa* 'punish', *fängsla* 'imprison', *beordra* 'command', and *uppfostra* 'educate/rear', all with a rather stern tone.

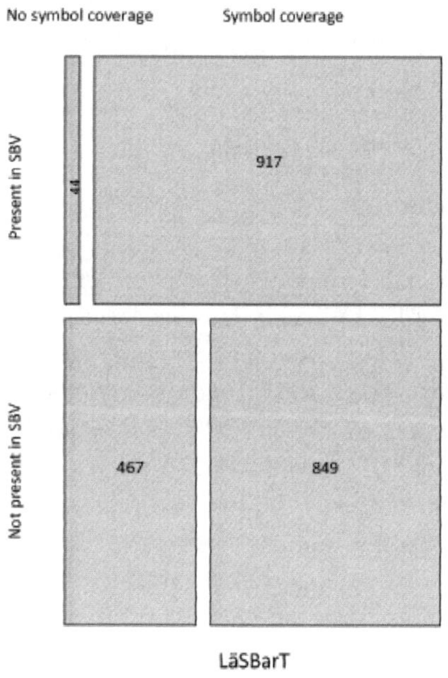

Figure 1: Overall ratio of LäSBarT verbs, presence in SBV and symbol coverage

5.2 Nouns

We found that 24 % of the noun lemmas in LBL and SBV lacked symbol coverage, and that there was a wide range in adjusted frequency, varying from 232.84 down to 1.06. Without making any formal categorization, it is clear that the words with highest adjusted frequency are abstract words, such as *samband* 'connection', *brist* 'lack', *sammanhang* 'context', and *allvar* 'seriousness'. Some of the nouns are meaningful only as elements of multiword expressions, such as *skull* 'sake' or *vis* 'manner', while others seem to be ephemeral words from news reports. One third are hapax, and 24 % of all are compound nouns.

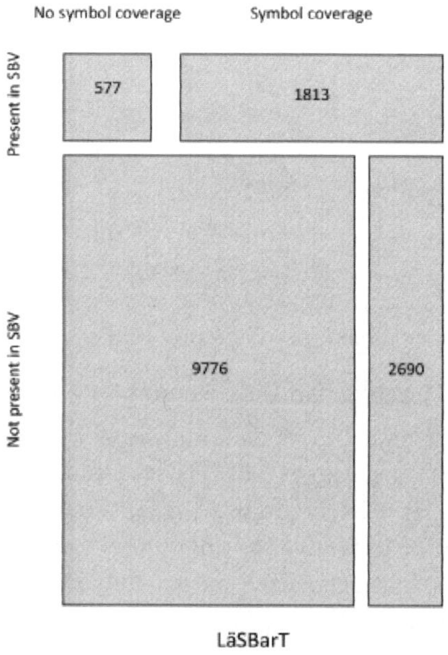

Figure 2: Overall ratio of LäSBarT nouns, presence in SBV and symbol coverage

5.3 Adjectives and adverbs

For adjectives, the proportion of lemmas without symbol coverage was as high as 29 %, while 40 % of the adverbs lacked symbol support. Differences in part-of-speech tagging for the two corpora, at the procedural as well as the annotational level, might however have influenced these results. Verb participles are for instance often subject to inconsistent tagging.

6 Augmenting the AAC lexicon

The next step was to investigate to what extent SALDO could be of assistance when augmenting

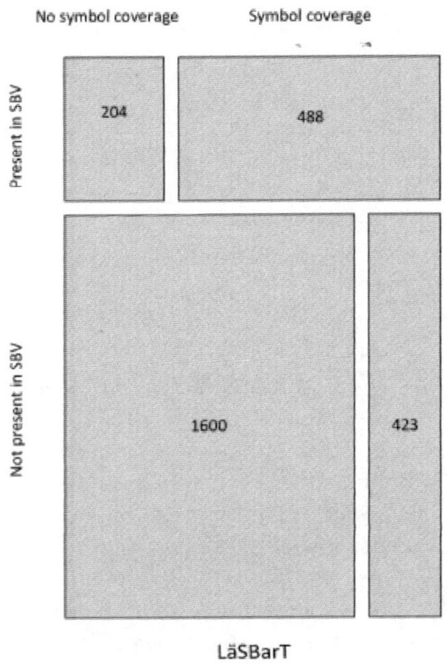

Figure 3: Overall ratio of LäSBarT adjectives, presence in SBV and symbol coverage

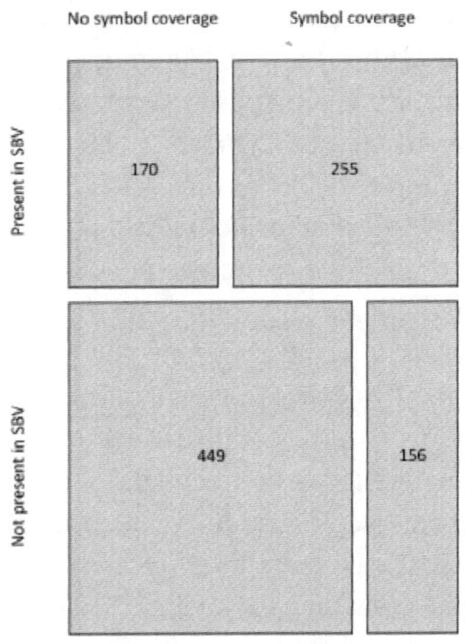

Figure 4: Overall ratio of LäSBarT adverbs, presence in SBV and symbol coverage

the AAC lexicon with additional concepts. Another interesting question concerned the feasibility of decomposing compounds into simplex words, each analysed against SALDO and provided with information necessary for correct symbol representation. Each entry in the set of lemmas present in both LBL and SBV, but without representation in the symbol lexicon, was compared against SALDO. As the concepts in SALDO are related by the mother-child relation, we could get the necessary lexical-semantic associations for further analysis of probable candidates for symbol representation. These could be either existing symbols, related as hyperonyms or synonyms, or a combination of two or more concepts.

As was stated earlier, a rather high proportion of noun lemmas missing in the symbol database were characterized as abstract nouns. We have for instance the noun lemma *kapitel* 'chapter', which had an adjusted frequency of 105.71 in SBV and a relative frequency of 1.03×10^{-4} in LBL. From our core vocabulary database we get that the only existing entry is identified as *kapitel 1/1*, i.e. lemma identifier 1 and lexeme identifier 1. The next step is to consult SALDO, where a look-up of *kapitel* gives two matches: *kapitel..1* with the semantic descriptors *avsnitt* + *bok* 'section + book', and *kapitel..2*, with the semantic descriptor *kyrka* 'church'. Given the fact that in the primary corpus material, the word is unambigous, we allowed to illustrate the concept just by combining the symbols for *avsnitt* 'section' and *bok* 'book', both existing in the AAC database.

Concerning ompound nouns, which made up the largest portion of lemmas occurring only in LBL and not in SBV, (66 % of the 14,856 noun lemmas), decomposition into simplex words made it possible to achieve information enough for further elaboration into symbol representations. An example, illustrating this procedure, is the word *huvudkontor* 'head office'. It is not present in the symbol vocabulary, but we find it directly by a look-up in SALDO with the semantic descriptors *kontor* 'office' and *främst* 'major', both with symbol coverage in the database.

The last example is another compound noun, *affärsägare* 'shop owner', a word that does not exist in SALDO. The compound analysis tells that this word has two constituents with a linking morpheme, namely *affär+s+ägare*. Since we already have the symbol illustrating the most common concept for *affär* in the primary corpus material, we use that. There is, however, no symbol in the database for *ägare*. Turning to SALDO,the word *ägare* 'owner' has only one descriptor *äga* 'to own'. We are now able to illustrate this concept by two symbols in combination, namely *affär* and *äga*, which by further analysis could possibly be extended to *person* 'person' + *äga* 'to own' + *affär* 'shop'.

As mentioned earlier, the few verbs not existing in the symbol database were generally either hapax, or particle verbs. Even if we regard the hapax words in LBL as peripheral in the easy-to-read genre, the fact that they exist in the SBV make them candidates for further analysis and inclusion into an augmented symbol lexicon. For nouns, the situation is largely the same. In general, they have a higher relative frequency, in average 8.0×10^{-6}, and only one third of the total are hapax words. Adjectives and adverbs in this set of words have a mean relative frequency in *LäSBarT* of 1.0×10^{-5} and 4.4×10^{-5}, respectively. For adjectives, the hapax ratio was 30 % and for adverbs 20 %.

7 Conclusions

We found this to be a good way to produce a core vocabulary for Swedish. The suitability of this method was ensured not only by the fact that the ingoing entries were to be found in a corpus of simple texts, but also that they had a high degree of frequency and dispersion in a corpus balanced for genre and domain. It also turned out the the symbol coverage of these entries in the AAC language studied was impressively high for verbs (95 %), lower for nouns (76 %) and adjectives (71 %), and considerably lower for adverbs (60 %). This is completely in accordance with what we expected, since the basic verbs play a major role in communication. The fact that the nouns to a higher degree lack symbol support, was compensated for by the circumstance that a relatively high amount of entries could be found in or derived by information in a semantic lexicon.

Given that the results in this study are based on only one of several symbol languages, we would like to extend the research also to these, at first hand Bliss and more of the pictorial systems, such as PCS.

References

Susan Balandin and T. Iacono. 1998. A few well-chosen words. *Augmentative and Alternative Communication*, 14:147–161.

Meher Banajee, Cynthia Dicarlo, and Sarintha Buras Stricklin. 2003. Core vocabulary determination for toddlers. *Augmentative and Alternative Communication*, 19(2):67–73.

D Beukelman and P Mirenda. 2005. *Augmentative and alternative communication: Supporting children and adults with complex communication needs.* Paul H. Brookes, Baltimore, 3rd edition.

Lars Borin and Markus Forsberg. 2009. All in the family: A comparison of saldo and wordnet. In *Proceedings of the Nodalida 2009 Workshop on WordNets and other Lexical Semantic Resources - between Lexical Semantics, Lexicography, Terminology and Formal Ontologies*, Odense.

Christiane Fellbaum. 1998. A semantic network of english - the mother of all wordnets. *Computers and the Humanities*, 32:209–220.

Eva Forsbom. 2006. A swedish base vocabulary pool. In *Swedish Language Technology conference*, Gothenburg.

W. Nelson Francis and Henry Kucera. 1979. Manual of information to accompany a standard corpus of present-day edited american english for use with digital computers. Technical report, Department of Linguistics, Brown University.

Dee Gardner. 2007. Validating the construct of word in applied corpus-based vocabulary research: A critical survey. *Applied Linguistics*, 28(2):241–265.

David Hirsch and Paul Nation. 1992. What vocabulary size is needed to read unsimplified texts for pleasure? *Reading in a Foreign Language*, 8(2):689–696.

Stig Johansson, G. Leech, and H. Goodluck. 1978. Manual of information to accompany the lancaster-oslo/bergen corpus of british english, for use with digital computers. Technical report, Unversity of Oslo.

Katarina Mühlenbock. 2008. Readable, legible or plain words - presentation of an easy-to-read swedish corpus. In Anju Saxena and Åke Viberg, editors, *Multilingualism, Proceedings of the 23rd Scandinavian Conference of Linguistics*, Studia Linguistica Upsaliensia, ISSN 1652-1336; 8, pages 325–327, Uppsala, Sweden. Acta Universitatis Upsaliensis.

Inger Rosengren. 1972. *Ein Frekvenzwörterbuch der deutschen Zeitungssprache*. GWK Gleerup, Lund.

George Spache. March, 1953. A new readability formula for primary-grade reading materials. *Elementary School Journal*, LIII:410–413.

TEI Consortium. 2007. *TEI P5: Guidelines for Electronic Text Encoding and Interchange.* TEI Consortium, p5 edition.

Edward L. Thorndike and I. Lorge. 1944. *The teacher's word book of 30,000 words.* Columbia University Press, New York.

Åke Viberg, K Lindmark, A Lindvall, and I Mellenius. 2002. The swedish wordnet project. In *Proceedings of Euralex 2002*, pages 407–412, Copenhagen University.

M. West. 1953. *A General Service List of English Words.* Longman, London.

Widgit Software. 2011. Widgit homepage. http://www.widgit.com.

World Wide Augmentative & Alternative Communication. 2004. Communication is not a privilege. Technical report.

Experimental Identification of the Use of Hedges in the Simplification of Numerical Expressions

Susana Bautista and **Raquel Hervás** and **Pablo Gervás**
Universidad Complutense de Madrid, Spain
{raquelhb, subautis}@fdi.ucm.es, pgervas@sip.ucm.es

Richard Power and **Sandra Williams**
Department of Computing, The Open University, Milton Keynes MK76AA, UK
{r.power, s.h.williams}@open.ac.uk

Abstract

Numerical information is very common in all kinds of documents from newspapers and magazines to household bills and wage slips. However, many people find it difficult to understand, particularly people with poor education and disabilities. Sometimes numerical information is presented with hedges that modify the meaning. A numerical hedge is a word or phrase employed to indicate explicitly that some loss of precision has taken place (e.g., "around") and it may also indicate the direction of approximation (e.g., "more than"). This paper presents a study of the use of numerical hedges that is part of research investigating the process of rewriting difficult numerical expressions in simpler ways. We carried out a survey in which experts in numeracy were asked to simplify a range of proportion expressions and analysed the results to obtain guidelines for automating the simplification task.

1 Introduction

All public information services and documents should be accessible in such a way that makes them easily understood by everybody, according to the United Nations (1994). Nowadays, a large percentage of information expressed in daily news comes in the form of numerical expressions (statistics of economy, demography data, etc). But many people have problems with understanding such expressions -e.g., people with limited education or some kind of mental disability.

Lack of ability to understand numerical information is an even greater problem than poor literacy. A U.K. Government Survey in 2003 estimated that 6.8 million adults had insufficient numeracy skills to perform simple everyday tasks such as paying house-hold bills and understanding wage slips, and 23.8 million adults would be unable to achieve grade C in the GCSE maths examination for 16 year-old school children (Williams et al., 2003).

A first possible approach to solve this important social problem is making numerical information accessible by rewriting difficult numerical expressions using alternative wordings that are easier to understand. Some loss of precision could have positive advantages for numerate people as well as less numerate. Such an approach would require a set of rewriting strategies yielding expressions that are linguistically correct, easier to understand than the original, and as close as possible to the original meaning.

In rewriting, hedges play an important role. For example,"50.9%" could be rewritten as "just over half" using the hedge "just over". In this kind of simplification, hedges indicate that the original number has been approximated and, in some cases, also the direction of approximation.

This paper presents a preliminary study of the use of hedges when numerical expressions are simplified to make them more accessible. We have carried out a survey in which experts in numeracy were asked to simplify a range of proportion expressions to obtain guidelines for developing the numerical expressions simplification task automatically. As a first step towards more complex simplification strategies, we

Proceedings of the 2nd Workshop on Speech and Language Processing for Assistive Technologies, pages 128–136,
Edinburgh, Scotland, UK, July 30, 2011. ©2011 Association for Computational Linguistics

are trying to simplify numerical expressions without losing substantial information. Our study does not have a particular kind of disability in mind. Rather, we aim to simplify according to levels of difficulty defined in the Mathematics Curriculum of the Qualifications and Curriculum Authority (1999). Adaptation to particular types of users is beyond the scope of this paper.

2 Background

Text simplification, a relative new task in Natural Language Processing, has been directed mainly at syntactic constructions and lexical choices that some readers find difficult, such as long sentences, passives, coordinate and subordinate clauses, abstract words, low frequency words, and abbreviations. Chandrasekar et al. (1996) introduced a two-stage process, first transforming from sentence to syntactic tree, then from syntactic tree to new sentence; Siddharthan (2002) instead proposed a three-stage process comprising analysis, transformation and generation. In 1998, the project PSET (Carroll et al., 1998) employed lexical as well as syntactic simplifications. Other researchers have focused on the generation of readable texts for readers with low basic skills (Williams and Reiter, 2005), and for teaching foreign languages (Petersen and Ostendorf, 2007). There has been some previous work on numerical expressions but more for experts than for people who have difficulties with numeracy (Ellen Peters and Dieckmann, 2007), (Nathan F. Dieckmann and Peters, 2009), (Ann M. Bisantz and Munch, 2005), (Mishra H, 2011). However, to our knowledge, there have been no previous attempts to automatically simplify *numerical* information in texts.

A corpus of numerical expressions was collected for the NUMGEN project (Williams and Power, 2009). The corpus contains 10 sets of newspaper articles and scientific papers (110 texts in total). Each set is a collection of articles on the same topic — e.g., the increased risk of breast cancer in red meat eaters, and the decline in the puffin population on the Isle of May. Within each set, identical numerical facts are presented in a variety of linguistic and mathematical forms.

3 Experiment

Our survey took the form of a questionnaire in which participants were shown a sentence containing one or more numerical expressions which they were asked to simplify using hedges if necessary.

3.1 Materials

Our simplification strategies are focused at two levels: decimal percentages and whole-number percentages. For the survey we chose three sets of candidate sentences from the NUMGEN corpus: eight sentences containing only decimal percentages and two sets of eight sentences containing mixed whole-number and decimal percentages. The number of numerical expressions are more than eight because some sentences contained more than one proportion expression.

A wide spread of proportion values was present in each set, including the two end points at nearly 0.0 and almost 1.0. We also included some numerical expressions with hedges and sentences from different topics in the corpus. In short, we included as many variations in context, precision and different wordings as possible.

3.2 Participants

We carried out the survey with primary or secondary school mathematics teachers or adult basic numeracy tutors, all native English speakers. We found them through personal contacts and posts to Internet forums. The task of simplifying numerical expressions is difficult, but it is a task that this group seemed well qualified to tackle since they are highly numerate and accustomed to talking to people who do not understand mathematical concepts very well. Our experimental evaluation involved 34 participants who answered at least one question in our survey (some participants did not complete it).

3.3 Survey Design and Implementation

The survey was divided into three parts as follows:

1. Simplification of numerical expressions for a person who can not understand percentages

2. Simplification of numerical expressions for a person who can not understand decimals

3. Free simplification of numerical expressions for a person with poor numeracy

Each part of the survey is considered as a different kind of simplification: (1) simplification with no percentages, (2) simplification with no decimals and (3) free simplification.

For part (2), the set of sentences containing only decimal percentages was used. One of the two mixed sets of sentences with whole-number and decimal percentages was used for part (1) and the other for part (3). The experiment was presented on SurveyMonkey[1], a commonly-used provider of web surveys. The survey was configured so that participants could leave the questionnaire and later continue with it.

We asked participants to provide simplifications for numerical expressions that were marked by square brackets in each sentence. Below the sentence, each bracketed number was shown beside a text box in which the participant was asked to type the simplified version. Our instructions said that numerical expressions could be simplified using any format: number words, digits, fractions, ratios, etc. and that hedges such as 'more than', 'almost' and so on could be introduced if necessary. Participants were also told that the meaning of the simplified expression should be as close to the original expression as possible and that, if necessary, they could rewrite part of the original sentence. Figure 1 shows a screenshot of part of the questionnaire.

3.4 Underlying assumptions

A numerical expression (NE) is considered to be a phrase that represents a quantity, sometimes modified by a numerical hedge as in "less than a quarter" or "about 20%". We have restricted coverage to proportions -i.e., fractions, ratios and percentages. We had five hypotheses:

- **H1:** The use of hedges to accompany the simplified numerical expression is influenced by the simplification strategy selected. We consider the use of fractions, ratios and percentages like simplification strategies.
- **H2:** The use of hedges to simplify the numerical expression is influenced by the value of the proportion, with values in the central range (say 0.2 to 0.8) and values at the extreme ranges (say 0.0-0.2 and 0.8-1.0) having a different use of hedges.
- **H3:** The loss of precision allowed for the simplified numerical expression is influenced by the simplification strategy selected.
- **H4:** There is some kind of correlation between the loss of precision and the use of hedges, in such a way that the increase or decrease in the former influences changes in the latter.
- **H5:** As an specific case of H4, when writers choose numerical expressions for readers with low numeracy, they do not tend to use hedges if they are not losing precision.

[1] www.surveymonkey.com

4 Results

The results of the survey were carefully analyzed as follows. First, within each block of questions, a set of simplification strategies was identified for each specific numerical expression. These strategies were then grouped together according to the mathematical forms and/or linguistic expressions employed (fractions, ratios, percentages).

With a view to using these data to design an automated simplification system, these data have to be analyzed in terms of pairs of a given input numerical expression and the simplified expression resulting from applying a specific simplification strategy. For such pairings, three important features must be considered as relevant to choosing a realization:

- Whether any numbers in the expression are realized as one of the different types of available expressions (fractions, ratios, percentages).
- The loss of precision involved in the simplification.
- The possible use of a hedge to cover this loss of precision explicitly in the simplified expression.

To calculate the loss of precision, we defined Equation 1.

$$error = \frac{(simplifiedNE - originalNE)}{originalNE} \quad (1)$$

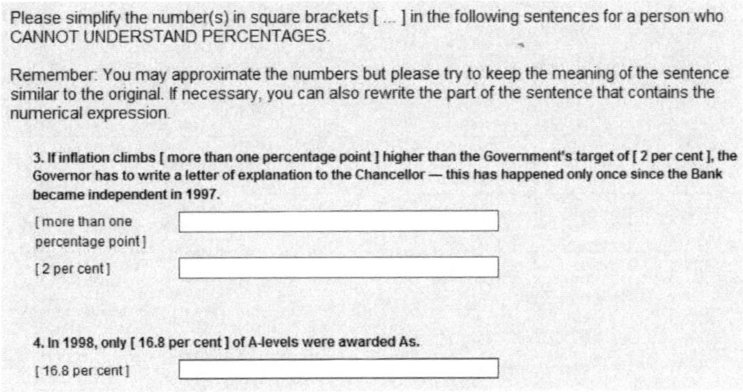
Please simplify the number(s) in square brackets [...] in the following sentences for a person who CANNOT UNDERSTAND PERCENTAGES.

Remember: You may approximate the numbers but please try to keep the meaning of the sentence similar to the original. If necessary, you can also rewrite the part of the sentence that contains the numerical expression.

3. If inflation climbs [more than one percentage point] higher than the Government's target of [2 per cent], the Governor has to write a letter of explanation to the Chancellor — this has happened only once since the Bank became independent in 1997.

[more than one percentage point]

[2 per cent]

4. In 1998, only [16.8 per cent] of A-levels were awarded As.

[16.8 per cent]

Figure 1: Screenshot of part of the questionnaire.

The set of pairings of input expression and observed simplification strategies, loss of precision and use of hedges as found in the results of the survey is given in Tables 1, 2 and 3. For each input numerical expression, the set of available simplification strategies is represented as three lines in the table. For each pairing, three columns are shown in the table. Empty cells represent that the strategy was not used. The first column presents the relative frequency of usage with respect to the total set of possible simplification strategies used for that expression. The second column captures the loss of precision involved, represented in terms of the ratio between the value of the difference between the original numerical value in the input expression and the numerical value that is conveyed by the corresponding simplified expression (using Equation 1). This ratio is also expressed as a percentage. The third column indicates the percentage of simplified numerical expressions that contained a hedge. All of them are mean values.

Each line represents one kind of simplification strategy used to simplify the original numerical expression. Another point to explain is that frequencies that belong to the same expression do not always add up to 100%. This is because a small number of others kinds of simplification strategies, like deletions or rewriting of the whole sentence, are not shown in the table. Moreover, we must keep in mind that not all participants answered each question of the survey.

Table 1 presents the relationships identified between the original numerical expressions and the simplification strategies (presented as lines) for the results of the first part of the survey (simplification of numerical expressions for a person who can not understand percentages). All the values are represented in percentages. Table 2 represents the same data for the second part of the survey (simplification of numerical expressions for a person who can not understand decimals) and Table 3 for the third part (free simplification of numerical expressions for a person with poor numeracy).

In the three parts of the survey, the percentage of simplifications that use hedges is slightly higher than that of those not using hedges especially in the second and third part of the survey. Adapting original numerical expressions by inserting hedges accounts for more than the 50% of cases. This reinforces our assumption that simplifications involving loss of precision may be better understood if an appropriate hedge is used.

4.1 Analysis of the Use of Hedges in the Simplified Numerical Expressions

In order to test hypothesis H1 (the use of hedges in the simplified numerical expression is influenced by the simplification strategy selected), we carried out a series of two sample *t-tests* where statistical significance was adjusted for multiple comparisons by using the *Bonferroni correction*. Results are presented in Table 4. When considering the entire survey (*Whole* column), there is no significant difference in the use of hedges in fractions and percentages. When analyzing the survey by parts we find similar results. There is no significant difference in the use of hedges in any strategy in the second (no decimals) and the third (free simplification) parts of

Num. Exp.		Frequency (%)	Error (%)	Hedge (%)
more than 1%	Fractions	18	0	67
	Ratios	6	0	100
	Percentages	18	17	50
2%	Fractions	6	0	50
	Ratios	18	-1	17
	Percentages	12	0	0
16.8%	Fractions	26	1	67
	Ratios	65	5	45
	Percentages	9	-3	0
27%	Fractions	82	-4	86
	Ratios	12	8	75
	Percentages	6	6	50
at least 30%	Fractions	41	0	93
	Ratios	35	13	67
	Percentages	3	0	100
40%	Fractions	53	12	50
	Ratios	29	0	10
	Percentages	6	0	0
56%	Fractions	82	-13	82
	Ratios			
	Percentages	6	-5	50
63%	Fractions	74	-3	84
	Ratios	24	0	75
	Percentages	3	0	0
75%	Fractions	32	0	0
	Ratios	29	0	0
	Percentages			
97.2%	Fractions	3	0	0
	Ratios	38	-8	23
	Percentages	18	1	50
98%	Fractions	6	0	0
	Ratios	12	0	0
	Percentages	3	0	0
Average	Fractions	39	-1	53
	Ratios	24	2	41
	Percentages	7	1	30

Table 1: Analysis of the data for 34 participants from the first part of the survey (simplifications intended for people who do not understand percentages). All values are percentages. The first column represents the frequencies of use for each simplification strategy. The second column shows the error as the loss of precision involved in the simplification. And the last column displays the use of hedges in the simplifications.

the survey, but in the first part (no percentages) we find significant difference between fractions and ratios ($p<0.0006$). These results do not support the hypothesis, as there is not a direct relation between the use of hedges and the selected strategy.

We performed another *t-test* adjusted by using the *Bonferroni correction* on the simplification strategies and central and peripheral values to test hypothesis H2 (the use of hedges to simplify the numerical expression is influenced by the value of the proportion, with values in the central range (say 0.2 to 0.8) and values at the extreme ranges (say 0.0-0.2 and 0.8-1.0) having a different use of hedges). In this case there is also no significant difference. The results show that the use of hedges is not influenced by central and peripheral values, rejecting our hypothesis H2 with a p-value $p=0.77$ in the worst case for the percentages strategy.

A new *t-test* adjusted by using the *Bonferroni correction* was done to test hypothesis H3 (the loss of precision allowed for the simplified numerical expression is influenced by the simplification strategy selected). Table 5 shows significant differences between each simplification strategy and each kind of simplification. In the *Whole* column we can observe that the loss of precision in fractions is significantly different to the one in ratios and percentages. In the first part (no percentages) there is a significant difference between ratios and the rest of simplification strategies. In the second part (no decimals) there is

Num. Exp.		Frequency (%)	Error (%)	Hedge (%)
0.6%	Fractions	6	25	50
	Ratios	9	22	33
	Percentages	47	21	100
2.8%	Fractions	3	-29	0
	Ratios	24	6	63
	Percentages	47	7	63
6.1%	Fractions			
	Ratios	18	-4	50
	Percentages	50	-3	82
7.5%	Fractions	12	9	75
	Ratios	12	-10	0
	Percentages	50	7	41
15.5%	Fractions	15	-1	80
	Ratios	12	6	50
	Percentages	44	2	33
25.9%	Fractions	15	-3	100
	Ratios	12	-3	75
	Percentages	38	5	62
29.1%	Fractions	3	0	0
	Ratios	15	3	60
	Percentages	50	2	71
35.4%	Fractions	12	-5	100
	Ratios	15	-4	60
	Percentages	41	-1	71
50.8%	Fractions	44	-2	93
	Ratios	3	0	0
	Percentages	21	0	43
73.9%	Fractions	44	1	93
	Ratios	6	1	50
	Percentages	18	0	50
87.8%	Fractions	3	0	0
	Ratios	15	-1	60
	Percentages	47	1	88
96.9%	Fractions	3	0	0
	Ratios	12	-2	75
	Percentages	29	0	80
96.9%	Fractions	6	0	50
	Ratios	18	-1	67
	Percentages	21	0	86
97.2%	Fractions	3	0	0
	Ratios	18	-1	67
	Percentages	41	0	93
97.2%	Fractions	3	0	0
	Ratios	18	-1	83
	Percentages	32	0	91
98.2%	Fractions	3	0	0
	Ratios	15	-2	40
	Percentages	44	0	67
Average	Fractions	11	0	43
	Ratios	14	1	52
	Percentages	39	2	70

Table 2: Analysis of the data for 34 participants from the second part of the survey (simplifications intended for people who do not understand decimals). All values are percentages. The first column represents the frequencies of use for each simplification strategy. The second column shows the error as the loss of precision involved in the simplification. And the last column displays the use of hedges in the simplifications.

Num. Exp.		Frequency (%)	Error (%)	Hedge (%)
0.7%	Fractions			
	Ratios	6	43	100
	Percentages	9	43	100
12%	Fractions	6	-17	100
	Ratios	21	-8	71
	Percentages	21	-17	100
26%	Fractions	41	-4	57
	Ratios	12	-4	50
	Percentages			
36%	Fractions	41	-8	86
	Ratios	9	-2	67
	Percentages			
53%	Fractions	41	-6	50
	Ratios			
	Percentages	6	-6	50
65%	Fractions	21	-5	100
	Ratios	18	-1	33
	Percentages	3	0	0
75%	Fractions	15	0	20
	Ratios	9	0	33
	Percentages	3	0	0
91%	Fractions			
	Ratios	29	-1	50
	Percentages	6	-1	50
above 97%	Fractions			
	Ratios	32	0	64
	Percentages	6	2	100
Average	Fractions	18	-7	69
	Ratios	15	3	59
	Percentages	6	3	57

Table 3: Analysis of the data for 34 participants from the third part of the survey (free simplification intended for people with poor literacy). All values are percentages. The first column represents the frequencies of use for each simplification strategy. The second column shows the error as the loss of precision involved in the simplification. And the last column displays the use of hedges in the simplifications.

no significant difference between any strategy. And in the last part (free simplification) there is only a significant difference between fractions and ratios. These results seem not to support the hypothesis, as there is not a direct relation between the use of hedges and the loss of precision in the simplified numerical expression.

For hypothesis H4 (there is some kind of correlation between the loss of precision and the use of hedges), we looked for correlations between each part of the survey and each kind of simplification strategy. We carried out a non-parametric measure of statistical dependence between the two variables (loss of precision and use of hedges) calculated by the *Spearman's rank correlation coefficient*.

In general, the results show no correlation, so there is no linear dependence between the loss of precision in the strategy and use of hedges, rejecting our hypothesis. For example, there are cases with a weak correlation (e.g. in the second part of the survey for fractions with $r=0.49$, $N=17$ and $p=0.03$), and cases where there is a strong correlation (e.g. in the third part of the survey, with $r=1$, $N=18$ and $p<.0001$).

Finally, when we analyzed hypothesis H5 (when writers choose numerical expressions for readers with low numeracy, they do not tend to use hedges if they are not losing precision), we worked with each part of the survey to study the cases where the loss of precision is zero and what is the tendency of use of hedges.

- In the first part of the survey (simplification of numerical expressions for a person who can not understand percentages), considering our 34 participants, in a 46% of responses the loss of precision is zero, and for these cases only 11% used hedges.
- For the second part (simplification of numerical expressions for a person who can not understand decimals), considering our 34 participants, in a 16% of responses the loss of precision is zero and for these cases only 7% used hedges.
- And finally, in the last part (simplification of numerical expressions for a person with poor numeracy), considering the same participants, in a 23% of cases the loss of precision is zero in the simplification and for these cases only 6% used hedges.

With this data, it seems that we can accept hypothesis H5, that is, we found evidence for our assumption that when writers choose numerical expressions for readers with poor numeracy, they tend to use hedges when they round the original numerical expression, i.e when the loss of precision is not zero.

4.2 Original Numerical Expressions with Hedges

In our survey there were a few cases where the original numerical expression had a hedge. We have observed that if the original numerical expression has hedge almost always the simplified numerical expression contained a hedge. There is a special case, "above 97%" where we do not count the use of hedges because in this case the participants chose non-numeric options mostly and they rewrote the numerical expression with phrases like "around all".

Strategy	No Pct.		No Dec.	Free Simp.	Whole	
Fractions	A		A	A	A	
Percentages	A	B	A	A	A	
Ratios		B	A	A		B

Table 4: Results of t-test adjusted by Bonferroni correction for H1 (the use of hedges in simplified numerical expressions is influenced by the simplification strategy selected). Strategies which do not share a letter are significantly different.

Strategy	No Pct.		No Dec.		Free Simp.		Whole	
Fractions	A		A		A		A	
Percentages	A		A		A	B		B
Ratios		B	A			B		B

Table 5: Results of t-test adjusted by Bonferroni correction for H3 (the loss of precision allowed for the simplified numerical expression is influenced by the simplification strategy selected). Strategies which do not share a letter are significantly different.

In the remaining cases, the same hedge is nearly alway chosen to simplify the numerical expression.

4.3 Kinds of Hedges

With respect to the actual hedges used, we have identified two different possible roles of hedge ingredients in a numerical expression. In some cases, hedges are used to indicate that the actual numerical value given is an approximation to the intended value. Uses of *about* or *around* are instances of this. This kind of hedge is employed to indicate explicitly that some loss of precision has taken place during simplification. In other cases, hedges are used to indicate the direction in which the simplified value diverges from the original value. Uses of *under* or *over* are instances of this. In some cases more than one hedge may be added to an expression to indicate both approximation and direction, or to somehow specify the precision involved in the simplification, as in *just under* or *a little less than.*

In our analysis we studied which hedges were the most frequent in each part of the survey. Only hedges with more than ten appearances in total (including simplification strategies not present in the table) have been considered in Table 6. We observed that the three parts of the survey have three hedges in common: *about, just over* and *over*. They are used in different strategies for each kind of simplification. In the second part of the survey, where simplifications of numerical expressions for a person who can not understand decimals are done, is where more hedges are used, in special for percentages strategy. In the last part of the survey, where there is more freedom to decide how simplify the original numerical expression, participants used less hedges compare to the others parts.

No Percentages			
Hedge	Fractions	Ratios	Percent.
about	15	9	0
at least	8	5	1
just over	21	1	0
more than	9	3	0
over	6	3	2
Total	59	21	3
No Decimals			
Hedges	Fractions	Ratios	Percent.
about	8	12	6
almost	4	1	8
just over	13	3	39
just under	3	2	27
nearly	7	5	24
over	7	5	9
Total	42	28	113
Free Simplification			
Hedges	Fractions	Ratios	Percent.
about	6	5	1
just over	6	0	5
more than	4	5	0
nearly	4	0	2
over	11	2	3
Total	31	12	11

Table 6: Use of the most frequent hedges in each part of the survey

5 Discussion

As can be seen in the results, the use of hedges to simplify numerical expressions can be influenced by three parameters. The first is the *kind of simplification*. Our survey was divided in three parts depending on the mathematical knowledge of the final user. The second is the *simplification strategy* for choosing mathematical form (fractions, ratios, or percentages). In our data we observed some differences in the usage of hedges with ratios and their usage with fractions and percentages (see Table 4). The last parameter is the *loss of precision* that occurs when the numerical expression is rounded. We investigated the use of hedges vs. loss of precision with different tests hoping to define some dependencies, but there was no clear correlation between them, and it was only when we tried a deeper analysis of strategies and kind of simplifications that we found some correlations such as those we presented in Section 4.1.

When asked to simplify for people who do not understand percentages, or for people with poor numeracy, the participants use different simplification strategies and sometimes they use hedges to simplify the original numerical expression. As some participants commented, not only are percentages mathematically sophisticated forms, but they may be used in sophisticated ways in the text, often for example describing rising and falling values, for which increases or decreases can themselves be described in percentages terms. Such complex relationships are likely to pose problems for people with poor numeracy even if a suitable strategy can be found for simplifying the individual percentages. In some of the examples with more than one numerical expression being compared, some of the evaluators reported a tendency to phrase them both according to a comparable base. Thus we should consider the role of context (the set of numerical expressions in a given sentence as a whole, and the meaning of the text) in establishing what simplifications must be used.

6 Conclusions and Future Work

Through a survey administered to experts on numeracy, we have collected a wide range of examples of appropriate simplifications of percentage expressions. These examples of simplified expressions give us information about the use of hedges that our participants carry out to adapt the original numerical expression to be understood by the final user. We investigated the loss of precision that occurs with each hedge and the relation between the simplification strategy and the use of hedges.

Our aim is to use this data to guide the development of a system for automatically simplifying percentages in texts. With the knowledge acquired from our study we will improve our algorithm to simplify numerical expressions. We could determinate from the simplification strategy, kind of simplification and the loss of precision allowed, which will be the best option to adapt the original numerical expression to the final user and if that option uses hedges to understand better the original numerical expression. As a part of our algorithm, we will have to look at inter-rater agreements for identifying appropriate hedges.

As future work, we plan to carry out another study to determine a ranking of simplification strategies from collecting a repertoire of rewriting strategies used to simplify. This data should allow us to determine whether common values are considered simpler and whether the value of the original expression influences the chosen simplification strategy. So, given a numerical expression, we could choose what simplification strategy to apply and whether to insert a hedge. We could investigate whether the value of the original proportion also influences choices, depending on its correspondence with central or peripheral values.

We have also collected a parallel corpus of numerical expressions (original vs. simplified version). This corpus will be shared with other researches so it can be used in different applications to improve the readability of text. This could be a very useful resource because simplification of percentages remains an interesting and non-trivial problem.

Acknowledgments

This research is funded by the Spanish Ministry of Education and Science (TIN2009-14659-C03-01 Project), Universidad Complutense de Madrid and Banco Santander Central Hispano (GR58/08 Research Group Grant), and the FPI grant program.

References

Stephanie Schinzing Marsiglio Ann M. Bisantz and Jessica Munch. 2005. Displaying uncertainty: Investigating the effects of display format and specificity. *Human Factors: The Journal of the Human Factors and Ergonomics Society*, 47(4):777.

J. Carroll, G. Minnen, Y. Canning, S. Devlin, and J. Tait. 1998. Practical simplification of English newspaper text to assist aphasic readers. In *AAAI-98 Workshop on Integrating Artificial Intelligence and Assistive Technology*, Madison, Wisconsin.

Raman Chandrasekar, Christine Doran, and Bangalore Srinivas. 1996. Motivations and Methods for Text Simplification. In *COLING*, pages 1041–1044.

Paul Slovic Ellen Peters, Judith Hibbard and Nathan Dieckmann. 2007. Numeracy skill and the communication, comprehension, and use of risk-benefit information. *Health Affairs*, 26(3):741–748.

Shiv B. Mishra H, Mishra A. 2011. In praise of vagueness: malleability of vague information as a performance booster. *Psychological Science*, 22(6):733–8, April.

Paul Slovic Nathan F. Dieckmann and Ellen M. Peters. 2009. The use of narrative evidence and explicit likelihood by decisionmakers varying in numeracy. *Risk Analysis*, 29(10).

The United Nations. 1994. Normas uniformes sobre la igualdad de oportunidades para las personas con discapacidad. Technical report.

Sarah E. Petersen and Mari Ostendorf. 2007. Text Simplification for Language Learners: A Corpus Analysis. *Speech and Language Technology for Education (SLaTE)*.

Qualification and Curriculum Authority. 1999. Mathematics: the national curriculum for england. Department for Education and Employment, London.

Advaith Siddharthan. 2002. Resolving Attachment and Clause Boundary Amgiguities for Simplifying Relative Clause Constructs. In *Proceedings of the Student Research Workshop, 40th Meeting of the Association for Computacional Linguistics*.

Sandra Williams and Richard Power. 2009. Precision and mathematical form in first and subsequent mentions of numerical facts and their relation to document structure. In *Proceedings of the 12th European Workshop on Natural Language Generation*, Athens.

Sandra Williams and Ehud Reiter. 2005. Generating readable texts for readers with low basic skills. In *Proceeding of the 10th European Workshop on Natural Language Generation*, pages 140–147, Aberdeen, Scotland.

Joel Williams, Sam Clemens, Karin Oleinikova, and Karen Tarvin. 2003. The Skills for Life survey: A national needs and impact survey of literacy, numeracy and ICT skills. Technical Report Research Report 490, Department for Education and Skills.

Towards an on-demand Simple Portuguese Wikipedia

Arnaldo Candido Junior
Institute of Mathematics and Computer Sciences
University of São Paulo
arnaldoc at icmc.usp.br

Ann Copestake
Computer Laboratory
University of Cambridge
Ann.Copestake at cl.cam.ac.uk

Lucia Specia
Research Group in Computational Linguistics
University of Wolverhampton
l.specia at wlv.ac.uk

Sandra Maria Aluísio
Institute of Mathematics and Computer Sciences
University of São Paulo
sandra at icmc.usp.br

Abstract

The *Simple English Wikipedia* provides a simplified version of Wikipedia's English articles for readers with special needs. However, there are fewer efforts to make information in Wikipedia in other languages accessible to a large audience. This work proposes the use of a syntactic simplification engine with high precision rules to automatically generate a Simple Portuguese Wikipedia on demand, based on user interactions with the main Portuguese Wikipedia. Our estimates indicated that a human can simplify about 28,000 occurrences of analysed patterns per million words, while our system can correctly simplify 22,200 occurrences, with estimated f-measure 77.2%.

1 Introduction

The *Simple English Wikipedia*[1] is an effort to make information in Wikipedia[2] accessible for less competent readers of English by using simple words and grammar. Examples of intended users include children and readers with special needs, such as users with learning disabilities and learners of English as a second language.

Simple English (or Plain English), used in this version of Wikipedia, is a result from the Plain English movement that occurred in Britain and the United States in the late 1970's as a reaction to the unclear language used in government and business forms and documents. Some recommendations on how to write and organize information in Plain Language (the set of guidelines to write simplified texts) are related to both syntax and lexical levels: use short sentences; avoid hidden verbs; use active voice; use concrete, short, simple words.

A number of resources, such as lists of common words[3], are available for the English language to help users write in Simple English. These include lexical resources like the MRC Psycholinguistic Database[4] which helps identify difficult words using psycholinguistic measures. However, resources as such do not exist for Portuguese. An exception is a small list of simple words compiled as part of the PorSimples project (Aluisio et al., 2008).

Although the guidelines from the Plain Language can in principle be applied for many languages and text genres, for Portuguese there are very few efforts using Plain Language to make information accessible to a large audience. To the best of our knowledge, the solution offered by *Portugues Claro*[5] to help organizations produce European Portuguese (EP) documents in simple language is the only commercial option in such a direction. For Brazilian Portuguese (BP), a Brazilian Law (10098/2000) tries to ensure that content in e-Gov sites and services is written in simple and direct language in order to remove barriers in communication and to ensure citizens' rights to information and communication access. However, as it has been shown in Martins and Filgueiras (2007), content in such websites still needs considerable rewriting to follow the Plain Language guidelines.

A few efforts from the research community have recently resulted in natural language processing

1 http://simple.wikipedia.org/
2 http://www.wikipedia.org/
3 http://simple.wiktionary.org/
4 http://www2.let.vu.nl/resources/elw/resource/mrc.html
5 http://www.portuguesclaro.pt/

Proceedings of the 2nd Workshop on Speech and Language Processing for Assistive Technologies, pages 137–147,
Edinburgh, Scotland, UK, July 30, 2011. ©2011 Association for Computational Linguistics

systems to simplify and make Portuguese language clearer. ReEscreve (Barreiro and Cabral, 2009) is a multi-purpose paraphraser that helps users to simplify their EP texts by reducing its ambiguity, number of words and complexity. The current linguistic phenomena paraphrased are support verb constructions, which are replaced by stylistic variants. In the case of BP, the lack of simplification systems led to development of PorSimples project (Aluísio and Gasperin, 2010). This project uses simplification in different linguistic levels to provide simplified text to poor literacy readers.

For English, automatic text simplification has been exploited for helping readers with poor literacy (Max, 2006) and readers with other special needs, such as aphasic people (Devlin and Unthank, 2006; Carroll et al. 1999). It has also been used in bilingual education (Petersen, 2007) and for improving the accuracy of Natural Language Processing (NLP) tasks (Klebanov et al., 2004; Vickrey and Koller, 2008).

Given the general scarcity of human resources to manually simplify large content repositories such as Wikipedia, simplifying texts automatically can be the only feasible option. The Portuguese Wikipedia, for example, is the tenth largest Wikipedia (as of May 2011), with 683,215 articles and approximately 860,242 contributors[6].

In this paper we propose a new rule-based syntactic simplification system to create a Simple Portuguese Wikipedia on demand, based on user interactions with the main Portuguese Wikipedia. We use a simplification engine to change passive into active voice and to break down and change the syntax of subordinate clauses. We focus on these operations because they are more difficult to process by readers with learning disabilities as compared to others such as coordination and complex noun phrases (Abedi et al., 2011; Jones et al., 2006; Chappell, 1985). User interaction with Wikipedia can be performed by a system like the Facilita[7] (Watanabe et al., 2009), a browser plug-in developed in the PorSimples project to allow automatic adaptation (summarization and syntactic simplification) of any web page in BP.

This paper is organized as follows. Section 2 presents related work on syntactic simplification. Section 3 presents the methodology to build and evaluate the simplification engine for BP. Section 4 presents the results of the engine evaluation. Section 5 presents an analysis on simplification issues and discusses possible improvements. Section 6 contains some final remarks.

2 Related work

Given the dependence of syntactic simplification on linguistic information, successful approaches are mostly based on rule-based systems. Approaches using operations learned from corpus have not shown to be able to perform complex operations such the splitting of sentences with relative clauses (Chandrasekar and Srinivas, 1997; Daelemans et al., 2004; Specia, 2010). On the other hand. the use of machine learning techniques to predict when to simplify a sentence, i.e. learning the properties of language that distinguish simple from normal texts, has achieved relative success (Napoles and Dredze, 2010). Therefore, most work on syntactic simplification still relies on rule-based systems to simplify a set of syntactic constructions. This is also the approach we follow in this paper. In what follows we review some relevant and work on syntactic simplification.

The seminal work of Chandrasekar and Srinivas (1997) investigated the induction of syntactic rules from a corpus annotated with part-of-speech tags augmented by agreement and subcategorization information. They extracted syntactic correspondences and generated rules aiming to speed up parsing and improving its accuracy, but not working on naturally occurring texts. Daelemans et al. (2004) compared both machine learning and rule-based approaches for the automatic generation of TV subtitles for hearing-impaired people. In their machine learning approach, a simplification model is learned from parallel corpora with TV programme transcripts and the associated subtitles. Their method used a memory-based learner and features such as words, lemmas, POS tags, chunk tags, relation tags and proper name tags, among others features (30 in total). However, this approach did not perform as well as the authors expected, making errors like removing sentence subjects or deleting a part of a multi-word unit. More recently, Specia (2010) presented a new approach for text simplification, based on the framework of Statistical Machine

6 http://meta.wikimedia.org/wiki/List_of_Wikipedias#Grand Total

7 http://nilc.icmc.usp.br/porsimples/facilita/

Translation. Although the results are promising for lexical simplification, syntactic rewriting was not captured by the model to address long-distance operations, since syntactic information was not included into the framework.

Inui et al. (2003) proposed a rule-based system for text simplification aimed at deaf people. Using about one thousand manually created rules, the authors generate several paraphrases for each sentence and train a classifier to select the simpler ones. Promising results were obtained, although different types of errors on the paraphrase generation are encountered, such as problems with verb conjugation and regency. Our work aims at making Portuguese Wikipedia information accessible to a large audience and instead of generating several possible outputs we generate only one based on rules taken from a manual of simplification for BP.

Siddharthan (2006) proposed a syntactic simplification architecture that relies on shallow parsing. The general goal of the architecture is to make texts more accessible to a broader audience instead of targeting any particular application. The system simplifies apposition, relative clauses, coordination and subordination. Our method, on the other hand, relies on deep parsing (Bick, 2000) and focuses on changing passive to active voice and changing the syntax of relative clauses and subordinate sentences.

Max (2006) applied text simplification in the writing process by embedding the simplifier into a word processor. Although this system ensures accurate output, it requires manual choices. The suggested simplifications are ranked by a score of syntactic complexity and potential change of meaning. The writer then chooses their preferred simplification. Our method, on the other hand, offers the user only one simplification since it uses several rules to better capture each complex phenomenon.

Inspired by Siddharthan (2006), Jonnalagadda and Gonzalez (2009) present an approach to syntactic simplification addressing also the problem of accurately determining the grammatical correctness of the simplified sentences. They propose the combination of the number of null links and disjunct cost (the level of inappropriateness, caused by using less frequent rules in the linkage) from the cost vector returned by a Link Grammar[8] parser. Their motivation is to improve the performance of systems for extracting Protein-Protein Interactions automatically from biomedical articles by automatically simplifying sentences. Besides treating the syntactic phenomena described in Siddharthan (2006), they remove describing phrases occurring at the beginning of the sentences, like "These results suggest that" and "As reported previously". While they focus on the scientific genre, our work is focused on the encyclopedic genre.

In order to obtain a text easier to understand by children, De Belder and Moens (2010) use the Stanford parser[9] to select the following phenomena to syntactically simplify the sentences: appositions, relative clauses, prefix subordination and infix subordination and coordination. After sentence splitting, they try to apply the simplification rules again to both of the new sentences. However, they conclude that with the set of simplification rules used, it was not possible to reduce the reading difficulty for children and foresee the use of other techniques for this purpose, such as summarization and elaborations for difficult words.

3 Simplification engine

3.1 Engine development

The development of a syntactic simplification engine for a specific task and audience can be divided into five distinct phases: (a) target audience analysis; (b) review of complex syntactic phenomena for such an audience; (c) formulation of simplification guidelines; (d) refinement of rules based on evidence from corpora; and (e) programming and evaluation of rules.

In this paper we focus on the last two phases. We use the simplification guidelines from the PorSimples project, but these are based on grammar studies and corpora analysis for a different text genre (news). Therefore additional corpora evidence proved to be necessary. This resulted in the further refinement of the rules, covering different cases for each syntactic phenomenon.

The Simplification engine relies on the output of the Palavras Parser (Bick, 2000) to perform constituent tree transformations (for example, tree

8 http://www.abisource.com/projects/link-grammar/

9 http://nlp.stanford.edu/software/lex-parser.shtml

splitting). Each node of a sentence tree is fed (breadth-first order) to the simplification algorithms, which can simplify the node (and its sub-tree) or skip it when the node does not meet the simplification prerequisites. Breadth-first order is chosen because several operations affect the root of a (sub)tree, while none of them affect leaves.

A development corpus containing examples of cases analysed for each syntactic phenomenon is used to test and refine the rules. The current version of the corpus has 156 sentences extracted from news text. The corpus includes negative and positive examples for each rule. Negative examples should not be simplified. They were inserted into the corpus to avoid unnecessary simplifications. Each rule is first tested against its own positive and negative examples. This test is called *local test*. After reaching a good precision on the local test, the rule is then tested against all the sentences in the corpus, *global test*. In the current corpus, the global test identified sentences correctly simplified by at least one rule (66%), sentences incorrectly simplified due to major errors in parsing/rules (7%) (ungrammatical sentences) and non-simplified sentences (27%). The last includes mainly negative examples, but also includes sentences not selected due to parsing errors, sentences from cases not yet implemented, and sentences from cases ignored due to ambiguity.

3.2 Passive voice

The default case for dealing with passive voice in our simplification engine is illustrated by the pair of original-simplified sentences in example[10] (1). Sentences belonging to this case have a non-pronominal subject and a passive agent. Also, the predicator has two verbs, the verb *to be* followed by a verb in the past participle tense. The simplification consists in reordering the sentence components, turning the agent into subject (removing the *by* preposition), turning the subject into direct object and adjusting the predicator by removing the verb *to be* and re-inflecting the main verb. The new tense of the main verb is the same as the one of the *to be* verb and its number is defined according to the new subject.

O: As[The] transferências[transfers] foram[were:plural] feitas[made] pela[by the] empresa[company]. (1)
S: A[The] empresa[company] fez[made:sing] as[the] transferências[transfers].

Other correctly processed cases vary according the number of verbs (three or four), special subjects, and special agents. For cases comprising three or four verbs, the simplification rule must re-inflect[11] two verbs (2) (one of them should agree with the subject and the other receives its tense from the verb *to be*). There are two cases of special subjects. In the first case, a hidden subject is turned into a pronominal direct object (3). In the second case, a pronominal subject must be transformed to oblique case pronoun and then to direct object. Special agents also represent two cases. In the first one, oblique case pronouns must be transformed before turning the agent into the subject. In the second case (4), a non-existent agent is turned into an undetermined subject (represented here by "they").

O: A[The] porta[door] deveria[should] ter[have] sido[been] trancada[locked:fem] por[by] John. (2)
S: John deveria[should] ter[have] trancado[locked:masc] a[the] porta[door].

O: [I] fui[was] encarregado[entrusted] por[by] minha[my] família[family]. (3)
S: Minha[My] família[family] encarregou[entrusted] me[me].

O: O[The] ladrão[thief] foi[was] pego[caught]. (4)
S: [They] pegaram[caught] o[the] ladrão[thief].

Two cases are not processed because they are already considered easy enough: the syndetic voice and passive in non-root sentences. In those cases, the proposed simplification is generally less understandable than the original sentence. Sentences with split predicator (as in "the politician was very criticized by his electors") are not processed for the time being, but should be incorporated in the pipeline in the future.

Table 1 presents the algorithm used to process the default case rule and verb case rules. Simplification rules are applied against all nodes in constituent tree, one node at a time, using breadth-first traversing.

10 Literal translations from Portuguese result in some sentences appearing ungrammatical in English.

11 Some reinflections may not be visible on example translation.

Step	Description
1	Validate these prerequisites or give up:
1.1	Node must be root
1.2	Predictor must have an inflection of auxiliary verb *to be*
1.3	Main verb has to be in past participle
2	Transform subject into direct object
3	Fix the predicator
3.1	If main verb is finite then: main verb gets mode and tense from *to be* main verb gets person according to agent
3.2	Else: main verb gets mode and tense from verb *to be* finite verb gets person according to agent
3.3	Remove verb *to be*
4	Transform passive agent into a new subject

Table 1: Algorithm for default and verb cases

3.3 Subordination

Types of subordinate clauses are presented in Table 2. Two clauses are not processed: comparative and proportional. Comparative and proportional clauses will be addressed in future work.

id	Clause type	Processed
d	Relative Restrictive	✓
e	Relative Non-restrictive	✓
f	Reason	✓
g	Comparative	
h	Concessive	✓
i	Conditional	✓
j	Result	✓
k	Confirmative	✓
l	Final Purpose	✓
m	Time	✓
w	Proportional	

Table 2: Subordinate clauses

Specific rules are used for groups of related subordinate cases. At least one of two operations can be found in all rules: component reordering and sentence splitting. Below, letter codes are used to describe rules involving these two and other common operations:

A	additional processing
M	splitting-order main-subordinate
P	Also processes non-clause phrases and/or non-finite clauses
R	component reordering
S	splitting-order subordinate-main
c	clone subject or turn object of a clause into subject in another if it is necessary
d	marker deletion
m	marker replacement
v	verb reinflection
[na]	not simplified due ambiguity
[nf]	not simplified, future case
[np]	not simplified due parsing problems
2...8	covered cases (when more than one applies)

Table 3 presents the marker information. They are used to select sentences for simplification, and several of them are replaced by easier markers. Cases themselves are not detailed since they are too numerous (more than 40 distinct cases). Operation codes used for each marker are described in column "Op". It is important to notice that multi-lexeme markers also face ambiguities due to co-occurrence of its component lexemes[12]. The list does not cover all possible cases, since there may be additional cases not seen in the corpus. As relative clauses (*d* and *e*) require almost the same processing, they are grouped together.

Several clauses require additional processing. For example, some conditional clauses require negating the main clause. Other examples include noun phrases replacing clause markers and clause reordering, both for relative clauses, as showed in (5). The marker *cujo* (*whose*) in the example can refer to *Northbridge* or to *the building*. Additional processing is performed to try to solve this anaphora[13], mostly using number agreement between the each possible co-referent and the main verb in the subordinate clause. The simplification engine can give up in ambiguous cases (focusing on precision) or elect a coreferent (focusing on recall), depending on the number of possible coreferents and on a confidence threshold parameter, which was not used in this paper.

O: Ele[He] deve[should] visitar[visit] o[the] prédio[building] em[in] Northbridge cujo[whose] desabamento[landslide] matou[killed] 16 pessoas[people].
S: Ele[He] deve[should] visitar[visit] o[the] prédio[building] em[in] Northbridge. O[The] desabamento[landslide] do[of the] prédio[building] em[in] Northbridge matou[killed] 16 pessoas[people]. (5)

12 For example, words "de", "sorte" and "que" can be adjacent to each other without the meaning of "de sorte que" marker ("so that").

13 We opted to solve this kind of anaphora instead of using pronoun insertion in order to facilitate the reading of the text.

id	Marker	Op	id	Marker	Op	id	Markers	Op
de	que [that/which]	8MRAdv	h	se bem que [albeit]	Mmv	j	tanto ... que [so ... that]	[nf]
de	o qual [which]*	8MRAdv	h	ainda que [even if]	2Mm	j	tal ... que [such ... that]	[nf]
de	como [as]	[na]	h	mesmo que [even if]	2Mm	j	tamanho ... que [so ... that]*	[nf]
de	onde [where]	[nf]	h	nem que [even if]	2Mm	k	conforme [as/according]	3PRAcm
de	quando [when]	[na]	h	por mais que [whatever]	2Mm	k	consoante [as/according]	3PRAcm
de	quem [who/whom]	[nf]	h	mas [but]	[np]	k	segundo [as/according]	3PRAcm
de	quanto [how much]	[nf]	i	contanto que [provided that]	2Rmv	k	como [as]	[na]
de	cujo [whose]*	MAd	i	caso [case]	2Rmv	l	a fim de [in order to]	2PMcm
de	o que [what/which]	Sd	i	se [if/whether]	2Rmv	l	a fim de que [in order that]	2PMcm
f	já que [since]	Scm	i	a menos que [unless]	2RAmv	l	para que [so that]	2PMcm
f	porquanto [in view of]	Scm	i	a não ser que [unless]	2RAmv	l	porque [because]	[na]
f	uma vez que [since]	Scm	i	exceto se [unless]	2RAmv	m	assim que [as soon as]	5PMAcvr
f	visto que [since]	Scm	i	salvo se [unless]	2RAmv	m	depois de [after]	5PMAcvr
f	como [for]	[na]	i	antes que [before]	Rmv	m	depois que [after]	5PMAcvr
f	porque [because]	[na]	i	sem que [without]	Rmv	m	logo que [once]	5PMAcvr
f	posto que [since]	[na]	i	desde que [since]	RAmv	m	antes que [before]	PSAcvr
f	visto como [seen as]	[na]	j	de forma que [so]	5Mmv	m	apenas [only]	[na]
f	pois que [since]	[nf]	j	de modo que [so]	5Mmv	m	até que [until]	[na]
h	apesar de que [although]	Mmv	j	de sorte que [so that]	5Mmv	m	desde que [since]	[na]
h	apesar que [despite]	Mmv	j	tamanho que [so that]*	5Mmv	m	cada vez que [every time]	[nf]
h	conquanto [although]	Mmv	j	tal que [such that]	5Mmv	m	sempre que [whenever]	[nf]
h	embora [albeit]	Mmv	j	tanto que [so that] (1)*	[na]	m	enquanto [while]	[nf]
h	posto que [since]	Mmv	j	tanto que [so that] (2)	[na]	m	mal [just]	[na]
h	por muito que [although]	Mmv	j	tão ... que [so ... that]	[nf]	m	quando [when]	[na]

* gender and/or number variation

Table 3: Marker processing

3.4 Evaluation in the development corpus

Figure 1 provides statistics from the of processing all identified cases in the development corpus. These statistics cover number of cases rather than the number of sentences containing cases. The cases "incorrect selection" and "incorrect simplification" affect precision by generating ungrammatical sentences. The former refers to sentences that should not be selected for the simplification process, while the latter refers to sentences correctly selected but wrongly simplified. There are three categories affecting recall, classified according to their priority in the simplification engine. *Pending* cases are considered to be representative, with higher priority. *Possible* cases are considered to be unrepresentative. Having less priority, they can be handled in future versions of the engine. Finally, *Skipped* cases will not be implemented, mainly because of ambiguity, but also due to low representativeness. It is possible to observe that categories reducing precision (incorrect selection and simplification) represent a smaller number of cases (5%) than categories reducing recall (45%). It is worth noticing that our approach focus on precision in order to make the simplification as automatic as possible, minimizing the need for human interaction.

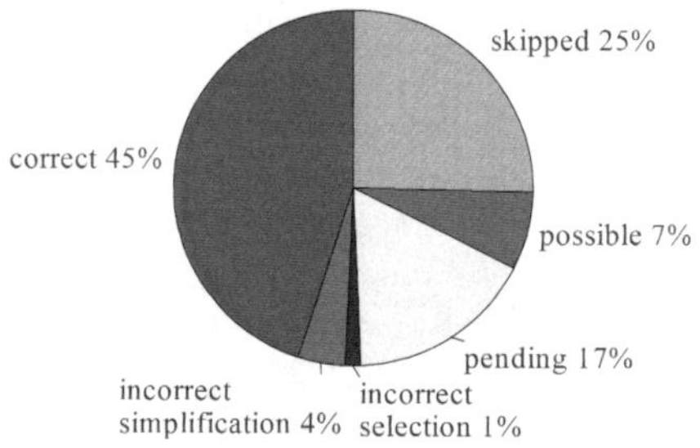

Figure 1: Performance on the development corpus

There are some important remarks regarding the development corpus used during the programming phase. First, some cases are not representative, therefore the results are expected to vary significantly in real texts. Second, a few cases are not orthogonal: i.e., there are sentences that can be classified in more than one case. Third, several errors refer to sub-cases of cases being mostly correctly processed, which are expected to occur less frequently. Fourth, incorrect parsed sentences were not take in account in this phase. Although there may exist other cases not identified yet, it is plausible to estimate that only 5% of known cases are affecting the precision negatively.

4 Engine evaluation

4.1 Evaluation patterns

The evaluation was performed on a sample of sentences extracted from Wikipedia's texts using lexical patterns. These patterns allows to filter the texts, extracting only relevant sentences for precision and recall evaluation. They were created to cover both positive and negative sentences. They are applied before parsing or Part of Speech (PoS) analysis. For passive voice detection, the pattern is defined as a sequence of two or more possible verbs (no PoS in use) in which at least one of them could be an inflection of verb to be. For subordination detection, the pattern is equivalent to the discourse markers associated with each subordination type, as shown in Table 3.

The patterns were applied against featured articles appearing in Wikipedia's front page in 2010 and 2011, including featured articles planned to be featured, but not featured yet. A maximum of 30 sentences resulting from each pattern matching were then submitted to the simplification engine. Table 4 presents statistics from featured articles.

texts	165
sentences	83,656
words	1,226,880
applied patterns	57,735
matched sentences	31,080

Table 4: Wikipedia's featured articles (2010/2011)

The number of applied patterns represents both patterns to be simplified (s-patterns) and patterns not to be simplified (n-patterns). N-patterns represent both non-processable patterns due to high ambiguity (a-patterns) and pattern extraction false negatives. We observed a few, but very frequent, ambiguous patterns introducing noise, particularly *se* and *como*. In fact, these two markers are so noisy that we were not be able to provide good estimations on their true positives distribution given the 30 sentences limit per pattern. Similarly to the number of applied patterns, the number of matched sentences correspond to both sentences to be simplified and not to be simplified.

Table 5 presents additional statistics about characters, words and sentences calculated in a sample of 32 articles where the 12 domains of the Portuguese Wikipedia are balanced. The number of automatic simplified sentence is also presented. In Table 5, *simple words* refers to percentage of words which are listed on our simple word list, supposed to be common to youngsters, extracted from the dictionary described in (Biderman, 2005), containing 5,900 entries. Figure 2 presents clause distribution per sentence in the balanced sample. *Zero clauses* refers to titles, references, figure labels, and other pieces of text without a verb. We observed 60% of multi-clause sentences in the sample.

characters per word	5.22
words per sentence	21.17
words per text	8,476
simple words	75.52%
sentences per text	400.34
passive voice	15.11%
total sentences	13,091
simplified sentences	16,71%

Table 5: Statistics from the balanced text sample

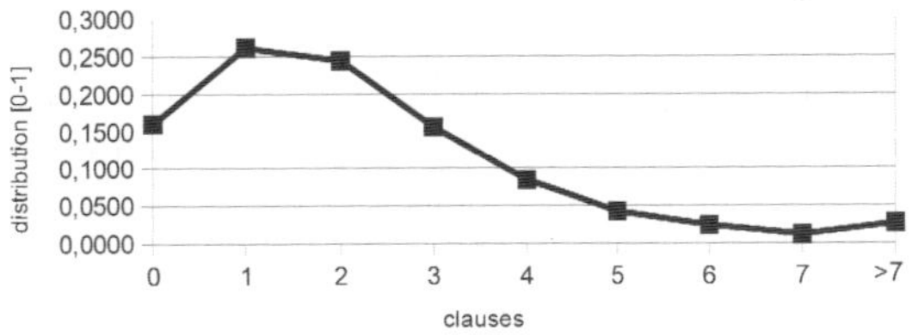

Figure 2: Clauses per sentence in the sample

4.2 Simplification analysis

We manually analysed and annotated all sentences in our samples. These samples were used to estimate several statistics, including the number of patterns per million words, the system precision and recall and the noise rate. We opted for analysing simplified patterns per million words instead of per simplified sentences. First, because an analysis based on sentences can be misleading, since there are cases of long coordinations with many patterns, as well as succinct sentences with no patterns. Moreover, one incorrectly simplified marker in a sentence could hide useful statistics of correctly simplified patterns and even of other incorrectly simplified patterns.

The samples are composed by s-patterns and n-patterns (including a-patterns). In total 1,243 patterns were annotated. Table 6 presents pattern estimates per million words.

Total patterns	70,834
Human s-patterns	33,906
Selection s-patterns	27,714
Perfect parser s-patterns	23,969
Obtained s-patterns	22,222

Table 6: Patterns per million words

Total patterns refers to the expected occurrences of s-patterns and n-patterns in a corpus of one million words. This is the only information extracted from the full corpus, while the remaining figures are estimates from the sample corpus.

Human s-patterns is an estimate of the number patterns that a human could simplify in the corpus. Unlike other s-pattern estimates, a-patterns are included, since a human can disambiguate them. In other words, this is the total of positive patterns. The estimate does not include very rare (sample size equals to zero) or very noisy markers (patterns presenting 30 noisy sentences in its sample).

Selection s-patterns are an estimate of the number of patterns correctly selected for simplification, regardless of whether the pattern simplification is correct or incorrect. Precision and recall derived from this measure (Table 7) consider incorrectly simplified patterns, and do not include patterns with parsing problems. Its purpose is to evaluate how well the selection for simplification is performed. Rare or noisy patterns, whose human s-patterns per sample is lower than 7, are not included.

Perfect parser s-patterns is an estimate very similar to selection s-patterns, but considering only correctly simplified patterns. As in selection s-patterns, incorrect parsed sentences are not included in calculations. This is useful to analyse incorrect simplifications due to simplification rule problems, ignoring errors originating from parsing.

Finally, *obtained s-patterns* refers to the estimate of correct simplified patterns, similar to perfect parser s-patterns, but including simplification problems caused by parsing. This estimate represents the real performance to be expected from the system on Wikipedia's texts.

It is important to note that the real numbers of *selection s-patterns*, *perfect s-patterns* and *obtained s-patterns* is expected to be bigger than the estimates, since noisy and rare pattern could not used be used in calculations (due the threshold of 7 human s-patterns per sample). The data presented on Table 6 is calculated using estimated local precisions for each pattern. Table 7 presents global precision, recall and f-measure related to *selection, perfect parser* and *obtained s-patterns*. The real values of the estimates are expected to variate up to +/- 2.48% .

Measures	**Precision**	**Recall**	**F-measure**
Selection	99.05%	82.24%	89.86%
Perfect parser	85.66%	82.24%	83.92%
Obtained	79.42%	75.09%	77.20%

Table 7: Global estimated measures

Although the precision of the selection seems to be impressive, this result is expected, since our approach focus on the processing of mostly unambiguous markers, with sufficient syntactic information. It is also due to the the threshold of 7 human s-patterns and the fact that a-patterns are not included. Due to these two restrictions, only approximately 31.5% of unique patterns could be used for the calculations in Table 7. Interestingly, these unique patterns correspond to 82.5% of the total estimated human s-patterns. The majority of the 17.5% remaining s-patterns refers to patterns too noisy to be analysed and to a-patterns (not processed due ambiguity), and also others n-patterns which presented a low representativeness in the corpus. The results indicate good performance in rule formulation, covering the most important (and non-ambiguous) markers, which is also confirmed by the ratio between both selection s-patterns and human s-patterns previously presented on Table 6.

An alternative analysis, including a-patterns, lowers recall and f-measure, but not precision (our focus in this work). In this case, recall drops from 75.09% to 62.18%, while f-measure drops from 77.20% to 70.18%.

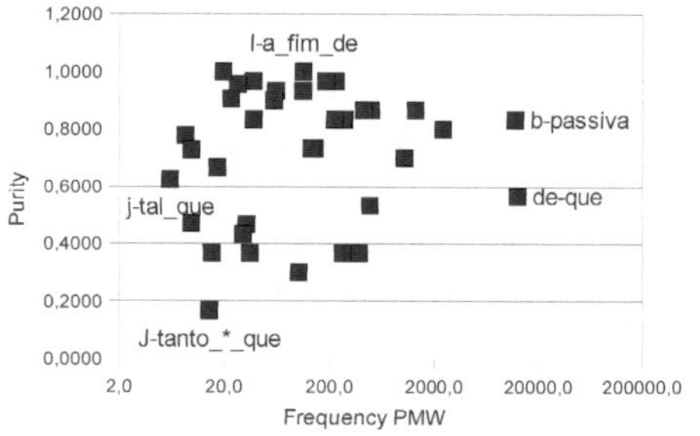

Figure 3: Pattern distribution

Figure 3 presents the distribution of patterns according to their frequency per million words and their purity (1 - noisy rate). This data is useful to identify most frequent patterns (such as passive voice in *b-passiva*) and patterns with medium to high frequency, which are easy to process (not ambiguous), such as *l-a_fim_de*.

5 Issues on simplification quality

This analysis aims at identifying factors affecting the quality of simplifications considered as correct. Hence, factors affecting the overall simplified text quality are also presented. In contrast, the quantitative analysis presented on Section 4.2 covered the ratio between incorrect and correct simplifications.

Three cases of clause disposition were identified as important factors affecting the simplified sentence readability. These cases are presented using the following notation: clauses are represented in uppercase letters; clause concatenation represents coordination; parentheses represent subordination; c_1 and c_2 represent clause/sentence connectors (including markers); the entailment operator (→) represents the simplification rule transforming clauses.

- "A(B(c_1 C)) → A(B). c_2 C": the **vertical case**. In this scenario it is more natural to read c_2 as connecting *C* to the main clause *A*, while c_1 connects *C* to *B*, as seen in (6). This is still acceptable for several sentences analysed, but we are considering to simplify only level 2 clauses in the future, splitting *C* from B only if another rule splits A and B first.
- "A(B)CD → ACD. c_1 B": the **horizontal case**. In this scenario, c_1 correctly connects *A* and *B*, but long coordinations following A can impact negatively on text reading, since the target audience may forget about *A* when starting to read *B*. In this scenario, coordination compromise subordination simplification, showing the importance of simplifying coordination as well, even though they are considered easier to read than subordination.
- **Mixed case**: this scenario combines the potential problems of horizontal and vertical cases. It may occur in extremely long sentences.

Besides clause disposition factors, clause inversions can also lead to problems in sentence readability. In our current system, inversion is mainly used to produce simplified sentences in the cause-effect order or condition-action order. Reordering, despite using more natural orders, can transform anaphors into cataphors. A good anaphora resolution system would be necessary to avoid this issue. Another problem is moving sentence connectors as in "A. c_1 BC. → A. B. c_2 c_1 C", while "A. c_1 B. c_2 C" is more natural (maintaining c_1 position).

O: Ela[She] dissertou[talked] sobre[about] como[how] motivar[to motive] o[the] grupo[group] de_modo_que[so that] seu[their] desempenho[performance] melhore[improves]
S: [He/She] dissertou[talked] sobre[about] como[how] motivar[to motive] o[the] grupo[group]. Thus, seu[their] desempenho[performance] melhore[improves] (6)

We have observed some errors in sentence parsing, related to clause attachment, generating truncated ungrammatical text. As a result, a badly simplified key sentence can compromise the text readability more than several correctly simplified sentences can improve it, reinforcing the importance of precision rather than recall in automated text simplification.

Experienced readers analysed the simplified versions of the articles and considered them easier to read than the original ones in most cases, despite simplification errors. Particularly, the readers considered that the readability would improve significantly if cataphor and horizontal problems were addressed. Evaluating the simplifications with readers from the target audience is left as a future work, after improvements in the identified issues.

6 Conclusions

We have presented a simplification engine to process texts from the Portuguese Wikipedia. Our quantitative analysis indicated a good precision (79.42%), and reasonable number of correct simplifications per million words (22,222). Although our focus was on the encyclopedic genre evaluation, the proposed system can be used in other genres as well.

Acknowledgements
We thank FAPESP (p. 2008/08963-4) and CNPq (p. 201407/2010-8) for supporting this work.

References

J. Abedi, S. Leon, J. Kao, R. Bayley, N. Ewers, J. Herman and K. Mundhenk. 2011. Accessible Reading Assessments for Students with Disabilities: The Role of Cognitive, Grammatical, Lexical, and Textual/Visual Features. CRESST Report 785. National Center for Research on Evaluation, Standards, and Student Testing, University of California, Los Angeles.

S. M. Aluísio, C. Gasperin. 2010. Fostering Digital Inclusion and Accessibility: The PorSimples project for Simplification of Portuguese Texts. Proceedings of the NAACL HLT 2010 Young Investigators Workshop on Computational Approaches to Languages of the Americas. : ACL, New York, USA. v. 1. p. 46-53.

A. Barreiro, L. M. Cabral. 2009. ReEscreve: a translator-friendly multi-purpose paraphrasing software tool. The Proceedings of the Workshop Beyond Translation Memories: New Tools for Translators, The Twelfth Machine Translation Summit. Ontario, Canada, pp. 1-8.

E. Bick. 2006. The parsing system "Palavras": Automatic grammatical analysis of Portuguese in a constraint grammar framework. Thesis (PhD). University of Århus, Aarhus, Denmark.

M. T. C. Biderman. 2005. Dicionário Ilustrado de Português. Editora Ática. 1a. ed. São Paulo

J. Carroll, G. Minnen, D. Pearce, Y. Canning, S. Devlin and J. Tait. 1999. Simplifying Text for Language-Impaired Readers,. In Proceedings of the 9th Conference of the European Chapter of the Association for Computational Linguistics (EACL), 269-270.

R. Chandrasekar and B. Srinivas. 1997. Automatic Induction of Rules for Text Simplification. Knowledge-Based Systems, 10, 183-190.

G. E. Chappell. 1985. Description and assessment of language disabilities of junior high school students. In: Communication skills and classroom success: Assessment of language-learning disabled students. College- Hill Press, San Diego, pp. 207-239.

W. Daelemans, A. Hothker and E. T. K. Sang. 2004. Automatic Sentence Simplification for Subtitling in Dutch and English. In: Proceedings of the 4th Conference on Language Resources and Evaluation, Lisbon, Portugal 1045-1048.

J. De Belder and M. Moens. 2010. Text simplification for children. Proceedings of the SIGIR Workshop on Accessible Search Systems, pp.19-26.

S. Devlin and G. Unthank. 2006. Helping aphasic people process online information. In: Proceedings of the ACM SIGACCESS 2006, Conference on Computers and Accessibility. Portland, Oregon, USA , 225-226.

K. Inui, A. Fujita, T. Takahashi, R. Iida and T. Iwakura. 2003. Text Simplification for Reading Assistance: A Project Note. In the Proceedings of the Second International Workshop on Paraphrasing, 9-16.

S. Jonnalagadda and G. Gonzalez. 2009. Sentence Simplification Aids Protein-Protein Interaction Extraction. Proceedings of the 3rd International Symposium on Languages in Biology and Medicine, Short Papers, pages 109-114, Jeju Island, South Korea, 8-10 November 2009.

F. W. Jones, K. Long and W. M. L. Finlay. 2006. Assessing the reading comprehension of adults with learning disabilities. Journal of Intellectual Disability Research, 50(6), 410-418.

B. Klebanov, K. Knight and D. Marcu. 2004. Text Simplification for Information-Seeking Applications. In: On the Move to Meaningful Internet Systems. Volume 3290, Springer-Verlag, Berlin Heidelberg New York, 735-747.

S. Martins, L. Filgueiras. 2007. Métodos de Avaliação de Apreensibilidade das Informações Textuais: uma Aplicação em Sítios de Governo Eletrônico. In proceeding of Latin American Conference on Human-Computer Interaction (CLIHC 2007). Rio de Janeiro, Brazil.

A. Max. 2006. Writing for Language-impaired Readers. In: Proceedings of Seventh International Conference on Intelligent Text Processing and Computational Linguistics. Mexico City, Mexico. Berlin Heidelberg New York, Springer-Verlag, 567-570.

C. Napoles and M. Dredze. 2010. Learning simple Wikipedia: a cogitation in ascertaining abecedarian language. In the Proceedings of the NAACL HLT 2010 Workshop on Computational Linguistics and Writing: Writing Processes and Authoring Aids (CL&W '10), 42-50.

S. E. Petersen. 2007. Natural Language Processing Tools for Reading Level Assessment and Text Simplification for Bilingual Education. PhD thesis. University of Washington.

A. Siddharthan. 2006. Syntactic simplification and text cohesion. Research on Language & Computation, 4(1):77-109.

L. Specia. 2010. Translating from Complex to Simplified Sentences. 9th International Conference on Computational Processing of the Portuguese Language. Lecture Notes in Artificial Intelligence, Vol. 6001, Springer, pp. 30-39.

D. Vickrey and D. Koller. 2008. Sentence Simplification for Semantic Role Labelling. In: Proceedings of the ACL-HLT. 344-352.

W. M. Watanabe, A. Candido Jr, V. R. Uzeda, R. P. M. Fortes, T. A. S. Pardo and S. M. Aluísio. 2009. Facilita: Reading Assistance for Low-literacy Readers. In: ACM International Conference on Design of Communication (SIGDOC 2009), volume 1, Bloomington, US, 29-36.

Workshop on Speech & Language Processing for Assistive Technologies

Demo Session

1 "How was School today...?" A Prototype System that uses a Mobile Phone to Support Personal Narrative for Children with Complex Communication

Rolf Black[1], *Annalu Waller*[1], *Ehud Reiter*[2], *Nava Tintarev*[2], *Joseph Reddington*[2]
([1]University of Dundee, [2]University of Aberdeen)

We will show a sensor based mobile phone prototype that supports personal narrative for children with complex communication needs. We will demonstrate how the phone is used to capture voice recordings and information about location, people and objects using RFID tags and QR stickers. The challenging environment of a special school for prototype testing will be discussed using real life experiences.

2 The PhonicStick: Interactive access to sounds for people with Complex Communication Needs

Ha Trinh, Annalu Waller, Rolf Black,
James Bennet
(University of Dundee)

The PhonicStick is a new sound-based speech generating device which enables nonspeaking individuals to access 42 English sounds and blend sounds into spoken words. The device can potentially be used both as a literacy learning tool and an interactive communication aid for people with literacy difficulties. We will discuss how NLP technologies, such as speech synthesis and predictive techniques, are utilised to improve the usability of the device.

3 Toby Churchill Ltd

David Mason[1], *James Bennet*[2]
([1]TLC, [2]University of Dundee)

Lightwriter® SL40. We will show one of the new SL40 Connect mobile phone enabled Lightwriters®. Lightwriters® are portable text-to-speech devices with dual displays, one facing the user and a second out-facing display allowing natural face-to-face communication. They are operated by keyboard and use a fast prediction system based on the user's own vocabulary. A certain degree of literacy is required to operate a Lightwriter®.

Lightwriter® SL40 with PhonicStick. We will show an SL40 development unit that is running a version of Dundee University's PhonicStick software. This project is an ongoing collaboration with the Assistive and Healthcare Technologies group in the School of Computing at Dundee.

VIVOCA. We will be describing a project with partners including the University of Sheffield and the Assistive Technology team at Barnsley District General Hospital. The project is developing and evaluating a novel device for supporting the communication needs of people with severe speech impairment that will address the limitations of the current technology. It builds on previous work by this team (funded by Neat) which has established user requirements and identified the technical developments required. The device, a Voice Input Voice Output Communication Aid (or VIVOCA) will take as input the unintelligible disordered speech of the users.

Proceedings of the 2nd Workshop on Speech and Language Processing for Assistive Technologies, pages 148–149,
Edinburgh, Scotland, UK, July 30, 2011. ©2011 Association for Computational Linguistics

4 SceneTalker: An Utterance-Based AAC System Prototype

Timothy Walsh[1], *Jan Bedrosian*[2], *Linda Hoag*[3], *Kathleen F. McCoy*[1]
([1]University of Delaware; [2]Western Michigan University, [3]Kansas State University)

SceneTalker is a prototype utterance-based augmentative and alternative communication system that uses scripts (and scenes within scripts) to organize prestored messages for highly routine goal-oriented public situations (such as going to a restaurant). Many aspects of the system design are inspired by a series of experiments on using prestored utterances in public goal-oriented situations when the prestored message did not exactly match what the user wanted to say. In addition to the script structures, we show system messages that are not anticipated to be perfect/complete for what is needed and strategies of use with stored messages that anticipate the communication partner's follow-up to utterances (adjacency pairs).

5 SIGHT System

Charles Greenbacker[1], *Seniz Demir*[3], *Peng Wu*[1], *Sandra Carberry*[1], *Stephanie Elzer*[2], *Kathleen F. McCoy*[1]
([1]University of Delaware; [2]Millersville University, [4]Tübitak Bilgem, Turkey)

The SIGHT system is intended to give people with visual impairments access to information graphics (e.g., bar charts) found in popular media. The system generates a textual summary that provides the chart's overall intended message and additional salient propositions conveyed by the graphic.

Author Index